TWO NATIONS

STEPHEN BATES read Modern History at Oxford before working as a journalist for the BBC, *Daily Telegraph*, *Daily Mail* and the *Guardian*, where he was in turn education editor, a political correspondent, European Affairs editor and, latterly, religious affairs and royal correspondent. He is now a full-time author. His previous books include: *A Church at War: Anglicans and Homosexuality*; *God's Own Country: Religion and Politics in the USA*; a biography of Herbert Asquith; a novel, *The Photographer's Boy*; and *The Poisoner: the Life and Crimes of Victorian England's Most Notorious Doctor*. His *1815: Regency Britain in the Year of Waterloo* appeared in 2015.

D0307838

By the same author

Non-Fiction:

A Church at War: Anglicans and Homosexuality

God's Own Country: Religion and Politics in the USA

Asquith

The Poisoner: The Life and Crimes of Victorian England's Most Notorious Doctor

1815: Regency Britain in the Year of Waterloo

Fiction:

The Photographer's Boy

Stephen Bates

TWO NATIONS

BRITAIN IN 1846

HEAD
of ZEUS

First published as *Penny Loaves and Butter Cheap: Britain in 1846*
in 2014 by Head of Zeus Ltd

This paperback edition first published in 2015 by Head of Zeus Ltd

1 3 5 7 9 10 8 6 4 2

A CIP catalogue record for this book is available
from the British Library.

ISBN (PB) 978-1-78185-354-2
ISBN (E) 978-1-78185-255-2

Typesetting by Lindsay Nash

Printed in the UK by Clays Ltd, St Ives PLC

Head of Zeus Ltd
Clerkenwell House
45–47 Clerkenwell Green
London EC1R 0HT

WWW.HEADOFZEUS.COM

Contents

For John King, BEM

Inspirational history master for forty-eight years at
St Bartholomew's School, Newbury
1964–2012

Introduction

British society in 1846 was changing rapidly. It was the height of the Industrial Revolution and its people were moving steadily and irreversibly from the countryside to the towns and cities. When they arrived there, they found new factories, working disciplines and methods of earning a living, but also squalid and foetid conditions. Almost all of the industrial cities that we know today were expanding, but London, the biggest conurbation in the world, was growing particularly quickly, stretching out and absorbing previously rural villages: Islington and Hampstead, Notting Hill and Hammersmith, Wandsworth and Putney. We would recognize the names of most of the streets and many of the buildings of the period survive, even those thrown up rapidly and imposingly across the suburbs to house the new middle and professional classes.* New Oxford Street had just been carved through the slums to connect the West End to Holborn and the first purpose-built five-storey blocks of flats in London were being built opposite St Pancras Old Church 'for improving the dwellings of the industrious classes'.

It was an age of innovation. The railways were spreading along routes they still follow today, enabling people to travel for distances and to places that they and their ancestors could

---

* A third of the houses in Britain today were built before the First World War, most of them during the Victorian period.

never have dreamed of visiting before. The Electric Telegraph Company was set up in 1846, allowing for the first time the instant transfer of information across the country. 'Why,' asked Francis Ronalds, the inventor of the telegraph, 'should not the Government govern at Portsmouth as promptly as in Downing Street?'[1] He meant that the invention could be used for passing orders to the fleet, but the Admiralty was not interested, though newspapers were. In a burst of creativity stimulated by the Industrial Revolution, inventors were developing new-fangled machines which would make life easier in the future: gas cookers, primitive washing-machines, agricultural machinery and ever bigger steamships capable of crossing the Atlantic. Within a few years, in 1851, the Great Exhibition would show off 100,000 exhibits from all over the world (but chiefly as a showcase for the industry of Great Britain) to six million visitors to the Crystal Palace, a glass and iron structure that was itself breathtaking to Victorians in its size and enterprise: nearly 600 metres long and 32 metres high, a demonstration of confidence and ambition, constructed in a few months – 'a sight,' said *The Times*, 'the like of which had never happened before.'[2]

In such a burgeoning, bustling society, government struggled to keep up with the pace of change, but it tried. This was the age of the inquiry and the royal commission, in which inspectors earnestly investigated every facet of Victorian life, looking into everything from sewers to cemeteries, and sought coordinated national solutions for many of the challenges and social problems thrown up by the relentless changes. Philosophical men thought they had found hygienic and efficient remedies in laissez-faire economics and utilitarian approaches to the great issues of the day, and many of their ideas about how society should be organized and conducted are still with us nearly two centuries on.

This was a country falling over itself to embrace the new and harness it. But it was also a time when many felt challenged by change, fearful that religious truths were being undermined and the old social order threatened. Even as the country raced forward, many looked back to an idyllic, pseudo-medieval past and sought to replicate a romantic image of it in their gothic buildings, their manners and their sensibilities.

And then, in the middle of this rush towards the modern age, came an enormous calamity, the worst natural disaster in the Western world since the Middle Ages: the potato famine in Ireland – a catastrophe which tested the government of Britain and found it severely wanting. Not only did a million people die, but a million emigrated, altering forever the face of five countries – Ireland, the United States, Canada, Australia and Great Britain – and affecting their relationships for generations. The famine had another effect too: it precipitated a political crisis in Britain in 1846 that permanently changed British politics and inaugurated economic policies that remained the goal of successive governments for a century to come.

At the heart of the decisions made in London in 1846 was one man: Sir Robert Peel, one of the most important and impressive figures in British political history. Having played a large part in turning the Tory party into a major electoral force following the Great Reform Act of 1832, he was then instrumental in splintering it, by the decision he took to repeal the Corn Laws. In doing so, he acted in defiance of the will of the bedrock of his party and thrust the Tories into parliamentary opposition for the following thirty years, the longest period out of government in their history. This political cataclysm realigned British parties for good: it led to the development of a new Conservative party and the creation of the Liberals out of the merger of the Whigs and Peelites, foreshadowing the politics of today. Peel strides across this narrative as the dominant personality of his time. Many of his contemporaries thought he was too; yet, if not a forgotten figure, his character is enigmatic and to us his personal style is remote and distant in both time and manner. For the best part of a century he remained a traitor to many Tories, and although he has been largely – though not entirely – rehabilitated in the last half-century, he remains obscure and elusive. Peel is a figure from a far-off past: a Tory, yes, and with conservative instincts, but the dominant head of a government which deliberately inaugurated some of the most far-reaching and long-lasting economic and political changes of the nineteenth century, many of them still with us today. When he died, people recognized the scale of his achievements. *The Times* wrote in its obituary:

> If it be asked who opened the gates of trade and bade the food of man flow hither from every shore in an uninterrupted stream, it is Peel who did it... No man ever undertook public affairs with a more thorough determination to leave the institutions of his country in an orderly, honest and efficient state.[3]

The Irish famine was a pretext for the abolition of the Corn Laws – which protected British agriculture and had kept the price of food high – but the decision to get rid of them was one Peel had already decided upon for other reasons. Their repeal had no significant or immediate effect on the starving populations of Ireland, or Scotland. In 1846, the decision over the Corn Laws – taken largely for economic purposes – had far-reaching political consequences; but it was also reached by a prime minister who was consciously motivated by a concern to improve the living conditions of a large swathe of the country's impoverished and voteless population, and thereby to remove the causes of discontent which might lead to revolution. Violent disorder was a constant and vivid fear for the ruling classes of the country in the 1840s, for Britain was by no means the tranquil and stable state that it appears from this distance. Peel's strength was to articulate the need to address directly the grievances of the poor, in a way that no previous prime minister had felt the need to do. As *The Times* said: if the Corn Laws had not been repealed, 'the whole realm of England might have borne a fearful share in [Europe's] storm of wreck and revolution' in 1848. Instead, that year England had an orderly Chartist protest demonstration in Kennington and a petition that called for parliamentary reform rather than revolution, peaceably delivered to Parliament by hansom cab, which MPs then ignored.

In many ways the Britain of 1846 is immeasurably different from our country today. It was a world of darkness and shadows, lit by gas lamps in some central city streets and candles in homes; a world of coal smoke and fogs in which starvation and absolute destitution existed alongside immense and heedless wealth and power; a world in which a single loaf of bread could cost a tenth of a man's weekly wage and children were still sent to work in factories and mines for twelve hours a day; a world of foul and pervasive smells and terrifying diseases far beyond the power of contemporary medicine to conquer. It was a time when criminals were still hanged in public; when vestigial police forces had to call in troops if there was disorder and when the best protection for a householder from the Bill Sikeses* of the world was thought to be a stout cudgel and window shutters. Most middle-class households were kept going by servants. Literacy, especially for women, was by no means universal and life expectancy in many cities extended scarcely into the twenties: it was a world of high infant mortality and sudden, inexplicable death. It was also an age of extraordinary artistic and cultural achievement, when respectable folk flocked to buy the next monthly instalment of Mr Dickens's latest novel, *Dombey and Son*, or crowded the theatres and penny gaffs to jeer at Sweeney Todd or laugh at Harlequin and his paramour Columbine;† when gruff, shabby old J.M.W. Turner was still exhibiting at the Royal Academy and the debonair young German composer Felix Mendelssohn was conducting the première of his great oratorio *Elijah* to a rapt audience at Birmingham town hall.

One hundred and seventy years have elapsed since then and yet that age is not so far away. To intrude a small personal but far from unique example: my great-grandparents, only three generations back, were alive then. In the 1840s, my father's grandfather, David Challis, was a young wine-merchant in Leicester, having like so many others joined the exodus from the country – from his family's farm, in rural north Essex, on which he had been born – to the town, and he lived just long enough to hold my father as an infant in his arms for a

---

* Bill Sikes is the murderous burglar in Dickens's *Oliver Twist*.
† Two traditional pantomime characters of the period.

photograph. On my mother's side, my great-grandparents were probably preparing to flee Ireland, perhaps because of the famine, and were heading east to London rather than west to the United States. The 1856 wedding certificate of William Alexander, a shoemaker aged 28 years, and Mary Sullivan, 20, a spinster, for their marriage at St George's Catholic Church, Southwark, solemnized 'according to the rites and ceremonies of the Roman Catholics', is the oldest family document we still have; William signed his name but his bride and both witnesses made their mark with crosses. These folk are not quite in the memory of anyone now living, but some of them were known to people alive until recently. They may not have appreciated it at the time, but all of them lived – like 26 million other British and Irish people – through one of the pivotal years in the nation's history: 1846.

1

Christmas 1845

'The only person fitted to govern the Country.'

QUEEN VICTORIA'S JOURNAL, 20 DECEMBER 1845

In the early afternoon of Saturday, 20 December 1845, Britain's former and future prime minister Sir Robert Peel travelled down to Windsor to meet Queen Victoria. He left Paddington by the 2 p.m. train and was in the royal presence at the castle an hour later: a journey and a punctuality that would have been impossible to imagine only five years earlier, before the railway had reached the town. Not long before, Peel had reluctantly resigned his office when the cabinet threatened to split over repealing the Corn Laws. After the Whig opposition had failed to form a government to replace him, the country was left without leadership for three weeks: a political crisis which only came to an end on that afternoon when Peel agreed to form a new administration. In doing so he probably scarcely imagined that he would precipitate one of the greatest governmental convulsions of the nineteenth century. The decisions he took over the next six months completed a national economic course – free trade – by which successive British governments would be guided for the following century, and inaugurated a policy of cheap food which the country has adopted ever since. But those decisions would split the Tory party Peel led with an acrimony and fury that would last for generations. Statues would be erected to the prime minister who had lowered the cost of bread across the country; but many in the Tory party would revile him as an arch-traitor to their dearest principles.

On that fine but windy afternoon, Peel found the young queen, 26 years old and pregnant with her fifth child, in a lively state of anticipation over whether he would agree to form a new government: 'Our excitement and suspense great,' she wrote in her journal that evening. 'After luncheon we saw Sir Robert Peel, who behaved most nobly and with a courage and devotion for one and the country which prove that he is the only person fitted to govern the Country. All he does is from a sense of duty because he considers it right and not from any party motive.'[1]

She had not always felt that way about Peel. Six years earlier, the queen had strenuously opposed him taking office as a replacement for the elderly Whig prime minister Lord Melbourne, who had been the teenaged queen's mentor during her first two years on the throne. But in the years since Peel had become prime minister in 1841, she had grown increasingly reliant on his advice and judgement, and so his decision to resign at the start of that December had thrown her into consternation. It was a huge relief to her that Lord John Russell, the leader of the opposition Whig party, had been unable (or perhaps just unwilling, given the leisurely way he had been sounding out party colleagues) to form a government instead. Russell had been to visit her that morning to give her the news in person – he had caught the 11 a.m. train – and a *Punch* cartoon would shortly encapsulate the event by showing the diminutive Russell as a uniformed page-boy clutching an oversized top hat being dismissed by the queen with the words: 'I'm afraid you're not strong enough for the place, John.'[2] Russell's party was indeed divided: of his close and powerful colleagues, Lord Palmerston was refusing to take any post other than the Foreign Office, and the young Lord Grey was refusing to serve at all if Palmerston became foreign secretary. But what had worried Victoria was the idea of having to get used both to a new, less congenial prime minister and to some radical reformers sitting on the government benches, such as the Anti-Corn Law League campaigner Richard Cobden. In her journal she wrote:

> At 12 Lord John Russell came and gave us his reasons for definitively declining to form a Govt... he is evidently v. glad not to make any further attempts as the last was so very difficult and he certainly never took the necessary authority over his followers. I feel thankful that all has turned out now as it has and that we have done everything in our power to give them a chance for they would have been driven to extreme opinions which certainly would have caused their downfall. The thought of possibly having Mr Cobden in the government was anything but pleasant.

The immediate cause of the political crisis at Westminster was rotten potatoes in Ireland. That autumn much of the potato crop, on which a large proportion of the Irish peasant population lived, had failed disastrously. It was failing in the rest of the country too and across the Continent, as a fungal blight called Phytophthora infestans spread through Europe in the wake of a wet summer, turning the tubers black and rotting them not only in the ground but even after they had been dug up sound and put into storage. Labourers in the rest of Britain, however, though badly affected, at least had other sources of food, a more varied diet and access as a last resort to local workhouse relief, which was more widespread than in Ireland. There, especially in the rural areas of the south and west, tenant farmers might grow other crops to pay the rent on their meagre smallholdings, but they had nothing else available to eat: about four million people out of a population of eight million ate only knobbly and unappetizing 'Connaught lumpers' – healthy men would consume up to twelve pounds a day each, it was said.[3] Without them, they and their families would starve to death. It was the only crop grown on two million acres of Irish soil. Now a third of the entire crop was turning to slime before the appalled eyes of a peasantry who, as every year, were relying on it to last them through the winter and well into the following summer. There had been blights before, and potatoes always ran short in the hungry months before July when the next crop was ready, but the rapidity with which the blight spread so soon after the harvest meant that a catastrophe was looming.

Word of Irish distress was only gradually seeping through to largely unsympathetic politicians and civil servants in London, men who viewed the Irish as an indolent, ungrateful and alien species ('more like tribes of squalid apes than human beings'[4]), grown idle in their reliance on such a basic crop, which 'foster[s] habits of indolence, improvidence and waste'. Peel was not like that – three decades earlier he had served for six years in Ireland as chief secretary of Lord Liverpool's administration, though he had never been back. Nonetheless, as urgently as he had seen the need to provide relief to the starving peasantry on both sides of the Irish Sea, he also saw the crisis as a prime opportunity to extend an economic policy that his government had already embarked upon: the lifting of tariff barriers on imported goods in order to facilitate free trade and enhance Britain's industrial prosperity to the further advantage of its international economic supremacy. The major remaining barriers to this policy were the Corn Laws, which imposed duties on imported grain and had been intended to protect the crop of home cereal-growing farmers. The tariffs they imposed were complicated and bureaucratic. Introduced by Lord Liverpool's Tory government at the end of the Napoleonic wars to safeguard home agricultural production, their intention was to protect the high price of corn for domestic farmers and landowners, by levying a sliding scale of import duties that were to be imposed if the price of home-grown corn fell below eighty shillings a quarter (a quarter being eight bushels, equivalent to 480 lb or 217 kg). In fact, eighty shillings a quarter was relatively expensive, and in the thirty years following 1815 the price of corn never rose this high, so the tariff on imports was always in place. Peel had already modified the scale in 1842, but the effect had been drastically to increase the cost of the most basic of foods. A single loaf of bread could cost tenpence, nearly a twentieth of the weekly wage of industrial workers and as much as a tenth of the wage of agricultural labourers – the very men who actually harvested the wheat.

Whatever the original motivation, by the 1840s these tariffs were seen as naked class legislation both by many industrial manufacturers and by the rising numbers whose income and prosperity did not come from the land, who thought they favoured the landed class over themselves and their employees. The intellectual tide was with them: most economists now favoured repeal as a step towards freeing trade. As these free-traders saw it, the Corn Laws were keeping prices

– and wages – artificially high and were a government interference with the open market. They were a drag on industry
and the cost of living for the poor: restricting their industri-
ousness, enervating their energies, potentially seducing them
into violent disorder – and on top of that, increasing the
wages they had to be paid. But many of the landed gentry who
supported the Tory party believed very differently: they saw
the Corn Laws as a vital protection for British agriculture and
their own prosperity. Great Whig landowners such as Lord
Palmerston – who also owned land in Ireland – felt the same.
Opposition leader Russell, however, was beginning to see the
tariffs issue as a useful means of dividing the government. This
meant the leadership of both parties was now committed to
repeal. But any change, particularly by a Tory prime minister,
would be politically toxic for his supporters. That Christmas
Tory MPs would be subjected to the full weight of the landed
gentry's fury.

'Rotten potatoes have done it all. They have put Peel in his
damned fright,' snorted the elderly Duke of Wellington, now
approaching his eighties but still a force in Tory politics.[5]
During the autumn Peel had sent scientific advisers to assess
the situation in Ireland and had sanctioned a secret operation,
channelled through Barings Bank so that American corn-
dealers would not be alerted, to buy £100,000 worth of maize
in the US to relieve domestic distress: supplies of sweet corn
that would arrive too late, in too small quantities, and which
the Irish did not know how to cook and did not want to eat.
They called it 'Peel's brimstone' because of its yellow colour.[6]
Back in London, Peel increasingly believed that it was the
Corn Laws that had to be tackled to reduce the cost of food;
a marrying of expedience with necessity – the use of a domestic

crisis to serve a long-term economic goal. What he had proposed to his colleagues in early November 1845 was an emergency reduction of the duty on imported grain, followed by the gradual removal of the tariff over four years: a procedure which was not only going to be cumbersome and bureaucratic, but would actually have little impact on the current crisis and would only aggravate his backbench critics rather than appeasing them. What the cabinet already knew was that he had decided that the Corn Law tariffs must be abolished altogether. Once suspended, they would never be reimposed. There had been straws in the wind for several years as the government had reduced other tariffs on many other food imports, including sugar. The principle of protection was being worn away. Only that spring Peel, sitting on the front bench and listening to Cobden eviscerating the principle of the Corn Laws yet again, had crumpled his notes and turned quietly to his colleague Sidney Herbert sitting beside him, saying: 'You must answer this, for I cannot.'[7]

But when he had broached the plan to phase out the tariffs to his fellow ministers early in November, during a secret cabinet meeting at his home in Whitehall Gardens (where the Ministry of Defence now stands), only three of them supported him. The rest were not happy and the prime minister was soon writing to the queen to warn her that his government might fall. Victoria, much influenced by her husband Prince Albert – himself a political progressive, who was fully supportive of the move towards free trade – sought to stiffen their resolve:

> The Queen thinks the time is come when a removal of the restriction upon the importation of food cannot be successfully resisted. Should this be Sir Robert's own opinion, the

Queen very much hopes that none of his colleagues will prevent him from doing what is right to do.[8]

It was at this point that Russell, alerted by rumours that Peel was planning repeal – and hence that there was a possibility of a government split – seized the initiative and issued a letter from Edinburgh to his constituents in the City of London. It was the most immediate way of making a policy announcement. He stated that he himself had decided that total repeal was the only way. Seeking to ride the tide of popular, urban, public opinion and without bothering to consult his colleagues, Russell stirringly announced:

The corn barometer is pointing to fair while the ship is bending under a storm. I used to be of opinion that corn was an exception to the general rules of political economy but observation and experience have convinced me that we ought to abstain from all interference with the supply of food… Let us, then, unite to put an end to a system which has been proved to be the blight of commerce, the bane of agriculture, the source of bitter divisions among classes, the causes of penury, fever, mortality, and crime among the people… The Government appear to be waiting for some excuse to give up the present Corn Law. Let the people by petition, by address, by remonstrance, afford them the excuse they seek.[9]

Peel was in a spot, in danger of being outflanked and pre-empted. Parliament was not in session, but now that the government was admitting that there was a crisis in Ireland and the opposition was demanding reform, Peel could scarcely do nothing, nor could he defend a tariff he no longer believed in. Gradually, his colleagues were coming round: a Tory government was at all costs better for the country, surely, than a Whig one. The Duke of Wellington stated: 'A good government for the country is more important than the Corn Laws, or any other consideration.' But two influential cabinet members, the Duke of Buccleuch and Lord Stanley, heir to a large part of Lancashire, told Peel that they would have to resign. Unfortunately, they did so on the same day that *The Times* published a scoop damagingly – and, as became clear, wrongly – announcing that the cabinet was unanimously in favour of repeal; Peel had yet to share his planned policy change with his party. With the government in disarray over such a fundamental shift, Peel resigned on 5 December 1845, leaving the way clear for Russell to form a ministry instead. The queen had hoped to send for her old adviser Lord Melbourne – the last occasion on which a British monarch tried choosing her own prime minister – but the old man astutely insisted that he was too ill to cross the sea to the Isle of Wight, where the royal family was inspecting the building of Osborne House, so the job of forming a government had fallen instead to Russell, the Whigs' Commons leader.

A fortnight later, though, and now he was unable to do so. At a time of acute political emergency, with the opportunity to become prime minister and carry free trade to a triumphant conclusion, he found his colleagues squabbling among themselves over which offices they should hold and refusing to serve if they did not get them. Russell, a diminutive figure with a high-pitched voice, had aristocratic influence (he was the younger son of the Duke of Bedford) but not political authority, and stepped back from the chance to govern and from the responsibility for carrying a divisive policy. The crisis could not be allowed to linger longer – if Parliament was to be recalled in January, notice had to be given – and so it was that Peel found himself at Windsor Castle on the Saturday afternoon before Christmas. He had been passed what his keenest Tory backbench critic Benjamin Disraeli felicitously described as the poisoned chalice, but Peel now seized it with relish. That morning, he had summoned his colleagues to a cabinet meeting scheduled for nine o'clock in the evening and, before leaving, penned a rapid note to Wellington: 'I am going to the Queen. I shall tell her at once and without hesitation that I will not abandon her. Whatever may happen, I shall return from Windsor as her Minister.'[10]

He knew what he had to do. The queen wrote in her journal:

He was much affected and excited and evidently indignant at the timid, and I must say shabby conduct of those who would never let Lord John Russell do what is right... He assured me that there was no sacrifice he would not make excepting his honour. This is noble, courageous and I must say chivalrous conduct... For the sake of the Crown and Country – that dear and great country – I pray that Sir Robert may remain at the head of the Government for yet many a year!

Fortified by her support, Sir Robert was on the train just after 4 p.m. and back at Paddington by 5.15. He would not have dissented from the queen's judgement that he was acting in the national interest – whatever the backbench members of his party might believe. He led them, but now he had not been chosen by them. His mood had changed too: energized and emboldened by the crisis and the queen's confidence, there would be no more hesitancy, or consultation. He would not waver like Lord John Russell and retreat from doing what was right, however unpopular it would be with his party. By contrast, that night Russell dined at Palmerston's house. The diarist Charles Greville was also there: 'I never saw people so happy, as most, perhaps all of them, are to have got out of their engagement.'[11]

At his meeting that same evening in Downing Street, Peel told his cabinet colleagues that he would meet Parliament alone if necessary and propose the measures he thought appropriate to deal with the crisis. He was met with silence, broken only when Lord Stanley repeated his dissent: he would support a suspension of the Corn Laws, so long as they were reimposed after the crisis had passed, but otherwise he would not break his word to the party to uphold their continuation. 'We cannot,' he said, 'do this as gentlemen.'[12]

That night, though, it was clear what would happen. The following morning's *Observer* newspaper warned:

> It is idle to blink at the question… with the total repeal of the corn laws the landlords and labourers will be enormous sufferers, the one by the reduction of their property, the other by the deprivation of the field for their labour. The farmers will perhaps suffer even still more for, lying as it were between these two classes they will, like the 'buffers' of a train of steam carriages, have to stand the shock of every collision.

Its editorial writer forecast demonstrations in the streets by disaffected landowners.[13]

There was agitation on the other side, too, and it was powerful. In its next edition, of 24 December, the Wednesday after Peel had resumed office, the bi-weekly *Manchester Guardian* was reporting a packed meeting of the manufacturers and mill owners of the city at the town hall on the previous day, to raise funds for the Million League Fund of the Anti-Corn Law League. The meeting was addressed by Cobden and his fellow MP John Bright, and the list of donations filled a densely typed column, even though the paper would only enumerate gifts of more than £50. Its harassed reporter, probably the editor Jeremiah Garnett, who was a keen supporter of the League, wrote that to list all the donors would fill the paper's space to the exclusion of other pressing news:

> we give every amount we heard announced of £50 and upwards but we found it impossible to write down the names and amounts of numerous subscribers and, from the rapidity with which the chairman read them out, no perfect list exists.[14]

The factory owners of the northern towns were an increasingly powerful and wealthy lobby and their mobilization by the League was focused, effective – and disconcerting to a landed aristocracy used to having its own way.

Stanley's comment in cabinet that evening was a gibe that must have stung, for Peel was acutely aware that his social origins were not as elevated as those of many in the party. He liked to describe himself as the son of a cotton spinner, though in fact his grandfather had built the large family fortune from calico printing in Blackburn, Lancashire. The prime minister was an immensely rich man by any standards: his father had settled more than £300,000 on him during his lifetime and bequeathed him £154,000 when he died in 1830. He owned 9,000 acres of prime agricultural land on the rolling plains of Warwickshire and south Staffordshire and had an annual private income in excess of £40,000: nearly £2.5 million by modern values. His father might have been a baronet – Peel had succeeded to the title too – but the family's status was derived from commerce rather than lineage. Peel himself had never worked in business. He had been raised on the family's Staffordshire country estate at Drayton, near Tamworth, and educated as a gentleman. Harrow had been followed by Christ Church, Oxford, an academic career which culminated in the first double first-class degree, in mathematics and classics, that the university had ever awarded. His political career had been built on administrative diligence and intellectual rigour, and he was disdainful of those in his party who could not follow where his mind led. Colleagues noted that one of Peel's favourite metaphors was drawn from hunting: 'heads see but tails follow.'[15] In an era when many backbench MPs valued their independence and resented party whipping, Peel rather expected his judgement to be respected and obedience to follow. 'The Right Honorable Baronet's horror of slavery,' said Disraeli waspishly, 'extends to every place, except to the benches behind him.'

The Tory backwoodsmen had long been suspicious of him because of his willingness to abandon fundamental party principles when he came to believe that situations had changed. They knew he was the most dominant politician in the country and that there was no one else on their front bench to match him, yet they increasingly resented his power – and now they were growing reckless. First there had been his betrayal of the

Protestant Ascendancy – the belief in Crown and Church that was one of the bedrocks of Toryism – when in the late 1820s he had abruptly switched from opposition to Roman Catholic emancipation to supporting it. Then there had been more betrayals, as they saw it, when Peel's government had reduced the duty on imported sugar, affecting British colonial sugar barons who had been required by a law of 1833 (but only implemented in 1840) to give up the slaves who worked their Caribbean plantations. He had already been tinkering with the Corn Laws in his 1842 budget and that too had increased their unease. Following that, his government had proposed increasing its grant to the Irish Catholic priests' training seminary at Maynooth, outside Dublin. Peel saw this as a means of winning over the Catholic clergy in rural Ireland, but the back-benches believed it was another betrayal of the Protestant Ascendancy. It was a time of extraordinary religious ferment, with the Church of England challenged by evangelicals on one side and beset by noisy conservative churchmen heading Rome-wards on the other. The passionate furore caused by the Maynooth grant, hard to understand today, was affected by a sense among its own backbenchers that the government was itself undermining the state's institutions. Was there no Tory principle he would not abandon? He had promised in 1844 that he had no plans for more changes to the Corn Laws, and now here they were again.

So Peel's plans for repealing the Corn Laws altogether produced resentment, anger and, increasingly that Christmas, fury. Peel really did not appreciate the visceral complaints of those in his party who did not spend their time poring over statistical tables and official reports, but who only knew where they stood on principle:

How can those who spend their time in hunting and shooting and eating and drinking know what were the motives of those who are responsible for the public security, who have access to the best information and have no other object under Heaven but to provide against danger and answer the general interests of all classes?

So he had written to his wife Julia in exasperation a few days before resuming office that December.[16] If they had studied the problems as he had, read up the arguments, commissioned the reports, gathered the facts and analysed them, they would have understood the danger the famine crisis posed to security in Ireland and the risk of violent upheavals in the country as a whole. Free trade would liberate the wealth and potential of the most industrially advanced country in the world. It would enhance the prosperity of its people and secure their contentment. He would explain these advantages carefully, logically, even ponderously – he was not a sparkling speaker – but if they could not see that, there was not much more he could do. He must act in what he saw as the national, not the party, interest. But it was the betrayal they did not like, even more than the policy. As Lord George Bentinck – the most furious of the backbench rebels, an immensely rich Nottinghamshire landowner and son of a duke, who had scarcely spoken during his eighteen years in Parliament and had previously loyally supported Peel – said: 'I keep horses in three counties and they tell me I shall save fifteen hundred a year by free trade, but I don't care for that; what I cannot bear is being sold.'[17]

It was intellect, not sentiment, which drove Peel. He came from the generation that had grown up in the wake of the French Revolution (Peel always read avidly about the subject) and the prolonged upheavals and economic dislocation of the Napoleonic wars – events which had terrified the British landed classes for more than fifty years and were a terrible warning of what might happen to them too. He, like them, had seen quite enough violent disorder at home over the previous decades, but unlike many of them, he no longer believed that repression was enough on its own to quell disturbances. The causes of discontent must also be addressed if it was not to fester and become worse. Not that he believed in appeasement – he was the minister who had introduced a police service in London in 1829, in the teeth of opposition from Tories who believed it was the right of freeborn Englishmen to defend their own property without interference with their liberties from a state police force.

During these decades, there had been political demonstrations put down by force, agricultural and industrial riots punished savagely, and even the assassination of a prime minister – Spencer Perceval, the man who had given Peel his first government job – shot in the lobby of the House of Commons itself in 1812. The queen had also been the target of a series of would-be assassins and Peel's own political secretary had been killed by a deranged assailant who mistook him for the prime minister in 1843. These were febrile times: ruthless cycles of economic prosperity and depressions had seen families impoverished and workers made destitute. There had also been waves of famine and regular epidemics of cholera and typhoid. Perhaps it was no wonder that he sought intellectual solutions to the unprecedented upheavals of a dangerous and burgeoning society, engulfed in rapid industrial and social change. On Sunday, 21 December, the *Observer* newspaper gave more prominent coverage to crime than it did to the political crisis: the murder of Sir Lawrence Jones, Bart. by brigands near Smyrna made the front page, as did an 'appalling' murder in Jersey, the attempted shooting of a gamekeeper at Dunmow and the grievous wounding of PC Turner (Number N210), who had been stabbed with a pig slaughterer's knife when, one dark night the previous week, he attempted to prevent two men stealing a sheep from a field in White Hart Lane, Tottenham. Had Turner's thick leather belt not deflected the blade, the newspaper said, the wound would have been deadly.

Peel, now aged 57, had been the most dominant political figure of the previous fifteen years. Even Disraeli, his keenest critic, remarked that he 'played upon the House of Commons like an old fiddle'. He was the man who had led the Tories back to power in 1841, nine years after the Great Reform Act had been expected to consign them permanently to opposition: a man of fierce intellect, competence and vision, prepared to make a career of politics, as many of his colleagues were not. But he had grown tired in office. The perpetual hard work away from his family, reading those lengthy reports, writing long-hand letters late into the night, relentlessly overseeing every aspect of government – without the aid of particularly competent or dynamic colleagues or a large civil service, decades before the invention of the telephone or typewriter – had begun to wear him down. He was suffering from crippling headaches 'like the noise of boiling water', nosebleeds and gout; he had ear-aches and was becoming deaf – the result of a shotgun blast too close to his ears while out hunting years before; and he was getting plump. These were not conditions likely to make a proud man feel more emollient towards his critics.

Peel knew he had little in common with many of his fellow Tories. He might be respected, but not admired. He was mocked for his provincialism: his Staffordshire accent, his dress sense and his eating habits. 'I was never so struck as yesterday by the vulgarity of Peel,' the diarist Greville had written ten years earlier. 'In all his ways, his dress, his manner, he looks more like a vulgar shopkeeper than a Prime Minister. He eats voraciously and cuts cream and jellies with his knife. [The Earl of] Jersey pointed this out to me. And yet he has genius and taste and his thoughts are not vulgar though his manners are to such a degree.'[18] Disraeli sneered after Peel's death:

> [He] always poot a question and to the last said 'woonderful' and 'woonderfully'. He guarded his aspirates with immense care. I have known him slip. The correctness was not spontaneous. He had managed his elocution like his temper: neither was originally good.[19]

In this, Peel was not alone: in the days before BBC English was broadcast across the land and received pronunciation became standard, many educated men spoke with regional accents. One of them was Peel's ministerial colleague and acolyte William Gladstone, whose recent biographer Roy Jenkins detected a faint Liverpudlian accent in a scratchy early recording made of the old man in the 1880s. Thomas Carlyle was more generous about Peel's voice. It was, he wrote, 'extremely good, low-toned, something of *cooing* in it, rustic, affectionate, honest, suitably persuasive'.

Peel's speaking style was fluent, but not charismatic. *The Times* said in its obituary after his death:

His egotism was proverbial but beside the excessive use of the first person it occasionally betrayed him into performances at variance both with prudence and taste... His style of speaking was admirably adapted for its purpose, for it was luminous and methodical, while his powerful voice and emphatic delivery gave almost too much assistance to his language, for it was apt to be redundant and commonplace. He had not the strong simplicity of expression which is almost a tradition of the old Whig school.[20]

Peel had never been gregarious. He was a shy man, despite decades in politics. Acquaintances had always found him cold; his smile, as the Irish politician Daniel O'Connell had famously once said, was like the silver plate on a coffin. Chilly, then, to those outside his family circle: for inside it he was a loving husband and doting father, and was warm and sardonic with his closest and most loyal friends. But he was also touchy, and sensitive of slights, unwilling to be mocked and unable to bend or conciliate. These were not attributes that would help him to win over the Tory party as he provoked its anger with his plans for the Corn Laws.

Peel did not like having his portrait painted and was dissatisfied with the results, which was curious for a man who built his own picture gallery at Drayton Manor and filled it with enormous paintings that he had commissioned of his contemporaries. Those paintings of Peel that were made were stiff and formal – the best of them, by John Linnell, strangely tentative; but they show a tall, handsome man with auburn hair, an aquiline nose and wary eyes. *The Times* described him as 'that tall, fair-haired, somewhat parrot-faced gentleman' and he was regularly caricatured in magazines such as *Punch*.[21]

But sadly, Peel seems to have turned down a request to have a daguerreotype portrait made in July 1846, so he remains the last prime minister not to have been photographed and – because we cannot quite see him (unlike many of his contemporaries) exactly as he was – he remains a figure from a distant, pre-modern age.[22]

∽

On the day that Peel travelled down to Windsor, one of the most keenly awaited books of the year was published. Charles Dickens's latest annual Christmas offering, *The Cricket on the Hearth*, which the author had only finished writing three weeks before, was not a patch on *A Christmas Carol*, published two years earlier – Dickens was finding it a strain to keep up the standard – but it still sold out, all 16,500 copies, within a fortnight: more quickly than the *Carol* had done in 1843. The story was preposterous and is now little read, but in an early example of cross-media marketing, it was helped along by immediate stage adaptations – the first at the Lyceum theatre in London on the day of publication and a further sixteen within a month.[23]

Reviews were mainly favourable. That weekend's *Observer* gave it four close-printed columns: 'his songs be as welcome to the hearths and homes of merry England as is the genial season of festivity which they usher in so gracefully'. There was just one notable dissenter. *The Times* described the book as 'a twaddling manifestation of silliness' – a judgement which later literary criticism has shared – but at the time that could easily be discounted because Dickens's considerable energies were absorbed that Christmas with the imminent prospect of editing a new rival paper in the New Year. The *Daily News*

– 'Liberal Politics and thorough Independence' – was to be the author's new plaything and mouthpiece, for which he would be paid £2,000 a year, more than any other editor except John Thaddeus Delane of *The Times*. He had been busy recruiting staff, including his improvident father John Dickens, who had been placed in charge of the reporters – a surprisingly successful appointment as it turned out and one that would long outlast his son's editorship. Peel's reappearance in the Commons in the New Year coincided with the first edition of the *Daily News*, and Dickens senior promptly took off for the West Country to distribute copies – to Exeter, Plymouth and back to London, all in a day. This was a feat made possible by the railway, and necessary because *The Times* had refused advertising for the new publication and blocked co-operation on distribution of the paper as well as the shared use of foreign freelance correspondents. Within three weeks of the paper's first appearance, though, Charles Dickens had decided that the daily grind of putting out a newspaper was not for him and had resigned. He would spend much of the year to come abroad in Switzerland and France, writing the draft of what would become his seventh novel, *Dombey and Son*.[24]

In Yorkshire that Christmas, other authors were also at work. In Haworth parsonage, the Brontë sisters were finalizing a selection of their own poems, which Charlotte was planning to send off for publication in the spring. On 2 January 1846, Emily wrote (and dated) her poem 'No Coward Soul is Mine': 'I see Heaven's glories shine/ And Faith shines equal arming me from Fear.' Later that month, Charlotte would write to the London publishers Aylott and Jones asking for an estimate of the cost of printing an octavo volume of 200 to 250 pages 'of the same quality of paper and size of type as Moxon's last edition of Wordsworth'.[25] They had spent some of the autumn choosing their pseudonyms: Charlotte was Currer Bell – after a local philanthropist – Emily, Ellis Bell and Anne, Acton Bell, their surname the middle name of their father's curate, Charlotte's future husband. The sisters would scrape together £31.10s to pay the cost of the poems' publication but, despite reasonable reviews, in the first year only two copies were sold. That winter, they also settled down to start writing *The Professor*, *Wuthering Heights* and *Agnes Grey* and caring for their brother Branwell, sunk deep in alcoholism. Charlotte would write *Jane Eyre* the following summer. It was to be an extraordinary literary year: R.S. Surtees was filling the gaps between hunting, shooting and fishing with his literary efforts, Mrs Gaskell was busy writing, and in 1846 Edward Lear would publish his nonsense poems as well.

∽

In Kent that December, Charles Darwin was enjoying 'raging discussions' with his friends at his home in the village of Down. The botanist Joseph Hooker came and brought with him a group of young naturalists and palaeontologists, including Edward Forbes, a geologist, who had an interesting theory about a sunken continent that might explain how plants of the same species had originally spread across the world. Darwin was astonished by the magnitude of the idea – an appallingly bold step 'to sink into the depths of the ocean within the period of existing species so large a tract of surface'. Others in the group were just as sceptical of Darwin's own developing thoughts on the transmutation of plants and animals: Hooker 'aloof from all speculation on the origin of species', still supporting 'the old assumption that each species has one origin [and] is immutable'. Forbes himself did not believe that the fossil record showed that animals evolved; any that did must do so because of God's will. This was not what Darwin wanted to hear. In the New Year, though, he would give five pounds towards the renovation of the local parish church and start to worry that the potato blight might have reached his own crop. The disease was, he thought, 'a painfully interesting subject'. In 1846 the Darwins would draw in their not inconsiderable resources and attempt to live on a thousand pounds a year, while still being 'as rich as Jews'; but they presumably did not need to economize as much as their handyman who, paid twelve shillings a week, was having to find an extra shilling out of that to pay for the rising cost of food for his family .[26]

*

Far away across the Atlantic, north of the Canadian mainland, two Royal Navy ships, the *Erebus* and the *Terror*, were spending the long Arctic winter at anchor, stuck in the ice and darkness off the south shore of Devon Island, to the west of Baffin Bay. They held the naval party led by Sir John Franklin, which had set out from Greenwich the previous May on an expedition to find a way at last through the Northwest Passage, which might open a route to the Pacific. The two sailing ships had been on a previous expedition here, but this time, to strengthen their chances, they were equipped with railway steam-engines to provide extra power and the latest screw propellers, as well as every modern convenience. The 134 men in the two crews had access to libraries with more than two thousand books. Each ship had a hand organ which could play fifty tunes automatically, including hymns. The officers had mahogany writing desks and there were instruments for making geological, botanical, zoological and magnetic observations. Before they left London, the *Illustrated London News* had written: 'The arrangements made for the comfort of the crews are excellent. The quantity of stores taken aboard is considerable.' There was tea and rum, 909 litres of wine for the sick, 4,287 kilograms of chocolate, 3,215 kilograms of tobacco and 4,200 kilograms of lemon juice. On board, for the first time on an expedition, there was also a daguerreotype camera to record the trip. It may have been the one which was used to take photographs of the officers shortly before their departure. Their ghostly faces peer out hauntingly from their portraits, now preserved in the National Maritime Museum at Greenwich, for these men would never again be seen by their fellow countrymen. Over the course of the next few years, they would all die agonizing and lonely deaths in the Arctic from starvation, exposure, disease, maybe cannibalism and, possibly, lead poisoning from the seals on the tins of food – another innovation – that the expedition had taken with them. Franklin himself, dressed in his rear admiral's uniform, complete with shiny buttons, decorations, epaulettes and a cocked hat, looks tired and distracted in his picture: a man, then aged 59, too old and unfit for the voyage, yet desperate to make it as his last chance for glory. His much younger fellow officers, Francis Crozier and James Fitzjames, look like the sort of ebullient young men you might meet in the bar of a rugby club on a Saturday night, were it not for their high winged collars and the black stocks tightly wound around their necks.[27]

During the voyage across the Atlantic a few weeks later, Franklin wrote a last letter to his wife: 'Let me now assure you, my dearest Jane, that I am amply provided with every requisite for my passage and I am entering on my voyage comforted with every hope of God's merciful guidance and protection.' He wrote also of the happiness he felt in his officers, crew and ship. Fitzjames himself wrote home: 'We are very happy and very fond of Sir John.' These were their last known messages. The letters were passed, along with five crew members who were already too ill to go further, to the crew of a transport vessel, the *Barretto Junior*, which had accompanied the expedition as far as Greenland. And with that the *Erebus* and *Terror* passed from view, heading west.[28]

By that Christmas one of the sailors on board the *Terror* was dying. We know, because the grave of Petty Officer John Torrington, together with those of two other early casualties of the expedition, was later found on Beechey Island, a small spit of gravel off Devon Island. They were the lucky ones: only scattered bones and remnants of equipment were ever discovered of the rest, including Franklin, Fitzjames and Crozier. When the three graves were excavated in the 1980s, the men's bodies were found perfectly preserved by the permafrost, still dressed in their uniforms, arms bound to their sides, jaws clamped by spotted neckerchiefs wound around their heads by a ship's undertaker, their eyes open, hair tousled and teeth bared. Torrington was a 20-year-old Mancunian, a slight, short man, not at all a burly sailor: just five feet four inches tall and no more than six stone in weight, with delicate features and long, clean, tapering fingers. He had died first, on 1 January 1846, and the autopsy that was carried out 138 years later showed his death had been caused by the effects of tuberculosis and pneumonia, exacerbated by lead poisoning. He had been taken on as a stoker, but his condition would have meant he had never been fit for that work, and he must have retired to his hammock quite soon after the ships left behind the last whaling vessels they had passed the previous summer – his last chance of being saved. By Christmas, Torrington would have been very sick indeed, probably suffering from delirium and mood swings, malnourished and feverish. When he died on New Year's Day, the crew were able at least to provide him with a wool-lined coffin and a tin plaque inscribed with his name, age and date of death. Why had he ever tried to go to sea and why was he picked for one of the most physically demanding jobs on board? Had it been the economic conditions at home? Had he wanted to escape Manchester and discover adventure? He found an isolated grave on a distant, barren shore instead.

༄

Back in London, Peel was feeling reinvigorated. 'It is a strange dream,' he wrote to his friend Princess Lieven. 'I feel like a man restored to life after his funeral service has been preached.' Prince Albert had discussed the developing political situation with him on Christmas Eve and wrote a memorandum afterwards:

> Sir Robert has an immense scheme in view; he thinks he shall be able to remove the contest entirely from the dangerous ground upon which it has got – that of a war between the manufacturers, the hungry and the poor against the landed proprietors, the aristocracy, which can only end in the ruin of the latter... He will deal with the whole commercial system of the country... removing all protection and abolishing all monopoly, but not in favour of one class and as

a triumph over another, but to the benefit of the nation, farmers as well as manufacturers.[29]

Peel was, for the moment, the subject of public acclaim for shouldering the burden of responsibility for handling the crisis. Sir Thomas Lethbridge, a Somerset landowner who was nonetheless an enthusiastic free-trader, wrote to the prime minister early in the New Year: 'Land, money and trade are all calling upon you. The great body of the people are ready for this Immense Change and you are the only Person in Existence that can do it.'[30] *The Times* also breathed a sigh of relief: 'Sir Robert Peel is minister again and the nation is reassured. The funds rise and manufacturers feel a little more encouragement to add to their stocks.'[31]

That Christmas night the businessmen of Manchester took their wives and families to the advertised performance of excerpts from Haydn's *Creation* and Handel's *Messiah* with 'upwards of 500 performers' at the Free Trade Hall. There were special late trains afterwards to take them back home to Rochdale, Oldham and Todmorden at 10 p.m. and Stockport at 11: 'all parties carried by one fare only'.

On the last evening of the old year, the queen mourned the loss of her pink and grey pet parrot, which had just died, but added that she had had a two-hour meeting with Sir Robert that day:

The sudden rise in the stocks is a sure and evident proof of the confidence in the government and from all sides (including Uncle Leopold* and the king of the French) we

* King of the Belgians.

receive letters of satisfaction. I have to thank God for so many blessings vouchsafed to us. We are well and our children are particularly flourishing. Most humbly, fervently and most confidently do I pray for the continuance of our great happiness.[32]

But the country would be very far from happy in 1846.

2
The Condition of England

> 'Two nations between whom there is no intercourse
> and no sympathy; who are as ignorant of each other's
> habits, thoughts and feelings as if they were dwellers
> in different zones or inhabitants of different planets;
> who are formed of different breeding, are fed by
> different food, and are ordered by different manners
> and are not governed by the same laws.'
>
> BENJAMIN DISRAELI, *Sybil* (1845), BOOK 2, CHAPTER 5

We can tell, dimly, what Britain looked like in the mid-1840s from the very earliest photographs which were taken during that period, shortly after the invention of the daguerreotype. The tiny pictures, whose images were reflected on copper plates coated with light-sensitive silver plating and iodine and then fixed with salt water, have a luminous, crystal, mirror-like clarity as they catch the light. It is like looking into a glass, darkly. They show immovable objects such as buildings and places better than moving people because of the time taken for the exposure. But even the tiny figures in the landscapes demonstrate how they dressed and held themselves. In the earliest picture known to have been taken in London, a view from Trafalgar Square looking down Whitehall, made by a Frenchman called de St Croix in the autumn of 1839, the buildings are easily recognizable, as is Le Sueur's equestrian statue of Charles I, which still stands there.[1] But this and other pictures

– Fox Talbot's calotypes (slightly fuzzier, but an improvement since views could be duplicated and printed on paper) of scenes around Westminster from the mid-1840s – show a grimy place with dirt-covered streets, blackened walls and a smoky atmosphere, making the sky look hazy. The people caught accidentally by the exposures are blurry, small and distant – top hats can be made out, and crinolines. Fox Talbot took pictures of his colleagues and of workers on the family estate in their waistcoats on sunny days at Lacock in Wiltshire. In Edinburgh at the same time, the painter David Octavius Hill and his young colleague Robert Adamson were setting up a photographic studio to take calotype portraits of Scottish worthies, but they were also carrying their camera equipment out of doors to make images of ordinary people on sunny days: soldiers at the castle and the fishermen of Newhaven and their wives, who gutted the catch and then hauled the fish in creel baskets up the hill to sell in the city.[2] The photographers' partnership was ended by Adamson's early death at the age of 26 in 1848, but by then they had taken at least 2,000 photographs. There is no shortage of imagery allowing us to stare the people of the 1840s squarely in the face, before ever getting to the paintings and illustrations of the era.

What the pictures cannot show, of course, is the smell of the period, which is probably the first thing that would strike a modern person who had somehow been transported back 170 years: a pungent mix of horse droppings and rotting refuse from the streets and coal smoke from thousands of chimneys above, or the sour odour of people with inadequate washing facilities and stale clothing. Nor can they show the relative darkness after nightfall of a land without electric or neon lighting. The streets of London and the main thoroughfares of other towns and cities were by now lit with gas – a much dimmer light than we are used to these days – but most private homes were not, and candles were still the form of lighting that illuminated rooms in the evenings. In 1846 the Canadian geologist and doctor Abraham Gesner invented kerosene – the mixture of coal, bitumen and oil shale, known as paraffin in Britain, that would soon be used in lamps to give a brighter light – but that was a decade or so away from domestic use.

The first photographs not only symbolize a new invention in an age bursting with innovations, enabling future generations to see directly what the country and its people looked like then and forever afterwards, but they also catch a country on the edge of modernity, in rapid transition from an older, largely agrarian society to a modern, urban and industrial one. This was the decade when railway lines spread rapidly, and migration from the countryside to find work in towns and cities accelerated. When the 1851 census of Britain was taken, it recorded that for the first time more people were living in towns and cities than in the countryside: just over half the population, compared with about a third fifty years earlier. The total size of that population had doubled since the start of the century – from 13 million to 26 million (less than half the current population size) – and during the 1840s alone it increased by about 10 per cent, even taking into account the sudden decline in the population of Ireland following the famine.[3]

In this rapidly urbanizing society, London was the biggest city in the world, reaching 2.5 million in 1846 – a doubling in size over the previous fifty years, making it two-and-a-half times larger than Paris, the next biggest European capital. Many of the manufacturing towns of the North of England and Midlands were also experiencing exponential growth in these years. Sometimes they were towns that had scarcely existed fifty years before, or small settlements which took off with the arrival of industry: Bradford's population in 1801 was 13,000 and by 1851 had reached 104,000; Manchester – which had only been incorporated as a borough in 1838 – saw its 75,000 inhabitants increase to 303,000 in the same half-century; Birmingham's 71,000 turned into 233,000.[4] This was a population which was not just expanding, but was on the move from its roots: the 1851 census, which recorded birthplaces for the first time, reported that 'in almost all the great towns the migrants from elsewhere outnumbered the people born in the town'. It was a young population too: 60 per cent of the country was under the age of 24 during the first half of the nineteenth century.

Life for those left in the country was harsh and primitive, in thrall socially and sometimes financially to the local squire or landowner, who could dictate the terms of life and liveli-hood. But the factory jobs in town offered little improvement: marginally better paid and more regular, maybe, but arduous, repetitive and dangerous, with long hours and often squalid living conditions. In the country, working hours were still governed by the hours of daylight and by the amount of work available seasonally; but factories needed to operate perma-nently to a different timetable. Hence strict disciplines were introduced into the workplace to inculcate punctuality in employees who lacked watches and were unused to keeping to time. This was why lateness or absence was severely punished and the most prominent features on the factory building were usually a clock and a bell.

Life expectancy, though improving, was poor, especially in the towns: in rural Rutland in 1842, the gentry might expect to live to the age of 52, tradesmen to 41 and labourers to 38; in Derby to 49, 38 and 21 respectively; and in Manchester to 38, 20 and 17. Young labourers in Bethnal Green at this time were dying on average aged only 16 and in Liverpool at 15.[5] * Overall, life expectancy in 1841 was about 40 years. In the cities, death rates had shot up during the intense industrialization of the 1830s: in Birmingham from 14.6 per 1,000 to 27.2 in the ten years between censuses, in Liverpool from 21 to 34.8, and in Bristol from 16.9 to 31.[6] The Victorians measured such things punctiliously.

By the early 1840s what old infrastructures there were in towns were buckling under the strains caused by rapid expansion. The new buildings thrown up to cater for the increasing urban population were basic and jerry-built. A succession of foreign visitors were impressed by the manufacturing energy and productivity, which often made them gasp, but appalled by the living conditions, filth and poverty. Here is Léon Faucher, a French journalist, writing after being shown around the slums of Liverpool under the protection of a policeman in 1844:

Imagine a sort of hole dug in the ground, between ten and twelve feet square, and often less than six feet high, so that it is difficult for a grown man to stand upright. These holes do not have windows; air and light come in only through the door, the top part of which is generally at street level. You go down as if into a pit, by a ladder or an almost vertical staircase. Water, dust and mud accumulate at the bottom. Since the floor is rarely paved and since no form of

* Life expectancy figures were seriously skewed by horrendous infant mortality rates: if you lived past early childhood there was a reasonable chance of lasting to 40.

ventilation is possible, it is perpetually dank and humid. In some places the cellar has two compartments, the second of which, normally used as a bedroom, only gets light through the first. Every cellar is lived in by three, four or five people.[7]

The same year, the German traveller J.G. Kohl stood on the banks of the Irwell in Manchester:

What an extraordinary spectacle! There stand rows and groups of huge manufactories, each consisting of numerous buildings which are sometimes bound together by one surrounding wall... See how eagerly these manufactories suck up through pumps and buckets the river water, which dirty as it is, is invaluable to them and which they pour back into the river in black, brown and yellow currents after it has served their purposes... The blue heavens above are hidden from us by the thick smoke of the huge factory chimneys which weave a close, impenetrable veil of brown fog between the city and the sky... The great establishments are built in various ways; some piled storey on storey, others on the straight line system in long successive rows; others like huge greenhouses, all on one floor lighted from the top. From these huge and oddly shaped buildings rise immense chimneys of all heights and diameters, many as tall as the steeples of St. Paul's and St. Stephen's and sometimes architecturally ornamented with stone garlands, bas-reliefs and pedestals... In the neighbourhood are seen the dwelling places of the work people, mean-looking little buildings, huddled in rows and clusters... These quarters are the most melancholy and disagreeable parts of the town, squalid, filthy and miserable to a deplorable degree. Here stand the abominable beerhouses, dram shops and gin palaces which are never without customers. Here the streets are filled with ragged women and naked children.[8]

In such slums the poor dwelt among excrement, overflowing from inadequate drains and open sewers and settling inches deep in basement rooms where families lived. Above ground, men employed to cart the waste away either dumped it in the nearest river or stream, or left it in great festering piles in the streets next to the tenements of the poor.

An even greater horror was the city burial grounds, where corpse had been piled on corpse for decades and barely covered over. The grisly details were exposed by George Walker, a London surgeon who became a campaigner for reform and whose 1839 book *Gatherings from Grave Yards* disclosed the abuses in the starkest terms. Municipal cemeteries presented an obvious solution to the problem, but they were opposed by both the Church of England clergy, who objected to the potential loss of burial fees, and the speculators building private cemeteries. Walker, with his earnestness and resolution to secure reform, year after year in the face of the inertia of these vested interests, became an archetypal Victorian lobbyist, though his name is little remembered today. Some churchyards rose up above the surrounding basements as more bodies were crowded in: Bunhill Fields in London had 100,000 corpses buried in four acres. The Church of England opposed reforms which would set up separate cemeteries away from its premises and so its city churchyards were bursting open. St Anne's, Soho, 'overlooked by houses thickly inhabited', had rotten coffin wood and fragments of bone lying about at ground level, and at St Giles-in-the-Fields partially decayed bodies still with flesh on the bones and human heads with hair attached could be seen on the surface. Gravediggers hacked through the coffins of recently deceased children to make way for more, and at the Enon Baptist Chapel on Clement's Lane, between the Strand and Holborn, Sunday school children told of clouds of winged insects rising from the graveyard and crawling all over the building in hot weather.[9]

These stories were replicated in many cities, but such areas existed alongside new buildings bursting with opulence and civic pride. The great classical edifice of Liverpool's St George's Hall was being built in the 1840s at the same time as Faucher was touring the city's slums – whose inhabitants were probably among those doing the building – and Birmingham's town hall, constructed along similar lines, in imitation of the Parthenon of ancient Greece, was also newly opened. Soon the cities of the North would be competing with each other for the erection of ever grander, larger, more imposing civic buildings. The noble, spec-built middle-class houses of the Regency period, the suburban villas designed by Decimus Burton and built by Thomas Cubitt, which still survive and give us a picture of nineteenth-century gracious living, were also being thrown up at this time, many of them with inadequate sanitation. The water supply even to these houses was intermittent and polluted and only a third of the properties in London were connected to the sewers at all. The drains were so badly constructed that the water often failed to run off and was left to stagnate in the pipes, or flood neighbouring basements.

It was another German visitor, Friedrich Engels, sent to Manchester from Düsseldorf in 1842 to spend time at a branch of his family company's cotton mills, on whom the industrial behemoth had its most profound and lasting effect.

He went home after two years, aged 24, to write his polemic *The Condition of the Working Class in England*, armed with copious notes, cuttings from the *Manchester Guardian* and a burning sense of the injustice of the economic woes that bore down on the labouring population:

> I wanted to see you in your own homes, to observe you in your everyday life, to chat with you on your condition and grievances... I have done so: I forsook the company and the dinner parties, the port wine and champagne of the middle classes and devoted my leisure hours almost exclusively to the intercourse with plain Working Men... you are right, perfectly right in expecting no help whatever from [the middle classes]. Their interest is diametrically opposed to yours... the middle classes intend in reality nothing else but to enrich themselves by your labour.

He contrasted the supposed pre-industrial life of skilled craftsmen, working with their families at home – 'a passably comfortable existence, leading a righteous and peaceful life' – with the economic competition and industrial grind which had worn them down. He said it had set class against class and locally born workers against Irish immigrants, who lived in even worse squalor than they did:

> the most horrible spot... lies... immediately south-west of Oxford Road and is known as Little Ireland... the race that lives in these ruinous cottages, behind broken windows, mended with oilskin, sprung doors and rotten door posts, or in dark, wet cellars, in measureless filth and stench, in

this atmosphere penned in as if with a purpose, this race must really have reached the lowest stages of humanity.[10]

More modern research suggests Engels was wrong, perhaps even racist, about that, succumbing to a traditional English prejudice. Even if their living conditions were dreadful, Irish immigrants were better educated and fitter than the English slum-dwellers who despised them and more enterprising than those who remained back home.

The working class was not one organic whole. There were also tradesmen and skilled artisans, many mobilizing to support the Chartist movement which was campaigning for political reform in the 1840s. They wanted not to overturn the parliamentary system – as the landed classes feared – but to be given the chance to have their, exclusively male, say in it: to vote in elections by secret ballot, safe from intimidation. Some of these and many others had turned to religion – evangelical denominations and sects were expanding, splitting, reforming and competing for both members and respectability – and they also joined the co-operative friendly societies, committed to mutual help.

The middle classes were also expanding. By the 1840s perhaps a million people could count themselves members of what would later be considered white-collar professions, although they were only a fifth of the numbers in labouring, agricultural or domestic service jobs. In cities such as London there were increasing numbers of clerks scratching away at ledgers in banks, counting houses, offices and law firms, in tedious secretarial jobs, adding lists of numbers, copying letters, legal documents and contracts in neat, copperplate longhand: men like Bob Cratchit in Dickens's *A Christmas*

Carol, who beavered away for fifteen shillings a week – though he was significantly underpaid, for clerks could expect upwards of £60 a year. The 1851 census would record 44,000 clerks, a number that would increase to 67,000 ten years later. Higher up the ladder, the professions were expanding too and establishing their own guilds and professional associations: the Law Society in 1843, the Institute of Mechanical Engineers in 1847, and more would follow in the years to come. These were bodies which would come to set their own entry standards and qualifications, and a man might rise in them (only men, of course) and through diligence, application and luck become wealthy and honoured – or, occasionally, disgraced. A clerk at the Bank of England in 1844 would be paid £100 a year by the age of 21, rising by £10 increments every year to a maximum of £250 (for comparison, the governor of the Bank received £400 a year and the directors £300). For this, a bank clerk's working hours were from 9 a.m. to 3.30 p.m., or until 5 p.m. with one-and-a-half hours for lunch. They might be sacked for being 'a smoking, singing, public house man' even outside working hours, but in 1845 the directors ordained that they might qualify for between six and eighteen days' annual holiday depending on seniority; the following year they were also banned from smoking cigars at work. When in 1844 one clerk, William Burgess, embezzled £8,000 from a client's account, he fled to Boston, was brought back from the US and sentenced to transportation for life.[11]

In every town and village there were small businesses: maybe 600,000 small shopkeepers and street sellers, servicing a middle-class population increasing in affluence, albeit sometimes precariously and without many checks and balances to limit the risks they were taking. New industries such as insurance and advertising were expanding fast, and there were opportunities for investing one's savings in railway shares and speculative schemes that could collapse as quickly as they inflated, thrusting aspiring families back down the ladder to penury as fast as they had risen.

Each morning and evening, the army of Bob Cratchits, from Islington, Pentonville and Hackney, would trudge to and from the City, while the professional men with families would catch the omnibus further out, from Bayswater, Brixton and Clapham. At home, their wives would employ housemaids to do the laborious and menial drudgery. Their houses were filling up with furniture and knick-knacks, symbols of status and prosperity: not just the necessities of life, but fripperies as well, such as pianos and wallpaper (often a fashionable green and accordingly laced with arsenic, which would give them headaches, make them sick and occasionally kill them). To furnish their aspirations they could draw inspiration from an increasing number of magazines and periodicals, all empha-sizing the virtues of home and family. But most of them did not own their own homes: perhaps 10 per cent of houses were owner-occupied, the rest being rented.[12] It was a society on the move, onwards and upwards.

And, whatever the indignant young Engels thought, not all the middle classes were ignoring the plight of the workers. They could hardly avoid them, living nearly cheek by jowl as many of them did, suffering from the same pollution, the same stinks, the same dirty water, and the same diseases and epidemics. These were huddled towns and cities. When Charles Dickens wrote *Oliver Twist* in 1836 and 1837, he was living in Doughty Street, near Holborn, in a comfortably middle-class area, with the barristers' garden at Gray's Inn at the end of the road. But in imagining Fagin's den of thieves and criminals, he placed it in Ray Street, just a few hundred yards and a ten-minute walk away, in Clerkenwell. By now, however, the professional and middle classes were seeking to escape: Dickens's worthy characters headed out to Camden Town, Islington and Hampstead north of the river and Walworth south of it to see their 'Aged P.' (as John Wemmick did in *Great Expectations*), or to go home to their wives and children. It was said of the Manchester middle classes that they 'reside chiefly in the open spaces of Cheetham, Broughton and Chorlton' – and who could blame them, considering the state of the nearby slums? William Cooke Taylor, in his *Notes of a Tour in the Manufacturing Districts of Lancashire* in 1842, had written:

> We have improved on the proverb, 'One half of the world does not know how the other half lives', changing it into 'One half of the world does not care how the other half lives.' Ardwick knows less about Ancoats than it does about China.[13]

But the middle class could not escape the cholera epidemics that erupted spasmodically from the early 1830s – the outbreak of 1832 expunged 18,000 people and the disease's return in 1848–9 would kill a further 53,000 in England and Wales – or the more endemic typhoid. Such frighteningly lethal illnesses were unpredictable in their arrival, spared no one rich or poor, were untreatable and could kill within hours. Charles Greville remembered Mrs Smith, the daughter of Lord Forrester, married to the heir of Lord Carrington:

young and beautiful, was dressed to go to church on Sunday morning, seized with the disorder, never had a chance of rallying and died at eleven at night... the dread of cholera absorbs everybody.[14]

Then there was the Earl of Clarendon's maid, who was eating gooseberry fool one evening and being carried off in a sealed coffin the following morning. Visit almost any Victorian town cemetery or church graveyard today and, amongst the grand tombs and mouldering statuary, you are likely to see poignant memorials to husbands and wives, children and babies lost to fevers, sometimes in quick succession, within weeks. Most believed that infection arose from miasmas emerging like mist from the ground, others that God had targeted the dissolute to teach them a lesson, though that was hard to sustain if one's children had died. The wrath of the Almighty was an evangelical creed so harsh that ultimately people recoiled from it. Alternatively, the protectionists, who were opposed to free trade, tended to think foreigners were to blame for spreading epidemics. Whatever the cause, reformers appreciated that disease had to be tackled, if only in the interests of economic efficiency: a debilitated workforce was an unproductive one.

And, if there was ignorance of the plight of the deserving, or undeserving, poor, it was not from want of being told. Dickens's early novels are full of comparisons between the rich and impoverished in his society. Reporters such as Cooke Taylor and James Kay wrote up their eye-witness reports in book-length detail and a succession of 'Condition of England' or 'purpose' novels were published through the decade. These were works like Mrs Gaskell's *Mary Barton*, written following the death of her baby son from scarlet fever in 1845, or Disraeli's *Sybil*, from which the famous 'two nations' reference is taken. All pointed up a fractious divided society.

There was poetry too: Caroline Norton's *A Voice from the Factories* and most famously Thomas Hood's 'Song of the Shirt' of 1843, first printed in *Punch*, about the plight of seamstresses:

> Work — work — work!
> My labour never flags;
> And what are its wages? A bed of straw,
> A crust of bread — and rags.
> That shattered roof — this naked floor —
> A table — a broken chair —
> And a wall so blank, my shadow I thank
> For sometimes falling there!
> ...
> Stitch! stitch! stitch!
> In poverty, hunger, and dirt,
> And still with a voice of dolorous pitch, —
> Would that its tone could reach the Rich! —
> She sang this 'Song of the Shirt!'[15]

This was from the magazine's early, radical phase in the decade following its launch in 1841, before it became complacent and respectable. A cartoon from 1846 catches the tone. It shows a poor but respectable woman with her painfully thin and evidently ailing daughter on a visit to a surgery, with the plump, well-dressed doctor patting the child on the head, saying as he does so: 'You must give her plenty of nice puddings, some calves' foot jelly – a little wine – a fowl or two

– take her to the seaside and, if possible, go with her to Baden Baden.'[16] The punchline is a little ponderous for modern tastes, perhaps, but the meaning is clear: such remedies were far beyond the family's capabilities.

Talk of class in the absolutist Engels sense was a new phenomenon in the 1840s (of course *The Condition of the Working Class in England* did not receive an English translation for more than forty years). The 'masses' and the middle class were not of one mind, or sensibility. The northern cotton manufacturers who flocked to meetings organized by the Anti-Corn Law League were among those most resistant to legislative attempts to limit the hours of child labour or improve factory conditions, on the grounds that this was an interference with their individual liberty and their workers' free will. There were clear gradations in their society, just as there were among the working classes.

The factory owners' fiercest persecutor was an evangelical Tory aristocrat, Lord Ashley, later Lord Shaftesbury, a man who, although now remembered as one of the great Victorian social reformers, was a prickly and self-righteous opponent. Ashley's disgust at what he called 'the Millocracy' seemed sometimes to verge on class hatred. He thought that they and their factories were deeply subversive of the social order – that they were exploitative of the workers, unlike paternalistic aristocrats such as himself – and inimical to Christianity. However evangelical the mill owners' roots were, he suspected them of promoting godlessness, if not popery. Before taking up the cause of improving working conditions, Ashley, whose wealth came from large family estates in Dorset, had never been near a factory in his life. His crusade at least partially had the aim of uniting the two Englands, of the aristocracy and the underclass, in a paternalistic compact against the millocrats. As he wrote in 1841: 'I have done much in hope to conciliate the landed gentry in [the mill workers'] behalf and approximate the parties who have common interests and "tell it not in Gath", a common enemy, the mill owner! He is the Jacobin of commerce.'[17] The element of retaliation – against Ashley and others who thought like him – in the Anti-Corn Law League's rhetoric and campaigning was inevitable.

In the 1840s the prolonged battle to improve working conditions, started in the 1820s, was beginning to obtain results. This was a raw struggle at the heart of the Industrial Revolution, between old ways of doing things – families had worked down mines or in craft industries for centuries – and new concerns for workers' moral welfare. It was between laissez-faire capitalism and supposed economic freedom, and the conviction that society could be ordered better. And it was also between the traditional, local administration of society, through the parish or the squire, and the sense that national rules laid down by government were now needed to combat abuse and direct the nation in a more orderly way. Over a period of twenty years cotton-spinning factories – where children scampered dangerously between the machinery clearing threads and unblocking tangles for twelve hours a day, risking life and injury for little money, no offer of education and precious little leisure – came to be regulated by the imposition of legal controls and inspections. These were nowhere remotely near what we would recognize as adequate or even particularly effective today, but they were remarkable for their time: a recognition by government for the first time that national regulations had to be established to control working conditions. There was an economic argument for this, to improve efficiency and order and prevent good employers being undercut by bad ones, but there was also a pre-eminent moral purpose, deployed by Ashley and others. This was to improve the way people lived, and to make them more responsive to God. Thus, in 1842, the Mines Act prohibited women and children from going underground, partly because of the sense that this was not a suitable industry for them to work in, but more pressingly because the nation had been shocked by reports of women colliers working semi-naked and wearing trousers next to men, and children as young as six being sent to sit in the darkness and open the doors in the shafts for coal wagons as they passed. Alongside this, the campaign to limit working shifts for children and women in factories to ten daytime hours took several attempts, but the reform was eventually passed in 1847.

✑

The 1830s and 1840s were a period when a nascent civil service was called in by government to conduct inquiries into the state of the nation. Their reports poured out: one reason why we now know so much about what it was like. Commissions recorded conditions in factories and mines, child labour, the state of city cemeteries, the working of the poor law and workhouses,* prisons and schools, handloom weavers,

---

* The much-hated Poor Law of 1834 was designed to reduce the cost of supporting the unemployed and poverty-stricken, by forcing those seeking help to apply to workhouses where they would be made to undertake manual labour. Previously such people had been supported by grants – 'outdoor relief' as opposed to incarceration – raised through parish poor rates that were levied on the local property owners. This new system was regarded by its supporters as more efficient and cheaper. The nineteenth-century arguments about the deserving and undeserving poor have striking

sanitation and Irish land tenure, tithes and ecclesiastical fees, lunacy and bankruptcy. All were designed to solve immediate crises or ongoing problems by marshalling statistical evidence and deploying factual information. By such means, it was confidently believed, dispassionate national solutions could be discovered and applied scientifically and logically in legislation across the country. It was the sort of weighing and measuring of the nation's problems that had not been attempted before.

Such empirical approaches were derided by Dickens ('Facts alone are wanted in life,' says Mr Gradgrind in *Hard Times*) and by Thomas Carlyle in his essay *Chartism*: 'you might prove anything by figures'. But it was the sort of information that was invaluable to government and to ministers such as Peel, seeking to frame legislative solutions to new social problems. These reports, such as Edwin Chadwick's *Sanitary Condition of the Labouring Population of Great Britain*, published in 1842, were extraordinarily thorough documents, painting a vivid picture of aspects of contemporary British life and pointing to ways of ameliorating it. Chadwick's 400-page report, garnered over two years of thorough research and laced with striking examples of deprivation and squalor, laid bare the conditions in the cities, paved the way for more research (he was immediately commissioned to investigate the graveyards scandal), and led to legislation to improve public health and the administration of towns and cities. Chadwick's report was forensic in its detail, from the redesign of sewer pipes (oval-shaped ones would be more efficient) to

---

resonances with today's debates over welfare, even if the solutions adopted have evolved.

the disposal of sewage waste in Edinburgh, and his conclusions were inescapable. Bad sanitary conditions increased the mortality rate and wasted the workforce, and improvements would prove worthwhile and cost-effective:

> These adverse circumstances tend to produce an adult population short-lived, improvident, reckless and intemperate and with habitual avidity for sensual gratifications... these habits lead to the abandonment of all conveniences and decencies of life and especially lead to the overcrowding of their homes which is destructive to the morality as well as to the health of large classes of both sexes... the expense of public drainage, of supplies of water laid on in houses and of means of improved cleansing would be a pecuniary gain, by diminishing the existing charges attendant on sickness and premature mortality.[18]

Chadwick had found that many towns and boroughs had a jumble of competing boards and authorities, often rivalling each other and jealous of their powers: St Pancras had nineteen, Birmingham three separate sets of commissioners and four boards of surveyors, all at loggerheads.[19]

Reformers such as Chadwick were heavily influenced by utilitarian efficiency theories along the lines of the prescriptions of the philosopher Jeremy Bentham (1748–1832). Bentham's Panopticon was a striking example. This was the 'all-seeing eye' which, when applied to prison design, as it was at Pentonville in 1842, proposed a building with long sight-lines where convicts could be constantly, clearly and efficiently monitored. It was 'a new mode of obtaining power of mind over mind in a quantity hitherto without example'.

Chadwick, a Manchester-born lawyer and workaholic, impatient with colleagues less diligent or professional than himself, argumentative, and happy to accumulate sweeping personal powers, had been a close friend of Bentham, so it is not surprising that his solutions were also utilitarian ones. When applied more abstractly, they meant the enforcement of national systems of regulation and bureaucracy, overseen by central administrators such as... well, Chadwick could think of no one better than himself. Over time he would serve as a commissioner for the Poor Law, Rural Constabulary, Health of Towns, London Sanitation, Sewers, the General Board of Health and the Crimean Sanitary Commission. Reports such as his were not bland expositions – they were pointed and, in effect, polemical. What is more, they ushered in gradual improvements in sanitation and health in towns and cities, and among factory workers. They made for clean and efficient solutions for legislators trying to frame national laws and for central governments taking over ever wider responsibilities for the running of society, as well as paying for it through taxation. Thus inspectors fanned out across the country, visiting factories, laying down standards, zealously initiating prosecutions, knowing that they would be held responsible themselves if things went wrong. This was all very well: it led to a system of government inspection that prevailed for more than a century. But it also led to a mentality that the gentlemen in Whitehall always knew best and bred rigidity, complacency and also a certain desiccated lack of humanity.

This was most vividly demonstrated in the workhouses that sprang up across the country following the passage of the 1834 Poor Law, legislation enacted by the Whig government which had just passed the Reform Act in a mood of administrative efficiency and cost-saving. 'We are busy introducing system, method, science, economy, regularity and discipline,' as Lord John Russell wrote to Chadwick at the time.[20]

The workhouses were designed to be grim – refuges of last resort for the destitute, the sort of places that no one would go if they had an alternative. They were run on rigid, cheerless lines: they intentionally had Spartan living conditions, often inadequate food, hard, repetitive work, and – most resented of all – the segregation even of married couples, from each other and from their children. No longer would the poor be allowed to receive aid as 'outdoor relief' at home (although this provision was not abolished). Instead, they would be corralled and incarcerated where they could be kept an eye on and made to work. The workhouses were, as one assistant commissioner put it, designed to be of prison-like appearance, 'intended to torment the poor' and instil 'a salutary dread of them'. They were for the 'less eligible' and aid would only be received now in return for work: 'no relief shall be given to the able-bodied, or to their families, except in return for work and that work as hard as it can be made... and that workhouse as disagreeable as it can be made,' as the economist Nassau senior wrote to the minister Lord Brougham in 1833.[21]

So feared was it that, even 140 years later, my mother, the youngest child of Victorian working-class parents, could speak with a shudder of ending up in the workhouse as if it still existed: the system had long gone but the building itself still stood gauntly on the hill above Newbury, Berkshire, where we lived. It was a maternity hospital by then, but still cast a baleful shadow over the town below. The system was brand-new in 1837 when Dickens started writing his powerful critique of it in *Oliver Twist* – the image of grim, ancient buildings usually portrayed in adaptations of the novel is anachronistic – and, so far as government and its local administrators were concerned, it was not only efficient, but cost-effective as well. The cost of poor relief fell by more than a third, from £6,736,000 in 1831 to £4,603,000 in 1835, and was little more than that in the early 1840s at the time of the most severe depression of the era.

More than 350 workhouses were built across the country in the 1830s, most of them in country towns and rural areas, where they soon got a bad name from those who were unappreciative of their utility – mainly those who needed to use them, rather than those paying for them. They soon provoked scandals, in fact as well as fiction, which were ruthlessly exposed by *The Times* newspaper in its campaign against the system. The worst was at Andover in north Hampshire where, in 1845, the inhabitants were found to be so starved that they were gnawing the rancid animal bones that they were supposed to be pounding into dust for fertilizer as their daily work. That the bones may even have included human ones, culled from the local churchyard, only made the exposure of what was going on more horrific. One inmate, Samuel Green, aged 61, admitted to the inevitable eventual inquiry:

> We looked out for the fresh bones by the look of them and then we used to be like a parcel of dogs. Some were not so particular about the bones being fresh as others. I like the fresh bones... sometimes I have had one that was stale and stunk and I eat it even then... because I was hungered, I suppose.[22]

The Andover workhouse was a ghastly regime, run by a Scottish retired artillery sergeant-major and Waterloo veteran called Colin McDougal and his sluttish wife. They were under the benevolent supervision of the chairman of the misnamed board of guardians, the local vicar Christopher Dodson. Not much guardianship was undertaken. Dodson had, however, recently been presented by the board with a service of plate costing £270 in testimony of his able and zealous services – equivalent, it was pointed out, to the cost of keeping a pauper for five years. The reason the inmates were so desperate was because McDougal had been stealing their food.

It was, Peel's home secretary Sir James Graham insisted, 'a workhouse squabble in the South of England'.[23] The commission of inquiry found that McDougal's conduct had been marked with undue severity and, crucially, a disregard for decorum:

> that he was on several occasions, once even while reading prayers to the inmates, seen in a state of intoxication, that he was utterly deficient in many of the qualities which are of essential importance in the difficult position which he filled, viz. fairness and impartiality, a due sense of truth, a well-regulated temper and proper habits of self-control.

Despite this finding, the Rev. Dodson and the board refused to sack him, though McDougal eventually resigned. The vicar himself stayed on for another thirty-two years, unrepentant to the last and seemingly unconcerned that abuses continued. The Andover minutes record that, in heavy snow in the winter of 1846, a one-legged labourer called William Few dragged himself, his wife and three children ten miles across the North

Hampshire downs from the windswept and remote upland village of Faccombe to seek relief, only to be turned away because he was not considered sufficiently a pauper. That Christmas of 1846 those same minutes state:

> Mr Hugh Mundy proposed that, as Christmas Day falls on a Friday, a bread and cheese day, and as no subscription could be raised to give the inmates roast beef and plum puddings on that day, the diet of Tuesday consisting of meat etc be substituted for that of Friday. Which proposition was not seconded.[24]

Mundy was the man who had exposed the bone-grinding scandal the year before, so there may have been some ill-feeling among his colleagues. Perhaps the Rev. Dodson went home after the meeting to dine off his dinner service. Meanwhile, the 'imposing and commodious' Andover workhouse had satisfactorily reduced the cost of relief to the local parishes from £12,715 to £8,272, a saving of 35 per cent.

At least McDougal did not kill anyone, perhaps more by luck than judgement, but others did, seemingly without penalty. There was the case of Joseph Howe, another former sergeant-major, in charge of the Eton workhouse, who brutally mistreated an inmate called Elizabeth Wyse when she tried to look after her sick two-year-old on Christmas Day in 1840. He dragged her away from her child and locked her overnight in solitary confinement in an unheated cell. While enduring a temperature of −29 degrees – the coldest night for decades, it was said – she soiled the floor. Her punishment was to be locked in it again the next day and made to clean the cell with her hands. The story got out, to *The Times*, and Howe was fined £10 (around £600 today), at which point it came to light that he had killed a small boy when in charge of the Brackley workhouse only the previous year, by pouring boiling water over him. That had not forced his dismissal. He told the unlikely story that he had thought the water was cold and that enabled him to move on to Eton to take another post. Such men make Mr Bumble – the workhouse beadle in Dickens's *Oliver Twist* – look positively benign.

∽

The man who exposed the Eton scandal was a clergyman, the Rev. Sydney Godolphin Osborne, who was a remarkable campaigner for justice for the agricultural poor, people whose lives were as desperate as any factory worker's. Osborne, the third son of Lord Godolphin, had married into one of the great liberal dynasties of the day, the Grenfell family, and was related to yet another, the Kingsleys. He was the vicar of Durweston in Dorset for more than thirty years. Both his background and his home were close to Lord Ashley's but the two did not get on, partly because Ashley disapproved of Osborne's high churchmanship and partly because he resented having to share credit for campaigning to end abuses with the clergyman.

Osborne's aristocratic self-confidence helped him to take on local landowners who came to loathe him for his regular correspondence to *The Times* publicizing their activities and abuses. Osborne, a tall, cadaverous figure with an Old Testament beard, also served almost as a roving correspondent for the newspaper, taking himself to Ireland to investigate the famine ('when is our turn to come?' he wrote home to the paper, thinking of the Dorset peasantry and their potatoes) and later even to the Crimean War to inspect Florence Nightingale's hospital and comfort the dying there. He also campaigned for women's rights, free trade and improved sanitation.[25]

Farm labourers in Dorset at that time were generally paid seven shillings a week for married men and between two shillings and six shillings for single men and lads. By comparison, a factory worker in town might get twelve shillings a week, a collier eighteen shillings and a skilled man such as a wire-drawer a pound. For an agricultural labourer, pay would rise to ten shillings at harvest time for a fourteen-hour day and then there might be a gallon of the farmer's worst cider – the stuff his family and friends wouldn't drink – thrown in if he was feeling generous. Cottage rents were a shilling a week, so there was little cash to spare. They might, however, occasionally be sold meat by the farmer from sick sheep and cows slaughtered only when the animals were diseased and dying 'afore they are cold dead', for which they might be charged four pence a pound. It was eaten, one labourer explained to Osborne, because ''tis the only meat we ever sees'.

He wrote up the testimony of another labourer as a first-person account in an article for a magazine in 1848:

> They expect us to do the work of meat-fed men, on wages which won't find meat. Then, sir, they are all against crowding the stock and say they can't thrive amidst bad smells; why, bless you, they crowds us in our cottages till we scarce have room to turn and as for smell – eight or ten forever sleeping in one room, who have most of them been at hard work all day, the land undrained above us and the ditches full of the stuff we can throw nowhere else – why,

if smell hurts a pig or a sheep, the squire has not a ram or a boar which could live a week in health where most of us live; they never think of bringing gentlefolks round to see how they lodge us; they don't care to see that we are kept in good air and in well-drained dwellings.

When once an angry farmer confronted him in Blandford shouting, 'If it was not for "the cloth", I'd take you by the nose and lead you down the street!', Osborne faced him down, retorting: 'Don't worry about "the cloth", just you try it!'

This was the Dorset from which the Tolpuddle Martyrs had been transported a few years earlier for trying to organize themselves into a trade union, and the society into which Thomas Hardy was born in 1840. It was a bleak life with a seething undercurrent of periodic violence. A *Punch* cartoon of 1844, 'The Home of the Rick Burner', shows a desperate farm labourer with four starving children in rags around him in their empty and dilapidated cottage contemplating the corpse of his wife. At his shoulder swirls the faint image of a horned devil carrying a fiery brand, inciting him to insurrection. The message: that there might be reasons for his resort to criminality.[26]

Agricultural labourers had risen up against their declining wages and living conditions in the wake of the introduction of new threshing machinery on farms right across the south of England in the early 1830s. They had smashed machines, burned hayricks and destroyed barns. 'Damn it, let it burn,' said one labourer watching a barn ablaze at Orpington in Kent (according to *The Times*). 'I wish it was the house; we can warm ourselves now; we only want some potatoes: there's a nice fire to cook them by.'[27] The so-called Swing riots, named after the anonymous letters sent to landowners signed by the fictitious Captain Swing – 'mark this, thou despot!' – had shown the depth of rural resentment.

The reform of the matrix of savage ancient game laws in 1831 had made matters worse, not better. Game that had been caught on farmers' land was no longer reserved to the aristocracy, but was now the property of landowners or those who bought a game licence. But tenant farmers as much as labourers could now be punished if they trapped birds or other wild animals for food, or poached them for sale, or even killed them for destroying their crops on land they farmed but did not own. Another *Punch* cartoon of 1844 shows a peasant, head bowed, bound and gagged, beneath an altar on which stands a hare. Beside it an ermine-clad and coroneted earl stands with a raised sword bearing the inscription 'According to Law', while in the background a phalanx of other aristocrats look on approvingly. Meanwhile, in the distance the peasant's family trudge off to the workhouse under a thunderous sky melodramatically split by lightening. The caption reads: 'The Game Laws, or the Sacrifice of the peasant to the hare.'[28]

When – inevitably – there was a parliamentary inquiry in 1846, MPs heard tales of farmers and their peasantry watching helplessly as their crops were laid waste each summer by birds and hares reared to be shot in landlord battues.[29] A Mr Chambers of Beechamwell, Norfolk, who rented 3,000 acres, told the MPs that game destroyed £1,000 worth of his crops each year and he could do nothing about it. Labourers accused of poaching by hated gamekeepers could expect heavy punishment. A farmer named Woodward of Kempsey in Worcestershire gave evidence that two of his ploughboys, aged 14 and 16, 'very good boys', had killed a rabbit encountered in their work and received six weeks' imprisonment, leaving him without anyone to plough his fields. In 1844 the *Aylesbury News* had carried an indignant report about a labourer named Eborn accused of poaching by a 'duke-made parson magistrate', the Rev. G. Chetwolde, who had seen the man pick up an empty snare. Eborn, who had no previous convictions, was known to be of good character. He had lived in the same cottage for twenty years and was unemployed. Eborn swore the trap was not his, but it did him no good: he received a sentence of thirty-two weeks' imprisonment, leaving his wife to starve. Parson justices like Chetwolde were, understandably, particularly hated.* A surviving 'Swing' letter warns one Hampshire clergyman:

> Your name is down amongst the Black hearts in the Black Book and this is to advise you and the like of you who are parson justices to make your wills. Ye have been the Blackguard Enemies of the People on all occasions, Ye have not yet done as ye ought...[30]

That the letter is perfectly correctly spelled, in a neat, legible hand, makes it all the more chilling.

A tenant farmer on the landowner Lord Forester's estate in Shropshire gave evidence that his son, out shooting rats, had been caught by a gamekeeper who accused him of aiming for his lordship's partridges, though there was no evidence that he

---

* Parson justices often served as local magistrates as a consequence of their local social (and financial) status. Like other magistrates, they were officially chosen and sworn in by the lord lieutenant of the county, on behalf of the Crown. They were often loathed and despised because of their harshness and their perceived support for the landed gentry and the status quo.

had. John Bright, the Anti-Corn Law League campaigner and Radical MP, who had set up the inquiry as part of his campaign against the aristocracy (itself part of the parliamentary campaign to abolish the Corn Laws), asked him: 'How often does Lord Forester shoot upon your farm?' 'Never but once a year... they come about a quarter to eleven and I generally see the game cart going away towards half-past three.' 'Then you consider it is for the sake of these six hours' sport you are encumbered with all this damage?' 'Yes, I do.' It was a hard life even for tenants.

This was how many of the rural and urban poor lived, scraping a living when in work, thrown into destitution when times were hard. Not all employers were neglectful or bad. In the Rhymney Valley in South Wales, the Marquess of Bute built two-storey cottages in the Palladian style for the men who worked his blast furnaces – it was called Butetown – and at Cyfarthfa Row in 1840, William Crawshay provided the workers from his ironworks with fifty terraced houses with gardens – buildings still habitable 130 years later. When a nearby ironmaster called Baily, with a reputation for mean-ness, built a terrace for his workers on the hill behind his house at Nantyglo, however, he made sure that none of the buildings had windows overlooking his property.

There was a strong paternalist element in the provision some employers made for their workers. The Ashworths of Bolton provided the workers at their cotton-spinning factory with housing, gave them holidays, encouraged education and paid sufficiently high wages that their wives did not have to work. But they also insisted on cleanliness – a change of shirt twice a week – attendance at church or chapel every Sunday, sobriety and sexual morality. There were schools, a library and a cook-shop selling bread and pies. A visitor to the Ashworths' estate village at Egerton in 1849 gleefully reported:

[it was] as sweet, wholesome and smokeless as it could be were its denizens the most bucolic hinds of Devon... Here is no grime nor squalor. The people are hard-working labourers, but they live decently and fare wholesomely. There is no ragged wretchedness to be seen, no ruinous and squalid hovels... a gratifying spectacle of the manufacturing system working under favourable auspices.[31]

At Flockton near Wakefield, Milnes Stansfeld had not only provided cottages for the miners who worked in his collieries, but there was a horticultural society, a cricket pitch and gymnastic apparatus. There was even music appreciation for the adults so that 'collier boys can be heard in the streets singing and whistling the beautiful airs from Handel, Haydn, Mozart and Spohr'.

Nor were all landowners vengeful in defence of their game. Buckinghamshire's Sir Harry Verney, moved by the story of Eborn, spoke out against the evils of the game laws: 'any system which renders our rural population criminal must be highly injudicious to the best interests of society'. Labourers, he told Bright's committee, 'instead of being valued and esteemed are viewed as surplus population, to be shipped off, or got rid of in any way'. If the game was allowed to be controlled by the farmers, they would not lose so many crops, would be more prepared to invest in improving the land, and would therefore employ more labour and so reduce rural poverty. Verney – who was not alone among the great landowners in calling for reform of the game laws – even defended poachers: they were not the dregs of society, he said, but very often 'men of considerable enterprise and intelligence'.*

One such, William Gowing, 'the greatest poacher in England' from Saxmundham in Suffolk, gave evidence to the committee that the main causes of poaching were starvation wages and dread of the workhouse:

> There is a door for the man, a door for the woman and a door for the children... Then he says, I will use my endeavours to get a little game, to keep out of the union-house as I might as well be caught under the game laws and get committed for two months' hard labour as to go into the union-house.[32]

One of the MPs defending landowners' rights, Grantley Berkeley ('I think a great deal of the prosperity of the agricultural districts is induced by pheasants and partridges,' he had said), asked Gowing: 'The gaol is such comfortable quarters then?' To which the poacher poignantly replied: 'They cannot hear the cries and screams of their children, nor the

---

* When Verney proposed to the magistrates of Buckinghamshire a motion pointing out to the government the 'injury caused to the inhabitants of the county by the preservation of game in great abundance', only five others supported him. One local newspaper suggested his proposal should be reprinted every week for three months so that he could receive 'the heartfelt thanks of hundreds of sturdy sons of the plough'. But in the autumn of 1846 twenty-six poachers were jailed in the county in the last week of October and the first week of November. The obtuseness must have aggravated Verney, but the family owned 40,000 acres of the county and received an income of £100,000 a year from it, so he could probably afford to ignore local opposition.

complaints of their wives [as they do in the workhouse] – that is what vexes them.'[33]

The committee's report in August 1846 filled a thousand pages, but by that time the Corn Laws had been repealed, the League's impulse to kick landowners was waning, and the urgency of the Peasants versus Pheasants political battle was lost. Not that the battle in the fields and woods was over. The *Lynn Advertiser* that month reported on a 'Dreadful Rencontre with Knives' in a turnip field where a poacher was wounded in the side and the gamekeeper's face was 'literally hacked to pieces… Both men were so dreadfully wounded that it is not thought they could survive many hours.' The same month in Devon a farm watcher was shot: 'on a post-mortem examination a number of small shots were found lacerating most frightfully the liver and injuring the bone. The surgeon also found a piece of the deceased's watch-chain which had been carried into the wound.' The local newspaper report said: 'there is a great deal of poaching, the practice being rather favoured than resisted by the generality of farmers.'[34]

In 1842, during the previous economic slump, with factory workers thrown onto the streets and farm labourers destitute, Prime Minister Peel had thought it prudent to buy arms and ammunition to protect his family at Drayton, fifteen miles outside Birmingham, where rumours of trouble were seething. 'We had better say nothing about it,' he wrote to his wife that August. 'I think one of the rooms in the tower would be the safest place of deposit. The ammunition should be carefully kept near the arms and in a safe place.'[35]

3

Alas! The Foul and Fatal Blight

'Ireland! Ireland! That cloud in the west! That
coming storm! That minister of God's retribution
upon cruel, inveterate and but half atoned injustice!
Ireland forces upon us those great social and great
religious questions. God grant that we may have the
courage to look them in the face.'

WILLIAM GLADSTONE, LETTER TO HIS WIFE CATHERINE,
12 OCTOBER 1845

However many excuses are made for Britain's reaction to the
Irish famine that started in 1845 and that would turn into the
worst natural disaster in western Europe since the Black
Death, it is hard to escape the sense of callousness and
ineptitude with which the authorities mainly tackled it. It is
easy to say that a crisis of that magnitude would have
challenged any administration at any time, let alone one that
was in its managerial infancy and of amateurish competence
as the British civil service in Ireland was in the 1840s. It is not
true, however, that what was happening was not known or
appreciated on the British side of the Irish Sea. There were no
television news reports to tug the heartstrings and prick the
conscience, of course, but there were plenty of graphic reports
in the press and urgent appeals from both British and Irish
observers that allowed the authorities in London to know
what was happening. Gladstone's letter to his wife was about

wider Irish issues, but it certainly shows that the country was at the forefront of ministers' minds in the autumn that the potato crop began to fail. The first reports that there was blight in the crop came from the south of England in August 1845, and by mid-October, when the potatoes started being lifted in Ireland, it was clear that they were infected too. The *Phytophthora infestans* fungus had spread from America to Europe and flourished in a wet summer – as it still does today. Now it can be contained by chemical means and ridge planting, but in the mid-nineteenth century there was no remedy once it took hold. In Ireland a third of the crop was lost in 1845, then three-quarters in the following two summers.

Peel's government certainly tried to deal with what was happening, and it did far more than the Russell administration that succeeded it in the summer of 1846. Indeed, Peel embarked on a major change in economic policy in response to the crisis, which ultimately caused his government's downfall. But the famine was a pretext for a repeal of the Corn Laws which Peel had envisaged anyway, and removing tariffs on imported grain had virtually no effect in tackling the Irish crisis. Douglas Hurd, a former Conservative minister who is Peel's latest biographer, insists 'no one died of starvation while Peel was in power', which is stretching it: deaths from malnutrition-related diseases were undoubtedly occurring.[1] But it is certainly true that the whole philosophy of the British political class made them not only disdainful of the Irish, but also reluctant to intervene with the urgency that the emergency required – or, as the Whigs showed, unwilling on principle to act at all. There was a feeling that the Irish had brought their troubles on themselves through indolence and improvidence, but it was also not regarded as part of a government's duty to get deeply involved in helping them, beyond ameliorating the worst difficulties – and Russell's government would see little need to do even that, withdrawing aid while it was still urgently needed. Many English politicians believed, bluntly, that the Irish were trying it on for political reasons. The diarist Charles Greville met Lord Bessborough, the Whig Irish peer, in London on 13 January 1846: 'He says there will be no deficiency of consequence in the potato crop, none of the potatoes are entirely spoilt; the state of Ireland very bad in parts and requires coercive measures.' Bessborough, who owned estates in Kilkenny, at that stage one of the less badly affected parts of the island, would become Lord Lieutenant of Ireland when the Whigs came into government later in the year.

Whether the British administrations would have done much more had the famine been as severe among the peasantry in England is a moot point. The failure of the potato crop after a very wet summer was first noticed in Britain on the Isle of Wight, then Kent, Lancashire and Scotland, but it was soon realized that Ireland, where it was the main food source, would be the centre of a particular calamity. Peel himself had been much moved and was privately philanthropic four years earlier when the weavers of the Scottish town of Paisley were thrown into destitution by that year's economic slump – which affected workers all across Britain – but he plainly saw it as the duty of wealthy landowners, rather than the national government, to sustain the local inhabitants. As he explained in the House of Commons in April 1846:

> If it were known that we undertook the task of supplying the Irish with food we should to a great extent lose the support of the Irish gentry, the Irish clergy and the Irish

farmer. It is quite impossible for the Government to support four million people. It is utterly impossible for us to adopt means of preventing cases of individual misery in the wilds of Galway or Donegal or Mayo. In such localities the people must look to the local proprietors, resident and non-resident.[2]

The trouble was that, although there were many large British estates in Ireland when the famine broke out, usually they were managed by agents for absentee owners living in England. Like their Irish landowning counterparts, some were sympathetic and helpful to their tenants when the emergency erupted, but nowhere near enough. There were complaints that the fertile and prosperous farming regions in the eastern counties of the island did little to help the west.

Peel actually knew better than most British politicians what the potato failure in Ireland would mean, as he had been Chief Secretary for Ireland during a previous famine in 1817. One occasion on which his habitual emotional coolness failed was during the Corn Law repeal debates when the protectionists were arguing that emergency measures were not necessary because there was no real suffering. The force of his words breaks through in the speech, on 27 March 1846:

Are you to hesitate in averting famine which may come, because it possibly may not come? Are you to look to and depend upon chance in such an extremity? Or, Good God, are you to sit in cabinet and consider and calculate how much diarrhoea and bloody flux and dysentery a people can bear before it becomes necessary for you to provide them with food?[3]

Such remarks tend to give the lie to Irish nationalist and Irish-American historians who still claim that the 'English' (they never say British) handling of the crisis amounted to a deliberate policy of genocide towards the Irish people. Assertions such as these have more emotion, and frequently sloppiness, than fact behind them.[4] Whatever happened afterwards when the Whigs took power – and their approach was characterized by incompetence, inhumanity and heartlessness rather than murderousness – Peel's administration attempted to alleviate the sudden emergency. 'We have a nation to carry, as it were, in our arms,' said Peel's home secretary James Graham: and it was true. In the first months of the famine, the British government spent £750,000 in relief, public works, loans and maize shipments to Ireland, which – considering that the government's national budget surplus that year was just £2.5 million – represented a not inconsiderable effort. The old Duke of Wellington later wrote to John Wilson Croker, the Tory critic of Peel: 'I cannot doubt that which passed under my own view and frequent observation day after day, I mean the alarms of the consequences in Ireland of the potato disease. I never witnessed in any case such agony.'

In the early 1840s, before disaster struck, Ireland had more than 8.175 million inhabitants – not too far short of half the population of England, Scotland and Wales, and nearly a third of the 26 million population of the entire British Isles. Compare this with today, when Ireland and Northern Ireland together have only a tenth of the UK's population – 6.4 million against the UK's 62 million, according to 2011 census data – and the relative size and significance of Ireland to the country as a whole in the 1840s is clear. By the time the potato blight waned at the end of the decade, approximately a million people had died of disease and starvation and, in the years to come, a million more (including my ancestors) would emigrate. The 1851 census recorded 6.5 million people living in Ireland; by 1861 it was down to 5.7 million.

During the early part of the famine, Ireland continued to export cereal crops including oats, wheat and barley from its larger farms and estates. From the autumn of 1845 into the second month of 1846, 258,000 quarters of wheat, 701,000 hundredweight of barley and a million quarters of oatmeal were shipped out of the country, together with 30,000 oxen, bulls and cows, 30,000 sheep, 100,000 pigs and assorted dairy products, also exported to England. This changed in the later years of the emergency, but it was questionable whether in the circumstances of the time such supplies would have helped greatly, short of a massive relief effort of the sort the local and British authorities were incapable of organizing. Even the shipments of Indian corn – maize – that Peel arranged to be surreptitiously bought on the British government's behalf by representatives of Barings Bank on the open market in America did not rapidly alleviate shortages. The purchase was not entirely altruistic: the purchase of maize helped ensure that international grain sales would not be disrupted and it was also hoped that the Irish might become accustomed to eating maize before famine struck again.

Potatoes were cheap, plentiful, filling and relatively easy to grow even on poor, damp soil. They had, over the previous fifty years, almost entirely supplanted a more balanced diet for the peasant families, especially in the south and west of the country. The primitive and impoverished rural areas compounded the problems of organizing aid and distributing food. Even when the maize from America eventually arrived in March 1846, there were not sufficient mills to grind it into a consistency that could be used as food, and anyway there was a shortage of ports on the west coast where ships could dock and unload their cargoes. The long voyage from the US meant that the corn was liable to overheat and sweat, so that it needed to be chopped or ground as soon as it arrived – ordinary milling was not enough – and Ireland lacked the facilities to do so. Sir Randolph Routh, who chaired the relief commission in Dublin, was writing to London that by May only a tenth of the imported corn had been ground – 30,000 bushels – 'and we shall have arriving 350,000 bushels'.[5] This flint corn needed grinding twice to make it palatable, but to the civil servants back in London this seemed excessively indulgent to the Irish: 'We must not aim at giving more than wholesome food,' Charles Trevelyan, the Treasury civil servant wrote to Routh. 'I cannot believe it will be necessary to grind the Indian corn twice... dependence on charity is not to be made an agreeable mode of life.'

The Irish peasantry did not initially like the cornmeal and were not used to cooking it. In the early stages of the famine William Wilde, a Dublin doctor (and later Oscar's father), was called in by the commissariat organizing food supplies to offer his advice, even though he was an ophthalmologist, not a nutritionist. He reported back that, not only did the peasantry not know how to cook the meal, they did not have the fuel to be able to do so:

the poor were totally unacquainted with the mode of preparing... Indian meal for food: indeed in many instances they ate the former raw. Some had no fuel, others were too hungry to carry it home and all were ignorant of the mode of preparing it either as stirabout or bread.[6]

In early 1847 Alexis Soyer, the French chef at the Reform Club in London, would be sent across to advise on how to make nutritious soups from his mobile kitchen in Dublin's Phoenix Park, but by then it was much too late. As Mr Bishop, the commissariat officer of West Cork, wrote back, the soup 'runs through them without affording any nourishment', while a doctor in Skibbereen, one of the worst affected towns in the area, complained that such a liquid food was 'actually injurious' to people suffering from dysentery.[7] For them, relief came too late.

The underlying long-term problem was related to the structure of Irish landholdings and tenancy arrangements, which meant that plots grew smaller as they were sublet from large tenants, then sublet again in ever smaller parcels, or subdivided when bequeathed among siblings. Sometimes whole families were subsisting on less than half an acre. If there was space for profitable crops, they were usually sold to pay the rent rather than sustain the family. Without heavy industry in much of the island, except for Ulster, the infrastructure of roads was poor and railways were as yet almost non-existent. Agricultural reform had been neglected – there was little parliamentary pressure or imperative for change at distant Westminster – many landowners were improvident where they were not insolvent, and periodic political discontent meant that the country's endemic poverty had been disregarded. There had been about two hundred commissions of inquiry into the state of Ireland over the previous half-century and many had warned of impending disaster, so there was no lack of awareness. But these inspectors were much better at detailing problems than the politicians were at dealing with them. Complacency, indifference and disdain for the alien Irish had meant there was no incentive to reform before it was too late.

With the failure of the crop on which the Irish peasantry depended to live, mass starvation loomed and there were other consequences too: the risk of disorder and disaffection, which weighed much heavier on British ministers' minds than famine relief. An internecine struggle was going on in Dublin in the autumn that the famine broke out between young nationalists and the old political leader Daniel O'Connell, the Liberator. 'The Great Dan' was a charismatic, dominating bull of a man with a voice like brass who had led the fight for Roman Catholic emancipation twenty years earlier and was heading the continuing campaign to repeal the Act of Union of 1801 and establish an Irish parliament.[8] O'Connell, though, was ailing and had just passed 70, weakened and disorientated by a recent prison sentence. He was being challenged by a more radical, younger faction, disillusioned by his refusal to confront the British. He had lost their respect when he had backed down three years earlier and called off a huge planned repeal rally against the Act of Union at Clontarf after the authorities banned it and threatened to use force against the demonstrators. O'Connell had called out 100,000 people at similar rallies earlier in the summer and the British still saw the threat of political disorder at least as keenly as the likelihood of famine. The Dublin-based Young Ireland movement, absorbed in its campaign, was slow to recognize the looming starvation. But O'Connell, a Kerry landowner, who had embodied the political aspirations of the Irish tenantry and raised the hackles of the English for so long, saw the threat immediately and began lobbying the government in London for aid. He was not the man likely to get the most sympathetic of hearings from his old enemy Peel, but as it became clear that the government planned to repeal the Corn Laws, he fully supported the move.

This contrasted with his long-standing rival William Smith O'Brien, aligned to the Young Ireland group, who suspected that repeal was an English plot to undermine Irish agriculture. He was all in favour of pressing ahead with a confrontational political campaign to restore the Irish parliament. O'Connell told him that famine relief should come first: 'While I desire Ireland's liberty, I desire also the preservation of her people.'[9] As the famine spread, the middle-class 'physical force' men of Young Ireland paraded at meetings in Dublin in their gold and green uniforms; they proclaimed no compromise on their political demands, while their newspaper *The Nation* insisted: 'Better a little blood-letting to show that there is blood [than] pining in the belief that all spirit is fled.' In April 1846, O'Brien took his principles to Westminster to the extent of refusing to serve on the Commons railways committee – and, although he voted for repeal of the Corn Laws, he privately told Peel he supported a maintenance of the tariff. By contrast, O'Connell was telling his followers: 'I will get all I can for Ireland and when I can I will take the rest.' To the zealots, that gradualism and moderation made him a pretend Irishman, no better than a west Briton, one of the 'luke-warm, milk and water, small beer lovers of their country'. To O'Connell, their speeches were the 'claptraps from juvenile orators'.

Against this background of political infighting, there was also rural violence and intimidation over evictions. In the first four months of 1846 the overstretched and underfunded constabulary knew of eighty cases of murder for which there had been only seven convictions. This violence was alarming to British politicians, though it took Peel to recognize that the famine had to be addressed if the lawlessness was to be tackled. The magazine *Punch* might have been socially radical at home, but even in the face of the famine its anti-Irishness was ugly. One 1846 cartoon shows 'Young Ireland in business for himself', a malevolent, grinning, pug-faced youth selling weaponry to an already heavily armed, evidently Irish, peasant standing next to a sign saying: 'Pretty little pistols for pretty little children.' There was, however, a shortage of political ideas, reflected in another *Punch* cartoon from the same time, showing Peel and Russell, both in footmen's livery, conversing complacently during a breather: 'What's to be done with Ireland, John?' asks Peel; 'I am sure I don't know,' replies Russell, nonchalantly picking at his teeth with a quill.[10]

As spring 1846 approached, most of the Irish had more pressing concerns: starvation was endemic across eleven counties. Bands of men were besieging food depots, mobs were congregating in towns such as Kerry, Galway and Kilkenny demanding help, and a provision ship was plundered at Mitchelstown on the River Fergus. Elsewhere, attempts to issue the first supplies of cornmeal – Peel's brimstone – also produced riots in the Limerick workhouse and at Waterford, where it was rumoured that the English had poisoned it and any who ate it would die.

Destitution was made worse as rents fell due and evictions began, removing any chance of peasant families recovering if the next harvest was good. Seed potatoes needed for the following year's crop were also blighted, so it was already realized that famine would inevitably stretch into a second year. Landlords were not averse to evicting tenants who could not pay their rent because of the famine, leaving them to walk the roads. Nor did they always need the excuse of a default, if they decided that their land could be more profitably culti-vated by other means, without the inconvenience of sitting tenants. In March 1846 a Mrs Gerrard, whose estate included the village of Ballinglass in County Galway, decided to evict the 300 tenants who lived there, even though they were not in arrears with their rent, in order that the area could be cleared for livestock grazing. The sixty-one houses were reported to be well built and maintained and the inhabitants had improved the land by draining a 400-acre bog. Nevertheless, they were thrown off their properties by a detachment of infantry and the houses were demolished:

the scene was frightful; women running wailing with pieces of their property and clinging to door posts from which they had to be forcibly torn; men cursing, women screaming with fright. That night the people slept in the ruins; next day they were driven out, the foundations of the houses torn up and razed and no neighbour allowed to take them in.[11]

When the incident was raised in the House of Commons a fortnight later, Sir James Graham, the home secretary, took refuge in the excuse that there were contradictory reports and he had no idea which was correct. However, the army veteran Lord Londonderry, a former ambassador to Vienna and Tory-supporting Ulster landowner, admitted the story was true:

the unfortunate wretches... mercilessly driven from the ditches to which they had betaken themselves for shelter. If scenes like this occur, is it to be wondered at that deeds of outrage and violence should occasionally be attempted?[12]

It was left to Lord Brougham, the Scottish lawyer and former Whig Lord Chancellor, to make the laissez-faire case. Undoubtedly, he said, it was the landlord's right to do as he pleased with his own property, and if he chose not to evict, that was merely an act of kindness:

> The tenants must be taught by the strong arm of the law that they had no power to oppose or resist… property would be valueless and capital no longer invested in cultivation of land if it were not acknowledged that it was the landlord's undoubted, indefeasible and most sacred right to deal with his property as he list.[13]

Turned off their land, with their cottages and hovels stripped of their roofs by bailiffs, the local constabulary or troops, families took refuge in ditches, cowering from the cold under makeshift covers of branches and mud, or making their way to local towns to beg for food. Even at the best of times, such people were impoverished: a survey in Donegal in 1837 had found that in one of the larger towns the 9,000 inhabitants had just ten beds, ninety-three chairs and 243 stools between them. Now they had nothing to carry with them, or sell. Those living near the sea might be able to supplement what food there was with fish, mussels or even seaweed, but inland, once the livestock had been slaughtered, families were found living off the decaying carcasses of dead horses and goats. There was nothing.

The government's relief efforts, supervised by an increasingly anguished Routh from Dublin, were not the only ones of course. Local boards of guardians set up committees to distribute food from depots, but were often short of money and provisions. Despite the growing evidence around them, they were sometimes staggeringly complacent. In January 1846, when a meeting was organized at Kilkee in County Clare – 'the room so filled with people that very few of the proprietors could gain access' – the committee's first action was to pass a resolution praising the local Catholic clergy for their zeal, its second a vote of warmest thanks to the chairman for his conduct of the meeting. Then the principal landlords of the district met separately and issued a statement saying that, because of their current difficulties, 'they neither can advance funds now, nor can they offer any sufficient security for the payment by instalments hereafter'.[14]

Workhouse overseers, interpreting the poor law with varying degrees of rigidity, obtuseness and incompetence, sometimes insisted that the only true paupers were their inmates and all others who wanted food would have to pay for it. Then, seeing a destitute Catholic population ripe for conversion, energetic evangelicals moved in with soup kitchens – 'souperism' – and, although most do not seem to have insisted that recipients should abandon the old faith, the implication of their aid was clear.[15] Organizations such as the Society for the Irish Church Missions, funded from England, set out to show the inhabitants of Connemara the error of their ways, and pamphlets such as *A Voice from Heaven to Ireland* were ready for distribution from early 1846. The Rev. Alexander Dallas, an Anglican clergyman from Hampshire, was particularly energetic in his crusade against the Anti-Christ of Popery, flooding the area around Clifden and

Oughterard with missionaries, including Gaelic-speaking converts. Scripture readings, schools and services followed, pointing up the undoubted fact that the famine was God's judgement on a heathen people. This, understandably, did not go down well with the Catholic clergy. Father Michael Gallagher of Achill complained to his bishop:

> Poverty has compelled the greatest number of the population to send their children to... proselytising villainous schools... one thousand children of the Catholics of the parish attending. They are dying of hunger and rather than dying they have submitted.[16]

The Quakers, too, would soon be setting up food kitchens in Dublin in early 1847. Many individual Catholic priests, such as the famous Father Mathew, who in happier times had been a crusader for temperance, tried to feed and succour their flocks and were outspoken in their lobbying for aid. Their tales were heart-rending: stories of families huddling together in ditches to die, of corpses found in the mornings outside their churches. And they were angry, too, at the profiteers and corn-merchants who demanded exorbitant prices for their grain and farmers who would not help their tenants: 'the capitalists in the corn and flour trade are endeavouring to induce government not to protect the people from famine but to leave them at their mercy,' Mathew wrote to London that August.[17]

In late 1846 the magnates of the City of London clubbed together to set up their own aid effort, called – with typical Victorian addiction to rolling sententiousness – the British Association for the Relief of the Extreme Distress in the

Remote Parishes of Ireland and Scotland. Queen Victoria herself donated £2,000 to the fund to help her Irish subjects, the Rothschilds gave £1,000, and the Duke of Devonshire, who owned an estate in Waterford, another £1,000. By that time, such philanthropy was increasingly needed because there was a new Whig government in London, headed by Lord John Russell, and governmental attitudes to famine relief in Ireland had hardened considerably.[18]

The famine brought out all the worst English attitudes to the Irish, with precious little by way of compassion. If the Benthamite philosophy had given rise to the workhouse doctrine, it also led much more lethally to the view that government had no place intervening in an emergency which was not, and should not be, its responsibility. Nor should the iron laws of laissez-faire economics, or of supply and demand, be contravened. Peel's Tory paternalism at least meant he believed the government had a limited responsibility to assist local efforts to alleviate suffering, for practical and humanitarian reasons, but no sooner were the Whigs in power in the summer of 1846 than relief was brought to an end. The Irish had long been looked on as devious, violent, lazy, subversive, untrustworthy, ungrateful – and Catholic – and this array of traditional and sometimes contradictory prejudices bolstered the official view that they had only themselves to blame for their God-given plight and would just have to knuckle down and get out of it as best they could. The statements of the time show an almost unbelievable callousness. Thus Sir Charles Wood, the new chancellor of the exchequer in Russell's government, to the Earl of Clarendon, the viceroy in Dublin:

Now, financially my course is very easy. I have no more money and therefore I cannot give it... Where the people refuse to work or sow, they must starve, as indeed I fear must be the case in many parts.[19]

The Russell government therefore stopped emergency food imports to Ireland immediately, just as the 1846 harvest was found to be failing even more disastrously than the previous year's, and made clear that they would not be resumed as that would interfere with private dealers' justified expectations of making a profit. As *The Times* would say in an editorial: 'There are times when something like harshness is the greatest humanity.'[20] If relief was needed, that was what local poor rates were for.

In this, the Irish peasantry had few voices in Britain to speak up on their behalf. Radicals and liberals were as harsh as anyone else. John Bright, the free-trade anti-Corn Law campaigner, said it was their own fault:

I believe it would be found on inquiry that the population of Ireland, as compared with that of England, do not work more than two days a week... wherever a people are not industrious and are not employed, there is the greatest danger of crime and outrage. Ireland is idle and therefore she starves: Ireland starves and therefore she rebels.

No less harsh, shamefully, was the *Manchester Guardian*, which compared the feckless Irish to the industrious English, without seemingly noticing the immigrant Irish workforce outside its own windows. The English, it stated, 'bring up their children in habits of frugality, which qualify them for earning their own living and then send them forth into the world to look for employment'.[21] *The Times*, which had campaigned so vociferously against the harshness of the Poor Law, devoted its energies to smearing O'Connell in a way remarkably reminiscent of more recent tabloid techniques. It sent its young reporter William Howard Russell, later to find fame as the paper's war correspondent in the Crimea, to investigate O'Connell's estate in Kerry and harried the old man with reports about his poverty-stricken tenantry and his own improvidence, apparently oblivious to the fact that many of those camping on his land were refugees who he was keeping from complete destitution.[22]

To implement its harsh neglect, the government had the perfect career civil servant: Charles Trevelyan, assistant secretary to the Treasury in London, placed in charge of Irish affairs. Brought up in the Clapham evangelical sect, connected by marriage or friendship with the great liberal families – he married the historian Macaulay's sister and knew the Wilberforces* – he was fond of reading the Bible aloud in his deep, sonorous voice and had a firm conviction of his incorruptibility, rectitude and correctness on every issue: qualities characteristic of a certain sort of evangelical then and since.[23] Macaulay, who was a friend and thought his temper very sweet, wrote of him:

> He has no small talk. His mind is full of schemes of moral and political improvement and his zeal boils over in his talk. His topics even in courtship are steam navigation, the

---

* The great and wealthy evangelical family of whom William, the crusader against the slave trade, was the best known.

education of the natives, the equalization of the sugar duties [and] the substitution of the Roman for the Arabic alphabet in Oriental languages.[24]

Trevelyan had already served in India, where the governor-general had said of him: 'That man is almost always on the right side of every question; and it is well that he is so, for he gives a most confounded deal of trouble when he happens to take the wrong one.'[25] At the age of 38, then, he was the most able man at the Treasury, diligent and punctilious – and the person most usually fingered with responsibility for implementing the policy of heartless neglect. He was the apostle of the belief that, as he wrote, the famine was a natural 'mechanism for reducing the surplus population', a sentiment Dickens's Ebenezer Scrooge had so bracingly asserted three years earlier during his miserly phase in *A Christmas Carol*. Trevelyan, trained from his youth for colonial public service, may well have imbibed this philosophy from one of his teachers at the East India Company College (now Haileybury public school), Thomas Malthus, the prophet of population disaster, but to this was added what seems to have been a congenital dislike for the Irish as well as a ruthless inhumanity and a staggering lack of imagination. He could not be stirred even when a delegation of Anglican clergymen got down on their knees to beg for relief to be sent to Ireland late in 1846. 'The judgement of God sent the calamity to teach the Irish a lesson, that calamity must not be too much mitigated,' he wrote. 'The real evil with which we have to contend is not the physical evil of the Famine, but the moral evil of the selfish, perverse and turbulent character of the people.' No wonder the name of Trevelyan has resounded with well-honed hatred down the years in Ireland, as his descendant, the BBC correspondent Laura Trevelyan, reported in covering events there even in recent years. In her family memoir, she wrote: 'His name is infamous in certain circles in Ireland, as I learned while working as a journalist on both sides of the border. The name Trevelyan retains a potency more than 160 years later.'[26]

Trevelyan dutifully implemented the Peel government's policy, but quickly adapted with relish to the much more congenial Whig approach. Sir Randolph Routh wailed to him in despair from Dublin: 'You cannot answer the cry of want by a quotation from political economy.'[27] As the Russell government assumed power, the commissary general was already warning that signs were bad for the coming harvest, but Trevelyan wrote back ruthlessly that if government aid was extended for a second season the population would just expect to be fed: 'The only way to prevent the people from becoming habitually dependent on Government is to bring the operations to a close. The uncertainty about the new crop only makes it more necessary.' To underline the point, he wrote again a few days later: 'Whatever may be done hereafter, these things should be stopped now, or you run the risk of paralysing all private enterprise and having this country on you for an indefinite number of years. The Chancellor of the Exchequer supports this strongly.'[28]

So the second year of the potato blight unravelled worse than the first and people did begin to die. 'No language can describe the awful condition of the people,' wrote a curate in Mayo that winter. 'They are to be found in thousands, young and old, male and female, crawling the streets and on the highways, screaming for a morsel of food.' In the *Cork Examiner* that Christmas a priest added: 'No description that I could give would for a moment adequately tell the misery, the wretchedness and the suffering of my poor people – they are in the most frightful state of destitution that can possibly be imagined.'[29] Warm and safe in London, the diarist Charles Greville spared a thought for the Irish, writing on 4 November:

> The state of Ireland is meanwhile most deplorable, not so much from the magnitude of the prevailing calamity as the utter corruption and demoralisation of the whole people, from top to bottom; obstinacy, ignorance, cupidity and idleness overspread the land. Nobody thinks of anything but how they can turn the evil of the times to their own advantage. The upper class are intent upon jobbing and the lower on being provided with everything and doing nothing.[30]

O'Connell, dying now, probably from a brain tumour, and estranged from the Young Ireland blowhards – 'vapouring about physical force and vindication by the sword [while] afraid to look at a poker' – was in despair. He knew now that there would be no help for his distressed countrymen from the Whigs. 'A nation is starving… and to the all prevalent famine is now added dysentery and typhus in their worst shapes,' he wrote in December 1846. 'What is to be done? What is to be done?'[31] Early in the New Year, he dragged himself to the Commons one last time, where Disraeli watched him struggling to make himself heard:

> Of great debility and the tones of his voice very still… it was a strange and touching spectacle to those who remembered the form of colossal energy and the clear and thrilling tones that had once startled, disturbed and controlled senates…

to the House generally it was a performance of dumb show, a feeble old man muttering from a table; but respect for the great parliamentary personage kept all as orderly as if the fortune of a party hung on his rhetoric.[32]

Only a great national act of charity, he told them, could save the lives of a quarter of the Irish population, food must be procured wherever it could be got at whatever expense. England ought to use her powers generously and magnificently to rescue the country as the Irish could do nothing for themselves. They ignored him and O'Connell wrote despondently to his old friend Patrick FitzPatrick: 'At a period when Parliament could not do half enough for Ireland, it is not disposed to do half as much as it can.' His doctor advised him to go abroad for his health and, accompanied by his Catholic priest, he set off on a pilgrimage to Rome, though he had only got as far as Genoa before he died three months later.

The English were disposed to do as little as they could for the Irish in 1846 and the trouble they stored up then has been with them ever since.

4

A Damned Dishonest Act

'I will not take the step with mutilated power and
shackled authority. I will not stand at the helm during
such tempestuous nights as I have seen if the vessel be
not allowed fairly to pursue the course which I think
she ought to take.'

SIR ROBERT PEEL, ADDRESS TO THE HOUSE OF COMMONS,
22 JANUARY 1846

When Parliament resumed in January 1846, Peel knew that he
had some explaining to do to the Tory backbenches about
why he had decided to repeal the Corn Laws, which they were
bound to see as a betrayal; but he underestimated how angry
some of them were. A minority were absolutely opposed,
many more remained to be convinced that repeal was the right
thing to do, some were agnostic on the issue, but relatively few
were prepared to back the prime minister regardless – and
many of them were already members of the government.
Could he win over the doubters? Over the previous five years
he had led the Tories gently through a series of tariff reforms
in order to extend free trade on coffee, glass, vinegar – in all,
more than 430 duties were abolished. But the Corn Laws had
achieved a talismanic status. If they went, the protectionists
believed, all would be lost: it was useless for the rural Tories to
talk of alleviating the sufferings of the poor with cheap food,
if the farmers were then put out of business and there was no

work to be had. If agriculture was undermined, then the country would collapse, foreigners would get rich at Britain's expense, and the bastions of British life – the landed gentry – would be destroyed. Tory MPs who had been at home in the shires for Christmas had been buffeted by their constituents' annoyance. But whereas many quietly shared Peel's view that there was no alternative to his leadership and that he was unassailable, a growing minority of irreconcilable protectionist Ultras, utterly opposed to the government, now began to believe that he had to go. They might not be able to stop repeal, but they could bring him down and, as the months went on, more came to share their view. As one of their newspapers, *The Standard*, said in February 1846: 'Even if it ends in defeat, a prolonged Parliamentary campaign would consolidate and discipline the true Conservative Party and direct it to its true leaders.' In the parliamentary debates that followed, it is quite possible to discern very similar arguments and tactics to those deployed much more recently in relation to Britain's membership of the European Union – another issue about foreign trade that has split modern Conservatives just as it did their ancestors.

Following the political crisis of November and December 1845, there was no disguising the fact that Peel had decided on abolition and that he had convinced most other ministers to go along with him. What he was going to propose was a phasing out of tariffs on imported corn over three years, though how that would solve the immediate crisis over the Irish famine was not explained, nor does he seem to have been asked. A more urgent, though interim solution – the temporary lifting of import duties to tackle the immediate crisis – was not seriously discussed either, because Peel, having decided that repeal was in the national interest, felt in honour unable to guarantee that the duties would ever be reimposed. Suspension of the Corn Laws might have been a more feasible way of proceeding politically: tackling the matter gradually to allow the landed interest time to get used to the idea and to realize that their livelihoods would not be destroyed. But Peel dismissed it, even at the risk of the political martyrdom that he seemed increasingly to embrace and eventually even to welcome. Extra-parliamentary pressure from the Anti-Corn Law League and maybe industrial unrest would undoubtedly have mounted and a temporary suspension would have been regarded as inadequate, but it might have kept the Tory party together. Peel, however, wanted to present repeal as an inevitable consequence of the economic policy on which the government had embarked, a logical culmination towards a free-trade future which would benefit the whole country commercially and thus, as a side effect, improve the condition of the poorest members of society and make them less prone to agitation and violent disorder. He wrote immediately after Christmas 1845 to Henry Goulburn, his chancellor of the exchequer:

> My wish would be not to give undue prominence to corn, but to cover corn by continued operation on the Customs Tariff… let us leave the tariff as nearly perfect as we can… I attach great importance to our doing and doing now, what yet remains to be done. Let us put the finishing stroke to this good work.[1]

Peel had managed, though with increasing difficulty, to carry the Tory party with him over previous U-turns and probably thought he would do so again. He anticipated difficulties, but, as he assured the queen, he believed opposition would be limited. Apart from loyalist Tory backbenchers, he could be clear that most Whig MPs would support repeal too, following Lord John Russell's public conversion to removing the Corn Laws in his pre-Christmas letter from Edinburgh. That was not the case with all the Whigs: Lord Melbourne, the queen's first prime minister and her old favourite, went down in her estimation by telling her too bluntly at dinner that Peel had embarked, Ma'am, on a 'damned dishonest act' – the authentic voice of the old landed aristocracy. She told him sharply to change the subject. Her loyalty and admiration – and, as importantly, that of her husband – were to her current prime minister now.

Peel was intellectually convinced that the move would not damage the country's prosperity and was able to articulate the case for it. He knew also that he had the strong support not only of the queen and her consort but also of many parts of the press, which was speaking of him in heroic terms as the only possible prime minister. He must have felt that he was the indispensable man, the undisputed leader of his party, the only man prepared to take office in the national interest following Russell's failure to form a government. He was privately contemptuous of the opposition leader. Above all, tactically, he may have thought, there was no one of sufficient talent in Parliament, least of all among the country squires and younger sons of the aristocracy on the Tory side, organizationally and oratorically able to lead a revolt and sustain it. Lord Stanley, the Lancashire magnate who had resigned from the cabinet, might have done so, but he would remain largely aloof from the debate. But if Peel thought there was no one else, he was wrong.

The protectionist wing of the Tory party had been organizing in the country for three years to defend the Corn Laws in response to the mounting influence of the Anti-Corn Law League among the manufacturers of the northern towns. The Anti-League, as it became known, even mirrored their tactics. This might have proved insufficient but for the emergence of two unlikely but energetic Tory leaders in the Commons itself.

Lord George Bentinck, the younger son of the Duke of Portland and member for King's Lynn, had been more interested in horse racing than speaking in the Commons. He had barely spoken in the chamber in his eighteen years as an MP: he had supported parliamentary reform and Catholic emancipation and had not associated himself with the protectionist lobby. He was, Disraeli later wrote in his hagiographic biography, an infrequent attender, one who 'took no part in debate and attended the House more as a club than a senate' and who had on more than one occasion turned up 'clad in a white great-coat which softened, but did not conceal the scarlet hunting-coat'.[2] Bentinck was a haughty, proud figure, with dark curly hair and mutton-chop whiskers in the fashion of the time, somewhat dandified and in his mid-forties. His energies had previously been focused on cleaning up corruption in horse racing: he had exposed Maccabeus, the winner of the 1844 Derby, as a fraud – a four-year-old in a race for three-year-olds. But now he was a man obsessed with a sense of betrayal by the prime minister. His dander was up and he brought the same concentrated, vengeful energy to bear on the Corn Laws as on racing fraudsters, honing his anger and invective, but also, unlike many of his colleagues, poring over statistics and trade figures to make his case and undermine Peel's arguments. Bentinck's hatred for Peel became visceral.

He was very far from being an accomplished speaker, so nervous that on debate days he would starve himself, nibbling on a piece of dry toast at breakfast, before placing himself in the chamber early in the day and waiting many hours for the chance to speak. It was a habit that Disraeli thought accounted for his frenzied, fervent manner when he did finally stand up: 'the disadvantage of general exhaustion... no doubt a principal cause of that over-excitement and apparently unnecessary energy in his manner of speaking, of which he was himself perfectly and even painfully conscious'. He certainly did not want to lead the protectionists, but his social position left him feeling he had little choice.

Then there was Benjamin Disraeli himself. More exotic and unlikely still as a leader of the die-hards than Bentinck, Disraeli was a man whose reputation as a novelist far outshone his progress as a politician. He had neither land nor title. Rather, he was an exotic metropolitan figure, dandified, with a taste for colourful clothes, sophisticated, witty, short of money if not impoverished, who had been several times passed over for government office by Peel on the grounds that he was unsound and unserious. Above all, if not actually a Jew, he was certainly Jew-ish. His father had converted to Christianity, otherwise Disraeli would not have been eligible for election or to swear the oath as an MP 'on the true faith of a Christian', as was then required (Jews would only be admitted to the Commons after the oath was amended in the mid-1850s). His name and saturnine, exotic appearance still made him suspect to many Tories: 'the Jew d'esprit', blackballed for membership by the Athenaeum.[3] Those who wished to belittle him and emphasize his antecedents spelled his name D'Israeli. This was a period when anti-Semitism was casual and pervasive – cartoons never failed to emphasize Disraeli's Jewishness at a time when *Punch* routinely depicted Jewish figures as hook-nosed, swarthy, grasping and alien 'Mr Nebuchadnezzars'. Disraeli was not the sort of person the landed Tories would have ever considered, had it not been for his sudden usefulness. He was someone who was emphatically 'not a member of our eleven', as one Tory said in those days when aristocrats recruited talented artisans for their private cricket teams; the member for Shrewsbury, he added, was merely 'a professional bowler we take round with us'. Disraeli by now was into his forties – two years younger than Bentinck – and in a hurry for political advancement. He had famously been howled down during his maiden speech nearly a decade earlier, but now he was to make his name with the Tory backbenches by attacking their own party leader, the man who was probably the most popular politician in the country. The combination of Bentinck's fervour, Disraeli's oratory and the Anti-League's organization would be devastating.

In his biography of Bentinck, Disraeli would write that they 'needed to prove to the country that they could represent their cause in debate and to this end all their energies must be directed. It would be fatal to them if the discussion were confined to one or two nights and they overborne by the leading and habitual speakers.' They both needed to prolong the argument, to give the opposition a chance to coalesce and grow.

Parliament reconvened after the state opening on 22 January 1846, the first time MPs had returned to Westminster since the previous August. In her artless way, the queen recorded in her journal that evening that it had been 'damp, rainy, dreadfully windy... had my hair dressed and lunched early. State coach with Duke of Buccleuch. I never saw a greater number of people out and all in such good humour. I got through my speech all right, though I always feel nervous. We got back by three...'[4] If the people were in good humour, that was probably worth recording since the queen had been the subject of assassination attempts along the Mall and had not always found such a favourable welcome on the streets. The *Manchester Guardian*'s report two days later suggested the crowd was unusually large, but that the sovereign had been 'generally cheered' as the state coach passed through the park. Inside the coach the atmosphere may have been a little strained as Buccleuch was one of two members of Peel's cabinet who had resigned rather than support repeal.

The royal speech was extremely short. It was delivered in the old Painted Chamber of the Palace of Westminster, most of which was still being rebuilt more than eleven years after the fire which had swept through it in 1834. The chamber was small and overcrowded, its walls still blackened and cracked, and with a temporary roof since the fire – peers routinely complained of being squashed in so tightly that they were unable to breathe. The *Guardian*'s report said it was full of peeresses and ladies of distinction 'dressed in all colours of the iris, glittering with jewels and many decorated with waving plumes. The number of peers, judges and foreign ministers was remarkable.' The queen, it said, delivered her speech 'in her usual distinct and pure enunciation', which sounds familiar.[5] What is striking is that the Corn Laws were not directly mentioned in the speech at all – a deliberate tactic by the government – though it was implicit in her statement:

the prosperous state of the revenue, the increased demand for labour and the general improvement which has taken place in the internal condition of the country are strong testimonies in favour of the course you have pursued. I recommend you to take into your early consideration whether the principles on which you have acted may not with advantage be yet more extensively applied.

Everyone knew what was meant, though that did not stop Tories from complaining afterwards that Peel's true intention was being hidden.

Later that afternoon and into the dark, wet January evening, Peel set out at length and in detail his reasoning for further reforms of excise duties. The Commons met in what was called the Lesser Hall at Westminster, a few yards from the Painted Chamber, approximately where the Central Lobby and the corridor to the House of Lords are now.[6] The Commons had taken over the eighteenth-century hall which the Lords had previously used while their chamber – also destroyed in the fire – was being rebuilt by Charles Barry along the gothic lines we know today. The large, high-ceilinged room, also with a temporary roof, was lit by candles, so it would have been gloomy and overheated, with a fusty atmosphere as the evening wore on. Most of the Corn Law debates in coming months went on late into the night, so the overcrowded chamber would have become stifling as the speeches dragged on and the drink MPs had been indulging in earlier took its effect. It is little wonder that tempers frayed, the rhetoric grew vehement and animosities became highly personal.

On this night the prime minister's speech was long, dense, laden with statistics and complicated as it rolled remorselessly on. Over the course of the two-and-a-half hours it took to deliver, it was met with a deepening, unhappy and ominous silence on the benches behind him. Peel's speaking style, in keeping with the time, though clear and precise, was orotund and ponderous. People noticed his declaratory approach, chest thrust out defiantly, hands clasped behind him and under the tails of his coat, as if to give a lecture. He clearly knew he had to defend his change of mind and did so first on the basis that circumstances had altered and that he was correcting the policy sincerely. This point was important to him in the wake of a career in which he had changed direction several times, and he knew critics on the benches behind him would accuse him of betrayal. He was acutely sensitive, very conscious of slights, even where none existed, and of condescension: his background, after all, was in trade, and he did not come from aristocratic stock. But, he insisted, people should not doubt his honour, or his integrity: it was a point he would return to time and again over the coming months and, the more he did so, the more his opponents challenged him on it and got under his skin. He insisted he could do no other than change course on the Corn Laws: 'I am led to the conclusion that the main grounds of public policy on which protection has been defended are not tenable, at least I cannot maintain them.'[7] Then, at some length and in detail, he spelled out the fact that previous tariff reform had not caused hardship, but improved prosperity; the reams of statistics about salt pork, wool, even lard must have been tedious to listen to. Then there was the rising price of food: 'Everything is rising rapidly in price and the people begin to show symptoms of discontent which may ripen into something more... we must not allow ourselves to be taken by surprise.' This was followed by a long explanation of the December political crisis and, at last, a peroration on sound Tory policy and his own indifference to office, so long as he was serving his country. This last section sounds both pompous and peevish, as if he was defying his critics to challenge his sense of duty:

> Sir, I will not take the step with mutilated power and shackled authority. I will not stand at the helm during such tempestuous nights as I have seen, if the vessel be not allowed fairly to pursue the course which I think she ought to take... I must, for the public interest, claim for myself the unfettered power of judging of those measures which I conceive will be better for the country to propose. I do not wish to be the Minister of England; but while I have the honour of holding that office, I am determined to hold it by no servile tenure. I will only hold that office upon the condition of being unshackled by any other obligations than those of consulting the public interests and of providing for public safety.

Lord John Russell followed, and then first up from the Tory benches was Disraeli, with the speech which made his name and probably gave more hope and encouragement than any other to the protectionists, battered by the weight and authority of the prime minister's rhetoric. The first thing you notice on reading the speech is the wit and fluency of Disraeli's style: couched in contemporary language, but with a wry, sardonic approach that seems much more recognizably modern than Peel's oratory. It must have been a relief to listen to a speech with jokes and resonant passages after the prime minister's lengthy discourse. Disraeli's manner of speaking was not declaratory, like so many others of the period, but low-key and, if not conversational (his voice would not have carried otherwise), straight-faced and ironic. If it seemed at all offhand, it clearly was not: he had obviously been taking notes. He knew precisely where to hit Peel – in his defensiveness and arrogance – and he stung. As the speech went on, much shorter than the prime minister's but still perhaps an hour long, the Tories stirred and started cheering. They were not used to Peel's authority being so derisively challenged – nor was Peel – and Disraeli gave them new hope.

The main line of attack was on Peel's rectitude and what Disraeli called 'his peculiar tone'; he would repeatedly throw the prime minister's words back in his face in a highly personalized critique. If Peel had wanted to change policy, he should have gone to the country and obtained a mandate rather than 'menacing' the party to follow him. Where Peel had spoken proudly and meaningfully of his long government service under four monarchs, Disraeli deployed ridicule:

What, sir, are we to think of the eminent statesman who, having served under four sovereigns, unable to complain of want of experience or royal confidence, who having been called to steer the ship on so many occasions and under such perilous circumstances, has, only during the last three years, found it necessary entirely to change his convictions on that important topic which must have presented itself for more than a quarter of a century to his consideration?

Peel was like the admiral of the Turkish sultan (and everyone knew how untrustworthy Turks were) who, having been equipped with a fine navy, steered them straight into the enemy's port to surrender, on the grounds that he had a sudden objection to war. He was like a coachman in directing the affairs of state (that must have hurt) – 'no more a great statesman than the man who gets up behind a carriage is a great whip'. 'He tells you this as his recommendation and he adds "follow me." Follow him! Who is to follow him, or why is anybody to follow him, or where is anybody to follow him to?' Peel could not expect to betray his party:

> What I cannot endure is to hear a man come down and say 'I will rule without respect of party, though I rose by party; and I care not for your judgement, for I look to posterity'. Sir, very few people reach posterity... Let men stand by the principle by which they rise – right or wrong... Do not because you see a great personage giving up his opinions, do not cheer him on – do not yield so ready a reward to political tergiversation.

The Tory benches erupted. It was magnificent invective, impertinent, calculated, contemptuous, unfair – and cynical. It was rich of Disraeli to speak of principle and he could have argued the opposite case equally well, and perhaps would have done had Peel only given him promotion earlier. He had not particularly aligned himself with the backbench country squires before, or shown much interest in the tariff question. But he had hit Peel in the solar plexus, at the roots of his self-regard, and the prime minister understandably could not see the funny side. He viewed Disraeli with contempt, although when the moment came later at which he could have destroyed him, he would not do so.

In both the Commons and the Lords that night, other backwoodsmen would attack repeal, but none had Disraeli's wit or gift for ridicule. In the Lords, the Duke of Richmond – patron of the Anti-League, owner of the Goodwood estate in Sussex, son of that duchess of Richmond who had given the ball in Brussels on the eve of Waterloo,* and himself a former aide-de-camp to the Duke of Wellington during the battle – denounced Peel in much more extreme terms. The prime minister was not manly, he was behaving unconstitutionally, abandoning his duty to his country. You can almost sense his face reddening:

> Whether or not we are to have these modern innovations passed into law, whether we are to be rendered dependent on foreigners for the supply of our population, whether we are to be constantly changing about because there happens to be some popular clamour... I will use every parliamentary means of opposition in my power – be it called fractious, I care not.

It was so far over the top that you can see why Peel called him privately 'that great goose Richmond'. Richmond's old general, Wellington, unhappy with the reform but loyal to Peel, sat up late into the night listening to the tirade, but then dismissed it as an unworthy attack on a prime minister acting

---

* This was the famous ball held on 15 June 1815, the night before the preliminary battle at Quatre Bras and three days before the final battle at Waterloo. The evening was interrupted by the news that Napoleon and the French army had crossed the border and were heading for Brussels. It is commemorated in a famous passage in Byron's epic *Childe Harold's Pilgrimage*.

in the best interest of the country. That would be the duke's default position: loyalty trumped doubt.

In the gallery, the Whig diarist Greville had a ringside seat that evening:

> Went to the House of Commons last night... Peel rose and spoke for about two hours. A very fine speech in a very high tone... He did not get a single cheer from the people behind him... except when he said that Stanley had always been against him... and then the whole of those benches rang with cheers... It was certainly not a speech calculated to lead to a reconciliation between him and the Tories and it is difficult to see how he will be able to go on after this session, supposing him to settle the Corn Bill. Then came an hour of gibes and bitterness, all against Peel personally from D'Israeli with some good hits, but much of it tiresome; vehemently cheered by the Tories, but not once by the Whigs. I never heard him before; his fluency is wonderful, his cleverness great and his mode of speaking certainly effective though there is something monotonous about it.[8]

This then was the flavour of the start of the parliamentary repeal process. Peel and Wellington knew now that they had a fight on their hands. Disraeli had become a hero to the backbenches overnight and leader of the opposition, but his speech, possibly because it was so late, did not draw particular comment in the morning. It did not impress Victoria, who would much later come to admire Disraeli at least as much as she now appreciated Peel. She wrote in her journal the following day:

Sir Robert Peel's speech, which is very long, is quite beautiful. He makes out such a strong case, very spirited and eloquent declaration, that he will not govern by party, but as he thinks it is best for the country. This is quite unanswerable... violent speeches from Mr Disraeli and Mr Miles, the Duke of Richmond a most absurdly violent speech.[9]

Is there just a hint of how strongly she was being influenced by her husband Prince Albert in all this? He was certainly closely engaged with Peel and thoroughly supportive of his policy, reading *The Times* each morning, corresponding with the prime minister several times a week and acutely aware of the minutiae of parliamentary tactics in the weeks to come.

The following week's *Observer* would lambast Richmond and 'his trained bands of misguided serfs' and relished pointing out that, despite being a Tory, he had actually served in Lord Grey's reform government in 1832: 'his present conduct, mischievous and unholy though it be in intention should excite no public alarm – it scarcely merits indignation – it is simply wicked and contemptible.'[10] The *Manchester Guardian*, voice of the cotton manufacturers, spoke of the 'bold and uncompromising avowals' in Peel's masterly and convincing speech, replete with important facts and sound principles, and, understandably, was convinced that the Corn Laws were all but repealed. The arguments of the protectionists were of the most feeble character:

The chance of maintaining an exclusive Corn Law is becoming daily less and less, the inevitable consequence in a country where public opinion is all powerful... however reluctant the landed interest, they cannot but feel that the death of monopoly is an accomplished fact – of which they may complain indeed but against which it is hopeless to contend.[11]

∽

The protectionists' arguments may have been useless to contend in the *Manchester Guardian*'s opinion, but now at least they had a cogent spokesman in the Commons, as well as a number of wealthy, vehement and influential opponents of appeal, such as Richmond and Bentinck. There was little doubt that the measure would pass in the Commons. Greville thought that the protectionists would manage 200 votes, the Peelites (as they were already being called, differentiating them from Tories) 180, and then the Whigs 200 to 300; but that still meant that the prime minister had lost the support of more than half of his party. The Tory opposition sometimes feels like the Major government's Maastricht rebels, with the exception that the 'bastards' of the mid-1990s did not have a leader who might one day become a prime minister himself. Of course, in 1846 the thought that Benjamin Disraeli would one day lead a majority Tory government would have been considered absurd, and indeed he had to wait almost thirty years to do so, by which time he was nearly seventy. Had the great split over the Corn Laws not occurred, the likelihood is that he would never have climbed, as he said, to the top of the greasy pole.

Over the coming months Peel would carry the repeal case in the Commons nearly single-handed. That is probably how he would have chosen to do it, confident that he was the only person with the authority and competence, conversant enough with the facts to deploy the arguments needed to do so. The queen's journal entries remain insouciant: for 23 January, 'Lord Exeter and Lord Hardwicke have both resigned which we are very sorry for, but which cannot be helped', but even she noticed that Sir Robert was looking increasingly weighed down in spirit as the debate wore on. It was the abuse he suffered that she found most deplorable.

Peel could have done with the support of his most able young cabinet colleague, William Gladstone, at that stage the colonial secretary, but unfortunately he had gone walkabout. His situation appears obscure if not absurd today: the previous year Gladstone, obsessively high-minded and absorbed by theological and church affairs, had resigned his ministerial post as president of the Board of Trade over the government's decision to increase the grant to the Maynooth Catholic seminary. This was not because he did not support the proposal – he did – but because he had previously produced a two-volume work in 1838 – *The State in its Relations with the Church*, 500 pages, written with characteristic energy in a month – against the principle of state support for the Catholic Church and felt that he could not desert that position with honour, despite the fact that he had now changed his mind. Even Gladstone eventually, fifty years on, found it hard to understand his own reasoning: 'I have difficulty in conceiving by what obliquity of view I could have come to imagine this was a rational or in any way excusable proposal.'[12]

But now there was another stumbling block. Peel had brought Gladstone back into the cabinet in December, following Stanley's resignation, and – in accordance with convention at the time (which was in place until 1918) – after his new ministerial appointment he was required to resign his seat and fight a by-election. Unfortunately, the patron of his Newark constituency, the Duke of Newcastle, was an ardent protectionist, so Gladstone had to seek another seat. Normally, for such a bright young talent (Gladstone was still only thirty-five) that would not have been a problem, but in the prevailing febrile atmosphere of the Tory party he would have to cast around for more than a year before eventually becoming one of the members for Oxford University, by which time Peel was out of office and he himself was accordingly no longer a minister.

During this period Gladstone was in any event in what his latest biographer Roy Jenkins describes as a mid-century frenzy. There was not only the political crisis and the crisis over Tractarianism within the Church of England to absorb him (see chapter 7), but also a family division. His sister Helen had converted to Catholicism in 1842 and gone abroad, from which fates Gladstone took it upon himself personally to rescue her (unsuccessfully as it turned out). More dangerously still, and potentially scandalously, he was beginning his nocturnal ramblings through London in search of prostitutes to rescue from their sin. And, in the margins of his diary, cryptic little signs were beginning to appear: crosses for when his inner turbulence was at its height and curious little whip-like symbols periodically highlighting what seem to have been either flagellations or self-mortification.[13]

The long-drawn-out parliamentary process through the spring and summer of 1846 grew increasingly bitter and personal on the Tory benches, exposing rifts that would never heal. The protectionist Duke of Newcastle ensured that his son, Lord Lincoln, a Peelite and friend of Gladstone's, would be defeated in the Nottinghamshire by-election and only spoke to him again on his death-bed five years later.[14] Instead of electing the son of the seat's patron, formerly a rising star in the party, the electors chose an unknown young protectionist named T. B. Hildyard. The farmers of the constituency enthusiastically campaigned for him, canvassed voters and even drove them to the polls. Lincoln spent thousands of pounds in a vain effort to get elected and Hildyard spent virtually nothing.

The internecine strife and anguish can be seen in a hyperventilating letter that the Tory politician and journalist John Wilson Croker wrote on 24th April 1846 to Sir Henry Hardinge, the governor general of India:

I am in as decided *opposition* as a private gentleman can be to the Queen's government... For all my affection for [Peel], I cannot excuse this late tergiversation and above all the deception of endeavouring to attribute it to the potato failure in Ireland...What the real cause of the change of opinion was I cannot *positively* assert. There was, perhaps, some *original* disposition to abstract free trade and the advancement of the manufacturing interests and some latent hatred of the 'proud aristocracy'. The fatal consequences are that Peel by betraying the precise and specific principle upon which he was brought into office, has ruined the character of public men and dissolved, by dividing, the great landed interest – the only solid foundation on which any government can be formed in this country... how are we to resist the attack on the Irish Church – the Irish Union? How to maintain primogeniture, the bishops, the House of Lords, the Crown? He has broken up the old interests, divided the great families and commenced just such a revolution as... in 1789.

The viciousness was striking. Bentinck cheerfully smeared another Peelite with accusations of marital infidelity. Peel's loyal follower Sidney Herbert berated his oldest and closest friend, Lord Malmesbury, who was supporting the Ultras, with conduct unworthy of a gentleman, one of the most powerful insults in an era when men still called each other out for duels. Accusations of bad faith and moral bankruptcy were spread on both sides. Greville said of Bentinck: 'From never having spoken, he now does nothing else. And he is completely over-doing it and like a beggar on horseback, riding to the devil.'[15] The government vainly offered money to buy off the farmers in the form of land improvement grants, but the bit was between the protectionists' teeth: as Sir John Tyrrell, a major landowner in Essex, said gleefully, it was 'such general opposi-tion as the boldest minister would hardly dare face'.[16]

Peel, sitting on the front bench listening for hours to personal attacks on himself, night after night, found support ebbing away. Time and again he was accused of betrayal, double-dealing, swindling and deceit. Farmers and landowners would be ruined. The Irish famine, the protectionists asserted, was not really serious – Bentinck argued that the potatoes were rotting only because they had been dug up too early; and Tory after Tory insisted there should be a general election to give a voice to those who doubted the prime minister's good faith – a rash demand in the circumstances and a bluff they well knew would never be called. The government's tactical error was to allow matters to get out of hand, just as it did in the Maastricht process a century and a half later. The initial debate – on a delaying protectionist amendment, to refer the reform to a parliamentary committee and then postpone hear-ings for six months – was dragged out over twelve nights.

More than a hundred backbenchers spoke in the debate, over half of them against the government. Gladstone, no admirer of Disraeli, would tell his biographer John Morley nearly half a century later that the parliamentary assaults on the prime minister had been 'quite as wonderful as report makes them, Peel altogether helpless in reply, dealing with them with a kind of righteous dullness'.[17]

In his speech on the fifth night of the debate, Peel was not helpless but became bogged down as he combatively ridiculed Tory backbenchers concerned for the domestic grease-producing industry or for the loss of flax production in a Somerset village which had actually ceased producing the crop twenty years before the tariff had been lowered. In answer to those complaining that poor tenants would be turned off the land that their ancestors had farmed for generations, he suggested that if landlords helped them to produce more crops everyone would be better off. He insisted that the measure was vital for Britain's economic future in the world, culminating in the peroration:

> This night you will select the motto which is to indicate the commercial policy of England. Shall it be 'advance' or 'recede'? Which is the fitter motto for this great Empire? Survey our position; consider the advantage which God and nature have given us and the destiny for which we are intended. The discoveries of science, the improvement of navigation have brought us within ten days of St. Petersburg and will soon bring us within ten days of New York... And is this the country to adopt a retrograde policy? Is this the country which can only flourish in the sickly atmosphere of prohibition? Choose your motto, Advance or Recede. Many

countries are watching the selection you may make. Deter-
mine for Advance and it will be the watchword which will
encourage and animate in every state the friends of liberal
and commercial policy... Can you doubt that the United
States will soon relax its hostile tariff and that the friends
of a freer commercial intercourse – the friends of peace
between the two countries – will hail with satisfaction the
example of England?[18]

In this, of course, Peel was much too hopeful, but as his
biographer Douglas Hurd asserts, the speech counts as one of
the founding documents of globalization and free trade.[19] But
was anyone still listening? By the time Peel sat down it was
nearly two o'clock in the morning and the debate still had
another fortnight to run. Queen Victoria thought the speech,
when she read it the next day, 'admirable and very long...
truly noble and spirited in such perfect temper'. Her husband's
enthusiastic support for Peel was noticed when Albert visited
the Commons on 27 January to watch Peel's speech from the
gallery – a breach of constitutional protocol that has never
been repeated by any member of the royal family and was all
the more sensitive because the prince was still regarded with
suspicion as a German by some Tories. They could not criti-
cize the queen, but they could certainly attack him, and they
did so. Albert cannot have stayed long – the queen's journal
for that day notes that he left for the Commons at 5.30 p.m.
and was back in time for dinner, while Peel's speech lasted
more than three-and-a-half hours – but he was there long
enough to be noticed and Bentinck drew malicious attention
to that fact when he spoke later in the debate. It gave, he said,
'the semblance of a personal sanction of Her Majesty' for a

measure that was opposed by the great majority of the landed aristocracy. The secret was out and it probably only made the protectionists feel even more recalcitrant.

Peel told the queen that a majority of 100 would be counted a success. The party's business managers began the debate thinking that a few dozen might rebel. By early February the estimate had risen to nearly 200, and when the vote was finally taken, at three o'clock on the Saturday morning of 28 February 1846, the government's majority was actually ninety-seven, which meant that only 112 Tories had supported Peel and more than twice as many – 231 – had voted against their leader. The majority was only guaranteed by the 227 Whigs who voted with the government on this occasion. In a House of 658 MPs, the writing was on the wall: Peel could be confident of the loyal support of only about a sixth of the MPs in the Commons. 'Deduct 40 official men and it would appear as if our independent strength did not much exceed 70 members,' Peel wrote gloomily to his friend Hardinge, the governor-general of India, a few weeks later.

Down at Osborne on the Isle of Wight, where Thomas Cubitt was building the royal family their new holiday home, Prince Albert wrote to the prime minister: 'This does not look like a strong government.' He consoled himself that it had moral strength 'which must tell more every day', but that was a very uncertain foundation. Victoria herself thought the majority 'a very large one, though we should have preferred, for appearances rather, three more, making up the 100'. Two months after she had thought the free-trader Richard Cobden a dangerous extremist, she now believed that his speech warning that, if there was an election, every borough with more than 20,000 people would vote for free trade was 'very wonderful'. The next day Peel's analysis of the vote arrived and she was no longer so sure: 'The division was certainly not very satisfactory, but then I am certain that a number of members voted against Sir Robert on this occasion, which they would not have done on any other.' And with that she wandered out into the garden to watch her husband plant a daphne bush, a magnolia and two japonicas in the new flower-beds – 'very rare and exotic plants'.

Peel had won the first round, but only with the massed support of the opposition Whigs. However, divisions on the Tory benches were now too bitter for there to be any assur-ance that the queen was right to think it was a one-off rebellion. For Disraeli, Bentinck, Richmond and the other conspirators, the object now was not to stop the repeal of the Corn Laws – they knew they could not do that – but, in a fit of fury, to bring down Peel and the government itself, which they no longer trusted to govern. It did not take long for them to discover a way to do it. And the time was fast approaching when the Whigs would join in to help them.

❧

The Duke of Wellington had spent the Christmas break writing lengthy letters to influential Tory friends and colleagues urging them to support the prime minister. He was now aged 76 and conceived it as his duty as an old soldier loyally to give his backing to queen and country: Russell had let her down, so it was now time to rally behind Peel. He sat down at Stratfield Saye, his country estate north of Basingstoke, and sent out laborious letters, sometimes five apiece to the doubters, and then responded to their replies, now with pen and ink rather than the cannon-shot and musket-fire with which he had defended the country of old. The message was consistent: the lady needed to be rescued from people like Cobden. When Lord Redesdale replied that it would be better for the Tories to go into opposition than cut their throats by carrying the measure, the duke retorted they needed to stand by the queen. The Duke of Beaufort, who was a relative of Wellington's, was given a lengthy exposition of how agriculture would benefit from repeal; it ended waspishly: 'I would likewise beg you to observe that the provisions of the Corn Law, however interesting, are not the only interest of this great country.' A good government, he insisted yet again, was more important than Corn Laws.[20]

Such a weight of authority from the party's senior statesman, one of the most admired men in the country, had some effect. It meant the protectionists could not count on him as a leader, but also that their alternative hope, Lord Stanley, would not lead them either against the duke himself. Stanley had no appetite for factional, die-in-a-ditch oppositionism, preferring to spend time with his Greek translations. He would, however, later become the longest-serving leader of the Conservative party – twenty-two years – and was three times prime minister (briefly on each occasion).

Wellington's effort was all the more steadfast because the duke's former private secretary, Colonel John Gurwood, had committed suicide that Christmas, and he had other things on his mind. Gurwood, who Wellington had known since he was a young officer during the Peninsula campaign more than thirty years before, had been increasingly erratic for some time. The duke had obtained for him the sinecure post of deputy lieutenant of the Tower of London at a reasonable salary of £800 a year a few years earlier, but Gurwood had become obsessive about the fashionable fad of mesmerism and also depressed and insomniac. Two weeks before Christmas 1845 Wellington wrote to him in his normal brusque style: 'My dear Colonel! I am sorry to learn that you are unwell. I should be very happy to see you here; you will find a warm house and great tranquillity.' But it was too late. On Christmas Day, in Brighton, Gurwood slit his throat.[21]

What the duke found even more alarming at such a time was that, unknown to him – and directly against all his instructions – Gurwood had been secretly collecting Wellington's papers and surreptitiously noting down his conversation in order to write a biography of him, as other friends of Wellington such as Lord Mahon were also doing. The duke was appalled. He knew that any biography, however hagiographic, would immediately appear in bowdlerized and fanciful versions across the Continent, so he had to get the papers back. It was a sensitive task at such a time. Gurwood's French wife denied that she knew anything about them and replied that if they had existed at all, her husband must have destroyed them. The correspondence grew acrimonious. The duke insisted: such a breach of confidence was anti-social and must put an end to 'all the charms of society, to all familiar and private communications of thought between men and men'. His letters grew longer and more agitated, but it was no good: Mrs Gurwood insisted she had not seen the papers and in the end he had to acknowledge the fact. Since they have never resurfaced, it is almost certainly true that Gurwood had burned them.

5

Fustian Jackets, Blistered Hands and Unshorn Chins

'Before the Majesty of their United Will, Whigs and Tories and all Dark and Deceitful Things will flee away as the shadows disappear before the rising sun.'

DECLARATION BY THE
BIRMINGHAM POLITICAL UNION, 1837

It was not so much the parliamentary opposition that unnerved politicians like Peel in the 1840s as the campaigns mounted outside Westminster in support of political reform. His speeches of this time are rich in references to the great masses of the people, the general interests of all classes, and the task of elevating the social conditions of those earning their daily bread by the sweat of their brow. The country had to be made cheap for living, he said. This was not a philanthropic concern, nor mere paternalism. It was, in his view, common sense and self-interest.

The country had seen a series of violent localized uprisings during the prime minister's lifetime and they were becoming more frequent with each dip in the economic cycle in the late 1830s and early 1840s. Disturbances had occurred in Newport in 1839, followed by the Rebecca agricultural riots across Wales over the following four years,* as tenant

---

* So called because the rioters called themselves 'Rebeccas', supposedly after the line in Genesis 24:60 which speaks of Rebecca leading thousands

farmers and labourers, often dressed in women's clothing to disguise themselves, attacked the buildings and tollgates of officialdom in protests against high prices, mechanization and taxation. There had also been the Plug riots of 1842, strikes in coal-fields and factories across the Midlands, the North and Scotland against wage reductions and redundancies, so called because the workers had removed the plugs from the steam-engines at their workplaces as they left. These had followed the Swing riots in the countryside in the early 1830s and the Peterloo massacre in Manchester during a political reform demonstration in 1819.* This was the army of what the Chartist leader Feargus O'Connor would call 'the fustian jackets, blistered hands and unshorn chins' of the working class in 1846.[1]

Masterless men and navvies in their thousands were tramping across the country, many of them Irish, coming from an island where violence was endemic. Local police forces, such as there were, often could not cope, and troops and militias had to be called in. Shots would be fired, men died and ringleaders were sentenced to hang, though such sentences were usually commuted to transportation. It could happen again and a more general uprising under charismatic leaders could repeat the worst depredations of the French Revolution of fifty years earlier. Even if ultimately it did not happen, that did not mean that this possibility was not in the minds of those in power in 1846.

---

of millions and possessing the gates of those who hate her.

* Fifteen people were killed and hundreds injured when a peaceful rally at St Peter's Fields, Manchester, was bloodily broken up by the local militia on horseback. Taking place four years after the Battle of Waterloo, it became known as the Peterloo massacre.

The House of Commons had been changed by the 1832 Reform Act: the franchise had been widened to include more householders, leaseholders and tenants, adding about 217,000 to the existing electorate of 435,000. But this remained a small proportion of the adult male population. Some of the more glaringly fraud-ridden and depopulated rotten boroughs had been abolished and their parliamentary seats redistributed to the previously unrepresented industrial towns, but the electoral system remained deeply corrupt. Candidates had to be men of wealth simply to get on the ballot, let alone fight an election, and MPs were not paid. Contests could be extremely expensive: returning officers charged fees – £1,065 in the Lindsey division of Lincolnshire in the 1830s, £752 in Berkshire, £522 in the City of London – even if the seat was uncontested, as many were. That was before taking into account policing costs and the bribes, inducements and entertainments for the electorate themselves. Local pub landlords had to be squared: one in Hertford in 1832 submitted an entertainment bill of £440.[2] The Irish journalist T. P. O'Connor wrote in his memoirs of elections in Athlone in the mid-1840s:

> the number of voters was small and therefore the amount of the bribe was high. [It] averaged £30 or £40 the vote and there were tales of a vote having run up to £100... with many of the people the periodic vote entered into the whole economy of their squalid and weary lives. Men continued to live in houses who had better have lived in lodgings because the house gave them the vote. The very whisper of a dissolution sent a visible thrill through the town.

Such sums could mount up and private resources or a wealthy patron – such as the Duke of Newcastle in Newark – were needed. In the 1841 election, winning over the 5,000 electors of Nottingham cost the two victorious candidates £12,000 and the losers a further £5,000. The Duke of Bedford told his younger son Lord John Russell that funding the election in Bedford in 1834 had cost £28,000: 'it makes my hair stand on end.' Also to be funded were the local toughs, paid to look after electors who were committed to vote for the candidate and, often, to attack those pledged to the other side. After the general election of 1847, Edward Seymour, who lost Horsham by nine votes, complained of his opponent: 'It is said he gave a thousand pounds for five votes! Certain it is that voters were made tipsy and locked up, besides all sorts of violence.' After the winner's declaration, there would often be legal disputes over the outcome, which also had to be paid for. Dickens satirized the process through the Eatanswill election in *The Pickwick Papers*, written in 1836, but as Norman Gash, the historian of the period, remarked, its picture is 'not so much an exaggerated as a pale and euphemistic version of the contemporary scene... in comparison with what actually happened in many constituencies, Dickens's account is under-drawn, conventional and staid'.[3]

Charles Greville dined with Abraham Robarts, the member for Maidstone, in 1835 and recorded their conversation about the constituency in his diary:

There are 1,200 voters: the dissenters are very numerous and of every imaginable sect and persuasion... the place very corrupt. Formerly (before the Reform Act) when the constituency was less numerous, the matter was easily and simply conducted: the price of votes was as regularly fixed as the price of bread... and this he had to pay. After the Reform bill he resolved to pay no more money as corruption was to cease. The consequence was that during his canvass none of the people who had formerly voted for him would promise him their vote. They all sulked and hesitated and, in short, waited to see what would be offered them... They have a sour feeling against what are nicknamed abuses, rail against sinnicures as they call them and descant upon the enormity of such things while they are forced to work all day long and their families have not enough to eat... the one prevailing object among the whole community is to make money of their votes. Power has been transferred to a low class of person, so low as to be dissatisfied and malignant, high enough to be half-instructed; so poor that money is an object to them... they may, on the whole, be considered disaffected towards existing institutions... but as their immediate wants are uppermost, their votes are generally at the disposal of the highest bidder, whatever his politics may be.

Robarts was actually only an MP for five years after the Reform Act (Greville claimed he had been an MP for seventeen years, but the Hansard record does not show that), so presumably his payments had gone to waste in losing contests earlier. His complaints about the venality and disgruntlement of his constituents might find at least a partial echo among some rueful politicians today.[4] Robarts's successor at Maidstone in 1837 was Benjamin Disraeli, who would himself write about a parliamentary election in *Coningsby*. By 1846 Disraeli, too, had moved on and was the MP for Shrewsbury

– many MPs moved from constituency to constituency, in search of safer seats or richer patrons, or after falling out with sponsors or voters. Peel himself represented five different places during a forty-year parliamentary career.

There were two national movements outside Parliament challenging the authority of politicians. The Anti-Corn Law League, organized by and partly centred on the northern manufacturers, campaigned largely for the single goal of repeal of the Corn Laws. Potentially rather more dangerous were the Chartists, a mainly working-class movement with a diffuse range of political demands. Both organizations had been founded in the late 1830s, and by 1846, while the League had gained in focus and influence, the Chartists had fallen to squabbling and internal divisions over tactics and strategy. This considerably weakened the movement's organization, but that was not necessarily obvious to politicians observing its leaders' rhetoric or its mass meetings. Their talk of 'an entire change in society... a complete subversion of the existing order of the world' was deeply threatening to those whose wealth came from the land and whose status depended on deference. The challenge was largely met by the suppression of meetings and the periodic arrest of Chartist leaders.

In fact the Chartists, so called from the National Charter Association with its programme of political reforms, presented their demands almost entirely by legitimate and decorous – indeed constitutional – means: the periodic peaceful presentation of petitions to Parliament. The demands of the Charter, drawn up in 1838 by the London Working Men's Association, seem entirely unthreatening, now that almost all of them have long ago been taken for granted: universal manhood (though not female) suffrage, secret ballots, equal electoral districts, payment of MPs, no property qualifications for candidates and – the only demand never agreed – annual parliaments. But it was the implications behind them, the potential loss of control, which frightened the political classes. 'The House of Commons is the People's House and there our opinions should be stated, there our rights ought to be advocated, there we ought to be represented, or we are SERFS,' the Chartists proclaimed in their original declaration.[5] And the rhetoric at their public meetings was often fiery. When Dr Matthew Fletcher, a Chartist from Bury in Lancashire, spoke of every man needing a loaded bludgeon 'as nearly like a policeman's as possible', or young George Julian Harney, who wore a revolutionary red liberty cap to show he meant business, demanded that 'before the end of the year, the people shall have universal suffrage or death', they tended to be taken at their word. Harney campaigned for a general strike – a grand national holiday, as it was gently called at the time – and demanded an insurrection as the only answer to people's grievances. Universal suffrage, he claimed, would bring universal happiness. He told a meeting in Derby in 1839:

Peaceably if we can, forcibly if we must... Time was when every Englishman had a musket in his cottage and along with it hung a flitch of bacon; now there is no flitch of bacon for there is no musket; let the musket be restored and the flitch of bacon will soon follow. You will get nothing from your tyrants but what you can take. Arm for peace, arm for liberty, arm for justice, arm for the rights of all and the tyrants will no longer laugh at your petitions.[6]

This was an England which never was and never would be, but those who listened to men like Harney were not to know that. Harney, who was twenty-one at the time he made this speech, would become editor of the Chartists' paper the *Northern Star* five years later and land in and out of prison over the coming years, before drifting towards an early form of socialism, being expelled from the Chartist movement, befriending Marx and Engels, and eventually moving to the United States.

But many Chartists were motivated just as strongly by Nonconformism and their religious allegiances. Mass meetings often opened with hymn-singing. The National Chartist Hymn Book, of which perhaps the sole surviving copy came to light in 2011, contained hymns that speak powerfully of social justice and are critical of both aristocrats and clergy.[7] They believed a just God would not permit their suffering.

The Chartists never managed to reconcile their divisions between the 'physical force' Chartists, including firebrands like Harney, and the 'moral force' constitutionalists who wanted to press for parliamentary reform peacefully, by the strength of argument and reason. The movement's problem was that, although its aims were drawn up by the latter (Francis Place, a London breeches-maker, and William Lovett, a cabinet-maker originally from Cornwall, were the chief movers in compiling the charter), its leadership was taken over by the former, notably by the Irish-born agitator Feargus O'Connor and whoever were his acolytes at any given time. O'Connor, who came from a wealthy Protestant Irish nationalist family and had been elected an MP for the Irish seat of Cork in the 1830s as a follower of O'Connell before being unseated, was of an entirely different background to the movement's founders. He was a charismatic speaker, but a prickly and difficult personality who succeeded in falling out with everyone who did not entirely share his own messianic vision of himself, or his rather hazy and wavering view of where the movement should be going. He was, said Lovett sourly, 'the great I AM'. O'Connor toured the country – and Europe – indefatigably, rousing crowds and inspiring fervent loyalty, but, it was said, did nothing and found fault with everything. The *Northern Star* was his newspaper, based in Leeds and selling 50,000 copies a time at its peak. That was a huge sale for its day, far outweighing that of *The Times* and other national newspapers, especially considering that each issue would have had probably up to a dozen readers. There were over 120 different Chartist newspapers at one time or another. But O'Connor even fell out with the *Northern Star's* editor Harney in the end.

It is a mistake to assume, because newspaper circulations were much smaller than today and there were fewer alternative sources of information, that political issues were not followed or debated by large sections of the population, including the working class. Parliamentary debates were extensively covered – there were already more than fifty reporters in the Commons in the 1830s, one of them the young Charles Dickens – and politics took up a considerable amount of editorial space. By the 1840s London papers could be delivered across the country by rail: Peel's January Commons speech, launching his campaign to repeal the Corn Laws, was delivered between 5.20 and 8 p.m., and by 5 a.m. the following morning the reports of it were on sale in London – and by lunchtime in Scotland. Local and regional papers often picked up reports from the national press, so that accounts in *The Times* would frequently be reprinted by papers elsewhere. They did not see their role as being simply to cover local events, and their readerships would obtain information about national and international events from them. As *Mitchell's Newspaper Press Directory* stated in 1846: 'The family resident in the country looks with the same eagerness to the delivery of the local paper as we in London do for the Times and other morning journals.' For each copy sold, there would be multiple readers: the *Leeds Mercury* estimated in 1839 that it had up to twenty readers a copy and the *Dover Chronicle* reckoned in 1841 it was seen by twelve readers for every paper sold. A cotton-trader at the Manchester Exchange or a gentleman in his London club would have a wide choice of papers to read every day: the Exchange took twenty-four copies of the *Morning Chronicle*, twenty-two of *The Times*, twelve each of the *Morning Herald* and the *Morning Post*, ten each of *The Standard* and *The Globe*, as well as twelve each of the *Manchester Guardian*, *Manchester Chronicle* and *Manchester Courier*, and an array of other local and regional papers – each having a distinct and polemical viewpoint on the issues of the day. Even those who could not read – though it is now thought that two-thirds of the adult population could read at least a little by this time – were able to follow what was going on: there were readings from the newspapers at public meetings, in halls and at hustings. *The Times*'s report of the Queen's Speech that January was read out the following evening at the Commercial Hall in Liverpool to an audience of 3,000, 'many of them gentlemen of wealth and influence'. Add to this specialist publications, weekly newspapers and broadsheets, and the intensity and range of the public debate becomes apparent.[8] There were even topical doggerel songs, hawked around the streets and tap-rooms:

> Oh! What advantage we shall reap,
> Penny loaves and butter cheap,
> Puddings in country, pies in town,
> And apple dumplings six for a brown,
> And the Queen declares if time should come
> That she should have another son,
> Stamped in gold should be upon his b—,
> Sir Robert Peel and the Corn Bill.

Chartism appealed to those who were excluded from the parliamentary process but were sufficiently educated to be literate: the skilled craftsmen and working classes of the industrialized towns of the Midlands and the North, tradesmen rather than shop-floor factory workers. Its membership lists are full of those in jobs susceptible to economic and seasonal fluctuations: weavers, tailors and shoemakers. Its support accordingly ebbed and flowed with the economy. Many were motivated by fear of destitution and the workhouse: the movement for political reform developed out of opposition to the new Poor Law. Many of the Chartists' concerns were more about reductions in wages and rising prices than with political reform, and the movement varied in tone from place to place, depending on who was in charge locally: decorous in Birmingham and London, more vehement and radical in Lancashire and Yorkshire. There were active groups in market towns such as Trowbridge and Carmarthen, but Chartism had little traction among the rural poor, who were more concerned with bread than ballots, or among the tenant farmers who might have led them. By the early 1840s, however, the Chartists claimed to have 500,000 members and 400 branches; more than 100,000 people were said to have accompanied its 1842 petition through London. It was a considerable force, but its political demands got nowhere with politicians.[9]

Crucially, the Chartist leadership did not see much purpose in seeking to make a strategic alliance with a more middle-class following and was actively hostile to the Anti-Corn Law League, which it saw, rightly, as an employers' organization whose interests were inimical to the working classes. Chartists even attended League meetings in order to break them up. When, in 1840, League organizers in Sunderland made overtures locally towards the Chartists, they received a dusty reply: 'You are the holders of power, participation in which you refuse us... you persecute us with a malignity paralleled only by the ruffian Tories. We are therefore surprised that you should ask us to cooperate with you.'[10] Nor were the League leaders any keener to dilute their campaign against the Corn Laws by association with ruffianly political reformers.

By 1845 O'Connor, having alienated virtually everyone else in the leadership and despairing of political reform, was turning his thoughts to ways of leading the movement in a different direction: towards the foundation of a co-operative land plan, to buy up country estates, divide them into two-, three- or four-acre plots, and resettle them with urban workers. More than £100,000 was raised in subscriptions, mainly in tiny amounts from factory employees wishing for a new start. Eventually six estates would be purchased in the name of the National Land Company, launched in October 1846. The first of them at Chorleywood in Hertfordshire became known as O'Connorsville.[11] The scheme was redolent of romantic notions of communal, rustic living and nostalgia for an idyllic rural past. But it was also infused with idealistic notions of freeing the working class from the slavery of the factory floor and giving them independence and security.

The Chartists petitioned Parliament for reform in 1838, then again in 1842 and would do so one last time in 1848, on each occasion having their demands rejected by progressively larger margins. The movement's final mass rally, on Kennington Common in London, was held on 10 April 1848. It was the first significant news event to be photographed anywhere in the world. There were revolutions in Europe that spring, and fears that the same thing would happen in London if the Chartists attempted to present their latest petition with violence. Scuffles in Trafalgar Square at a demonstration the previous month had led to many arrests, one of them of a young man detained outside Buckingham Palace after shouting 'Vive la République', who burst into tears when he was arrested. The queen fled to Osborne on the Isle of Wight on Lord John Russell's advice two days before the meeting.[12] Russell was by then the prime minister of a Whig government.

The newspapers warned of anarchy. *The Times* claimed in time-honoured fashion that the demonstrators were the tools of sinister forces: 'the true character of the present movement is a ramification of the Irish conspiracy. The Repealers wish to make as great a hell of this island as they have made of their own.'[13] Thousands of police, 8,000 soldiers, twelve cannon and detachments of marines and sailors were called up to protect Whitehall, and 150,000 special constables (including the future Napoleon III, then living in exile in London) were sworn in to assist if there was trouble. The centre of the capital was closed down. As it was, the event ended in bathos when the authorities stopped a planned march from crossing the Thames to present the petition and the crowd dispersed in the rain.

The daguerreotype camera, set up at a high vantage point from a distance as speakers addressed the gathering, depicted several thousand people, but clearly far short of the 500,000 O'Connor claimed – Russell's later estimate of 15,000 must have been much closer. The photograph was taken by a William Kilburn and is now in the royal archives at Windsor Castle. In it a respectably dressed crowd, many in top hats, are gazing towards a distant platform on which banners are waving in the breeze.[14] In the foreground is a man standing up on a dog cart watching the proceedings and next to him there is a carriage with a liveried coachman, so not all those present were necessarily horny-handed sons of toil.

Among the speakers on the platform was Feargus O'Connor. Having told the crowd that his life was at their command, as if he was preparing to die on the barricades, he instead shook hands with the police commander at the scene. The petition, with 5,700,000 signatures, was loaded into three cabs for delivery to Parliament. Safely on the Isle of Wight, the queen – who had given birth to her sixth child, Princess Louise, three weeks before – was kept informed of the day's events by telegraph: 'How wonderful! What a blessing!' she wrote artlessly in her journal that evening, forgetting how frightened and tearful she herself had been a few days earlier:

Lord John Russell evidently much relieved. F O'Connor was dreadfully frightened and thanked Mr May for telling him the procession would be stopped and shaking him by

the hand! The loyalty of all classes, the excellent arrange-
ment of the troops and police, the efficiency of Special
Constables, high and low, lords and shopkeepers – and the
determination to put a stop to the proceedings – by force if
necessary – have no doubt been the cause of the failure of
the meeting. It is a proud thing for this country and [I] trust
fervently will have a beneficial effect in other countries.
We dined together and I began reading a pretty little novel
by Mme Reybaud called Mme de Chageuil and then we
played...'[15]

Later it would be claimed that two-thirds of the names on
the petition were fraudulent or jokes: they allegedly included
Victoria Rex, Wellington, Punch and No Cheese. Chartism
was laughed to scorn. The *Manchester Guardian*, no friend of
the Chartists, joined in the lugubrious merriment, though not
without a sense of relief, later that week:

> The occurrences have thrown such an air of ridicule over
> the artificial agitation... as to deprive it henceforth of the
> mischievous character which at one time it appeared to
> possess. The previous swaggering and blustering by the
> gang of foolish fellows... furnish irresistible provocations
> to mirth [so] that it will be difficult in future to induce the
> public to regard the Chartist agitation as anything better
> than a foolish piece of pleasantry. The agitation is in the
> course of being fairly laughed out of the field.[16]

That did not stop the authorities arresting many of its
leading lights, including O'Connor, in the coming weeks, just
to make sure. They were clearly not that confident that the

movement had been scotched, but it never surfaced as such a threat again. Many of its most committed members moved abroad, to the United States and Australia.

Chartism had valid political grievances, some of which might even have been listened to if its leaders had presented them in a more conciliatory and effective fashion, as Place and Lovett, both of whom stood apart from the movement, had wished. It was ultimately defeated not by ridicule alone, but by its shortcomings of organization and tactics, by its failure to recruit respectable middle-class opinion (the middle classes, such as Queen Victoria's shopkeepers, joined the ranks of the special constables rather than the demonstrators in 1848), by the fact that Peel in particular had addressed some grievances with his banking and free-trade reforms in the mid-1840s, and – perhaps most of all – by the economic recovery of the early 1850s, which improved prosperity.

Unfortunately by then O'Connor's land redistribution scheme had also failed. The company was poorly organized and managed, and as plots of land – which became little better than allotments – were allocated by ballot, its structure was found to have contravened companies law. The two-acre plots could not sustain the families who came to live on them and the scheme eventually collapsed in 1851 under the weight of legal challenges and managerial incompetence. Those who had bought into it were left destitute, and O'Connor, increasingly erratic and sodden with brandy, would eventually be carted off to Dr Harrington Tuke's lunatic asylum in Chiswick after throwing punches at MPs in the Commons lobby.

By contrast, the Anti-Corn Law League became the second successful modern extra-parliamentary pressure group – after the campaign to abolish the slave trade, from which it drew some of its organizational methods and membership – and a model for the future mobilization of supporters and the shaping of public opinion in single-issue causes. It helped that its membership was well-heeled and respectable and that its leaders, especially the MPs Richard Cobden and John Bright, were astute and well focused, but if in the end it was pushing at an open door when Peel accepted its arguments and decided to abolish the Corn Laws, it was an open door that the League had largely created. It helped that their message was a positive and forward-looking one, focused, limited and clear: repeal would bring prosperity and benefits for all.

Although there had been earlier, scattered voices calling for the Corn Laws to be repealed, it was not until the trade depression of the late 1830s that industrialists, particularly in the North, began to focus on the issue. It was no coincidence that the League was founded among the textile manufacturers with their laissez-faire view of what was good for their trade. This was, essentially, the removal of barriers to both exports and imports – especially those tariffs and regulations imposed artificially by the state. This philosophy was becoming known as the Manchester school of economics, a term first coined by Disraeli. The Manchester men saw the Corn Laws as a prime drag on industry and the main cause of their having to pay higher wages. If to get them abolished they had to take on the landed interests and the aristocratic classes, so be it. Their rhetoric against the landed gentry was often harsh, contemptuous and threatening. Landowners' views, it was said, should count 'for no more than those of animals fattened for the Smithfield Show'.[17] The League was assiduous in trying to win over small tenant farmers and separate them from their landlords: 'to wring from their hands that political influence which they have so much abused,' a speaker told them at a meeting reported in the *Morning Chronicle* in April 1843.[18] When farmers and landowners claimed they would be ruined if the League got its way, they had some reason for thinking so and the Leaguers' provocative speeches played up to that. As Cobden – a Sussex landowner but also an economist and part-owner of a Manchester calico printing company (the same process that had brought the Peels their fortune) – later said: 'I am afraid that most of us entered upon the struggle with the belief that we had some distinct class interest in the question.'[19]

The League was formed in Manchester in the summer of 1838, a few months after Lovett and Place had drawn up their charter in London, but from the start the northern group was much better funded and organized. It was run by a council of large subscribers, each paying a £50 fee to have a vote, and it soon had large offices in Market Street, with a professional staff dealing with post and printing and sending out pamphlets and newspapers. A sympathetic journalist called Alexander Somerville (who was paid by Cobden) visited in 1843 and reported admiringly:

> From this office letters to the amount of several thousand a day go forth to all parts of the kingdom... I saw letters addressed to all the foreign ambassadors and all the mayors and provosts of corporate towns, inviting them to the great banquet which is to be given in the last week of this month... copies of all the parliamentary registries are kept so that any elector's name and residence is at once found and, if necessary, such elector is communicated with by letter or parcel of tracts... several men are at work making up bales of tracts each weighing upwards of a hundredweight and despatching

them to all parts of the kingdom… from sixty to seventy of these bales are sent off in a week, that is, from three to three and a half tons of arguments against the Corn Laws![20]

The League's accounts in the mid-1840s show £11,344.14s.1d spent on printing, £19,786.16s.10d on publications, including journalists' and printers' salaries, £2,645.16s.10d on deputations, and £4,813.15s.6d on renting premises in central London in the fifteen-month period to the end of 1844. It spent £1,498.15s.0d on postage during that time and its activities were greatly assisted and facilitated by the introduction of the penny post in 1840. It could afford to pay its travelling lecturers salaries of up to £170 a year, plus at least as much again in expenses. By contrast, when the National Charter Association was wound up in 1851, its remaining members struggled for six months to raise the £40 needed to pay off their creditors.

Cobden and his colleagues argued that free trade would increase national prosperity and that of its manufacturers – that it would lower the price of food, make British agriculture more efficient, improve trade with other nations and so make international peace more likely. Some of these arguments were specious, or at least highly optimistic and untried, but once Cobden had persuaded John Bright, a Rochdale cotton manufacturer and Quaker, to join, the League had a powerful dual leadership. Cobden acted as the tactician and persuader, Bright was the movement's passionate evangelist and orator, and soon they were both in the Commons. Cobden was elected MP for Stockport in 1841 and Bright became the MP for Rochdale two years later. They harried the government and operated tactically during debates: Cobden the cool rationalist, deploying the economic arguments, Bright coming later to denounce and ridicule the protectionists and attack their speeches messianically. Theirs was the self-righteous rhetoric of evangelicals, complete with Biblical references – 'Behold, I have heard that there is corn in Egypt; get you down thither and buy for us from thence, that we may live and not die!' from Genesis 42:2 – rather than the shrill threats of physical violence used by some Chartist orators. They insisted that the Corn Laws were immoral, anti-scriptural and anti-religious, opposed to the law of God – as they frequently told ministers of religion. But there were distinct and subtle threats too: the assiduous registration of voters in constituencies, attempts to remove their opponents from electoral registers and the naked class antagonism towards the protectionists. They were not above arguing both ways too: that repeal would either reduce wages, or that it would improve them, depending on their audience. Both men could also hit below the belt, and the vehemence and personal nature of their rhetoric was condemned by their opponents. Cobden repeatedly cast aspersions on Peel's good faith: 'Sir Robert Peel feels for Sir Robert Peel and not for you,' he told a crowd in 1845.[21] It was little wonder that their opponents were enraged by their high moral tone: *The Times* spoke of incendiary claptrap and the Cant and Cotton men. The arguments of Cobden and Bright reverberated out from the Commons: 'You speak with a loud voice when you are talking on the floor of the House and if you have anything to say that hits hard, it is a very long whip and reaches all over the kingdom,' said Cobden.[22]

The League published its own newspapers, brought up sympathetic journalists and sponsored a new magazine, *The*

Economist, launched in 1843, as its mouthpiece and the organ of free trade. The press, Cobden was told, was not 'a self-acting machine and wants an Almighty power of grease to set it going', so he set aside £500 of 'grease' a year to buy the editorial allegiance of a newspaper called *The Sun.* The League offered to pay half the *Morning Chronicle*'s costs for a series of reports about distress and poverty in the northern towns and farming districts, so long as they were written from an anti-Tory and anti-Chartist slant. It also promised to buy up and distribute free 3,000 copies of eight weekly papers if they carried editorials supporting the League's activities.[23] Both Cobden and Bright were frequent writers for the press in pursuit of the cause. The great manufacturers of the North queued up – as before Christmas 1845 – to subscribe large sums for the League's war chest, and there were events such as fund-raising bazaars and the sale of free-trade tea-pots, handkerchiefs and pin-cushions. Cheap pottery figurines from Stoke-on-Trent included Cobden and Bright among the celebrities of the day, and public meetings took place across the country – 136 meetings in London alone in 1843, some of them at the Drury Lane Theatre.

Unlike the agitators, lobbyists and the protectionists, Peel and his ministers – it almost goes without saying – disdained opportunities to buy the support of sympathetic newspapers, as they might have done. The prime minister expressed his 'horror of money transactions with newspaper proprietors'. If an editor took an editorial position he did not like, 'what remedy should I have but communication with the editor, remonstrance against the course taken, menaces probably of withdrawing my subscription? All this places me in the man's power.' As Sir James Graham, the home secretary, wrote in

1843, they would not 'buy the Press but... leave it to its own free agency, thinking on the whole that Government free from the trammels of a newspaper alliance fares better than one which renders itself subservient to this, the most degrading of all tyrannies'.[24]

Whether the League would have carried the argument without the pressure of the Irish famine may be more doubtful. Cobden thought so himself, though Peel had privately conceded the League's arguments in favour of the principle of free trade long before the famine ever broke out. Once repeal had gone through, the League wrapped up its affairs with a series of celebratory dinners across the country (the Victorians were great diners) and with subscriptions and testimonials to its leaders – a public appeal raised £80,000 for Cobden whose business had suffered from his political activities; its members then returned to the serious business of making money. They had no interest in wider social or political reforms and most were hostile to them. Throughout a lengthy parliamentary career which lasted into the late 1880s, Bright would oppose all labour law restrictions on employers and legislation to improve working conditions, because he thought them unreasonable restrictions on the rights of trade and – speciously – on the liberties of employees. 'All legislative interference with the labour market, all attempts of government to fix the wages of industry, all interference of a third party between employers and employed, are unjustifiable in principle and mischievous in their results,' he said. And again: 'I never professed to keep on my manufactory for the benefit of my work people, or for the sake of clothing my customers. My object is, by the expenditure of capital and by giving labour to a business, to procure for myself and family a comfortable income.'[25]

But the League had changed the political weather, and Bright recognized it. He told a meeting in Manchester in 1849:

The Anti-Corn Law League will henceforth stand before the world as a sign of a new order of things. Until now this country has been ruled by the class of great proprietors of the soil. Everyone must have foreseen that, as trade and manufactures extended, the balance of power would, at some time or other, be thrown into another scale. Well, that time has come and the rising of the League... was sufficient to have pointed out to any statesman that the power of the landed aristocracy had reached its height and that henceforth it would find a rival to which eventually it must become subjected. We have been living through a revolution without knowing it.[26]

That was optimistic – it would take several more generations for the aristocracy to realize that the game was up, long after Bright's death in 1889. The protectionists too had organized in direct response to the Anti-Corn Law League's campaigning.[27] The so-called Anti-League was set up in 1843 to defend the Corn Laws, well before the Irish famine crisis, to stiffen the resolve of Tory MPs and particularly of Peel himself, whom they rightly suspected of preparing to repeal them altogether. It arose from county agricultural protection societies and drew its support from tenant farmers, land agents, millers and corn-dealers, country bankers and rural clergy, and some – though by no means all – large landowners. They feared that if the laws were repealed agriculture and therefore the country and all its institutions, including the Church of England, would be destroyed, and what maddened them was that it would be a Tory government that did it. It had the support of influential conservative newspapers, including the *Morning Post*, which had been hostile to Peel all through his administration, and the *Morning Herald*, which came out against repeal in 1846. *The Times* itself was more ambivalent but finally supported the government. The Anti-League was well funded, chaired by the Duke of Richmond and other aristocratic landowners, and was linked to local county agricultural societies. It acted to secure declarations by shire Tory MPs against repeal and exerted electoral pressure on them. The sense of betrayal was strong, as Richmond said in the *Morning Post* in July 1846:

> The greater part of those who ought to have supported us but who criticized us and held aloof were those who for 10 years had been labouring to bring Sir Robert Peel into office. Men do not like to admit, and are slow even to believe, that they have toiled so long for nothing. Every motive of political ambition or personal interest inclined them to support him and even, strange as it may seem, to trust him.[28]

The Anti-League was strategically well placed, with local societies and influential farmers and landowners in many counties. There was a central organization with an office in London and local activists met up nationally each year at the Smithfield Show, which fortuitously occurred at the time of the government crisis in December 1845. Even so, many farmers out in the provinces had so far been reluctant to join them, being suspicious of political activism and, if they were tenants, worried about what their landlords might think:

people like them had been known to lose their tenancies if they voted the wrong way in elections. The Anti-League had been astute in placing tenant farmers to the fore in their activities, making them spokesmen at meetings and ensuring that they mentioned that landowners were supportive 'in purse and in person'. They sought to create the sense that everyone was of the same mind. Sir Charles Knightley told farmers in Northamptonshire:

> the most influential and powerful body of men – viz., the agriculturalists of this country – are determined to support them against the machinations of a conspiracy and the farmers of England are determined to act against it as one man.[29]

Even so, that December Peel had strong grounds for believing that he could discount such opposition. There was only a small group of Ultras in Parliament: maybe twenty, including men such as William Miles, MP for Somerset, Augustus Stafford O'Brien in Northamptonshire, and Charles Newdigate, the MP for Warwickshire. Most Tory MPs were reluctant to join them, especially if it meant overthrowing the prime minister. F.H. Dickenson, another Somerset member, spelled out his reasons in a letter to the League: the dangers of committing MPs to 'statements which might afterwards prove mischievous – the danger of the league not being guided discreetly – the impropriety of MPs having to do with getting up petitions – the danger of pursuing the same course as the Anti-Corn Law League while we abuse them for it'. Nor were all the great landowners hostile to repeal: many saw the advantages of free trade and accepted the Anti-Corn Law

League's argument that the reform would make agriculture more efficient and competitive – they were already taking advantage of scientific and technological advances to improve production and breeding stock. Many of them also, of course, loyally supported Peel and viewed the insurgency first with disdain and then with mounting exasperation. Even Lord Stanley, who owned large parts of Lancashire and had resigned from the government, refused to lead a revolt or to attempt to form an alternative Tory government on the Anti-League's behalf. He called on them to make a 'full and impartial consideration of all the consequences which may arise from breaking up the present government and the responsibility that must attach to those instrumental in breaking it up'. The Ultras by now were quite irreconcilable, however, and meanwhile Stanley preferred to spend more time on the racecourse and the hunting field and brushing up his translation of the *Iliad*.

Over Christmas and the New Year the Anti-League got to work, organizing mass meetings in the counties, which Tory MPs were honour-bound to attend, and issuing veiled threats while of course denying them. As Richmond had said:

> I think we are entitled to ask, not in the language of menace or threat, or even perhaps of any sort of reproach that we think the uncertainty of their opinions an evil of no uncertain magnitude... I have no doubt that they will speak out when they know the opinions of most of the respectable farmers in the country.[30]

The *Morning Post* diligently reported each county meeting, and MPs who attended were asked to promise 'strenuous opposition to any measure'. In Sussex, under Richmond's influence, the farmers passed a resolution to vote only for men 'who are well known to be friendly to the agricultural and landed interests of this country and who will offer an independent and unflinching opposition to any measure calculated to diminish the present amount of protection to domestic industry'. The lack of a leader to take Peel's place did not matter, said Richmond during a speech in Brighton: 'honest good intentions go far towards the government of mankind'.[31] He and others started calling for a general election to test opinion in the country.

By the time they returned to Westminster, the protectionists' numbers had grown to forty, still far short of enough to embarrass Peel, but more would slide into place as the debate dragged on over the coming months. The *Morning Post* reminded them of their promises to oppose reform night after night, instead of 'yawning over the newspapers and damning Cobden for his impudence'. As *The Times* said in January: 'A dire necessity of speech urges on the hapless protectionists. Fain would they pass in the crowd, vote and have done, but the "peine forte et dure" of agricultural indignation urges them on.'[32]

The Anti-League's part in opposing the repeal of the Corn Laws in 1846 is worth emphasizing as it has been largely overlooked by history, partly because Disraeli himself underplayed it – almost certainly deliberately – when writing about his and Bentinck's role in bringing down Peel. Perhaps he did not want the country squires to share the glory, but more likely it was because within a few years he himself was trying to eliminate the group as its rigid insistence on protectionism was no longer politically convenient, or practically sustainable.[33]

The protectionists themselves and especially their arguments have been discounted in the dramatic political story of the Corn Laws debates ever since, but they formed an influential and well-organized pressure group in the shires and a third extra-parliamentary force to be reckoned with by MPs. In the crucial vote on the repeal in 1846, 107 Tory county members would vote against their government, with only twenty-five in favour.

It was a period in which the parties were setting up their rival clubs along Pall Mall in the wake of the Reform Act. The Carlton Club, for the Tories, expanded rapidly after the architect Sir Robert Smirke built premises for it in 1835 – so much so that it had to move again eleven years later.[34] It engaged a French chef and became a place of refuge and plotting: 'that party scullery', according to one MP. The grandees of the party became trustees – dukes, marquesses and earls – and rank-and-file MPs found it somewhere to go, to dine after the Commons rose in the evening, to meet socially and to hold meetings. It could whip supporters and organize canvassing. Significantly, it was said that the unclubbable and self-conscious Peel himself had visited only once, just to view the building. For the Whigs, the Reform Club started at about the same time just down the road – Disraeli was briefly a member before he realized his mistake and the club returned his subscription – though there was some controversy over whether both Whigs and Radicals should be admitted to membership. They employed their own French chef, Alexis Soyer.

At the same time, the first party managers were informally in place. For the Tories it was Francis Bonham, a bachelor from an Anglo-Irish family, who had been an MP for Rye and a party whip, but now placed himself discreetly at the Carlton to listen to the gossip. He advised Peel on the trends in party opinion and became very good at forecasting likely votes and outcomes. 'For myself,' he told Peel, 'I am ready to devote my whole time out of the H. of C. to this work.' Lord John Manners remembered Bonham in his memoirs, years later:

> He was in 1841 an elderly man, dressed in a long brown coat and carrying a large strapped book, full of election-eering facts, figures and calculations... Sir Robert Peel's trusted agent in matters relating to elections and party management... my recollection of Mr Bonham is distinctly favourable – rough, faithful, honest, indefatigable, the depositary of a thousand secrets and the betrayer of none.[35]

Bonham told Peel that he was in the position of a looker-on who sees and knows more of the game than the players – the mark of the backroom political fixer through the ages. When Peel fell, so did he. So discreet was he that when he died he did not receive an obituary in *The Times*.[36]

On the Whig side, Bonham's equivalent was Joseph Parkes, a Birmingham solicitor and loyal Benthamite – like Chadwick, he had served on a royal commission, in his case investigating municipal corporations. He was described as 'quite up to the spirit of the age in practical and popular acquirements'. Unlike Bonham, he did merit a *Times* obituary in 1865:

> If anyone on his side of politics wanted information... Mr Parkes was the man to apply to. If he could not at once give it, he could get it. He was a most useful man in his party – useful not only because he was so well informed and had such a wide circle of friends but also because his

judgement was of the soundest and he was ever active and loyal in offices of friendship.[37]

His colleague was James Coppock, who started his career as a haberdasher's clerk and became a solicitor and first secretary of the Reform Club, a sharp man and not one to get on the wrong side of in litigation over a disputed election result.[38]

These were the men at the sharp end of party management in the 1830s and 1840s as Whigs and Tories more clearly distinguished themselves from each other and took on the glimmerings of their later shapes. In the rival extra-parliamentary movements of the 1840s, too, the country's politics had seen dynamic new forces at work: a tightly organized middle-class pressure group succeeding in influencing and even changing a central government economic policy; and a more disparate working-class movement, which did not manage to achieve political change in the short term, but whose ideas would eventually come to be accepted and influential in the later development of progressive politics.

For Chartism was, authentically, the first working-class political movement, forerunner of modern trade unions and the Labour party. Its influence can be seen in the educational and self-help societies that sprang from it; in the co-operative movement, formed from the Rochdale Society of Equitable Pioneers in 1844; in temperance organizations and nonconformist chapels, which became the refuges of respectable and serious-minded artisans and their families. Samuel Smiles, the Yorkshire journalist who would later write *Self Help*, the founding text of self-improvement, told a meeting in Leeds in 1845 that education was not a means of raising up a few clever and talented men but of elevating the whole class:

The grand object aimed at should be to make the great mass of the people virtuous, intelligent, well-informed and well-conducted and to open up to them new sources of pleasure and happiness... Education will teach those who suffer how to remove the causes of their sufferings and it may also make them dissatisfied with an inferiority of social privilege... It is the opprobrium of some of the most wretched and suffering classes in our land that they are contented with their condition. Theirs is the satisfaction of the blind who have never known light.[39]

∽

The *Manchester Guardian* was never going to be anything other than a supporter of the Anti-Corn Law League. Its offices were in the same street as the League's headquarters and its founder, John Edward Taylor – a young businessman who had brought the news of the Peterloo massacre to the London papers in 1819 and established his own newspaper to press the case for parliamentary reform two years later – was one of the earliest members. The paper's printer and co-editor Jeremiah – Jerry – Garnett had joined too. Presumably it was Garnett who was unable to hear, or keep up with, the list of donors read out during the giant League meeting in Manchester at Christmas 1845. Perhaps he should have sent John Harland, the Hull-born chief reporter, who had the best shorthand note in England and might have followed the meeting better. By then, Taylor had died, but his two sons would shortly take over the reins at the paper (and, keeping it in the extended family, Taylor's second wife's nephew, C. P. Scott, would later become the *Manchester Guardian*'s editor for more than fifty years, well into the twentieth century).[40]

The paper was far from the only newspaper in Manchester in the 1840s – there was the *Courier*, the *Times* and the *Advertiser* as well – but by hitching itself to the cotton traders and textile manufacturers it had become the most successful and influential in the city ('the cotton lords' bible'), sharing their views and prejudices and assiduously reporting prices on the new cotton exchange. Like his readers, Taylor had opposed factory legislation to reduce working time to ten hours a day because he believed the manufacturers could not afford it. He had also defended child labour as a necessary evil, better than starvation. Manchester journalism was a rough old trade, rife with jealousies and rivalries. Garnett had once been physically attacked in St Ann's Square by a rival editor and had fended him off with his umbrella. But its thorough coverage of the League and firm support for free trade meant it outsold even the London papers within its region, and in the South it was beginning to be noticed as one of the most important newspapers of the North of England. The first reference ever made to the *Manchester Guardian* in Parliament was when Peel spoke appreciatively about the fairness of its coverage in the Commons in 1842.[41] Frederick Engels liked the paper too, and drew on its reports in writing *The Condition of the Working Class in England* in 1844.

The paper was published bi-weekly, on Wednesdays and Saturdays, following the reduction of stamp duty on newspapers in 1836. The 75 per cent reduction in the tax had the effect of halving the cost of buying newspapers and, because the remaining tax counted as a stamp, allowed them to be posted free to a wider range of subscribers. Circulations rose rapidly, just in time for and contributing to the rise of the Chartist and Anti-Corn Law League movements, and they would rise again when the tax was removed altogether in 1855.

The *Manchester Guardian*, selling for fourpence (it had been ninepence before), with a circulation of up to 9,000 copies a day, offered readers eight pages of advertisements and tight, grey editorial type. Its contents were mainly local news, but it also had lengthy, verbatim reports of parliamentary debates and sensational court cases. The paper's press clattered away in the early hours of the morning and it was being distributed before the London papers arrived by train at lunchtime. Circulation was not the only measure of its influence. Copies were widely read on the cotton-exchange floor, in the inns and chop-houses of the city, and out among the factory owners, overseers and dissenting ministers of Lancashire and Cheshire. The reliability of its reporting meant that when it lost libel actions in 1823 and 1861, after exposing in the first case unsound bank-notes and in the second price-fixing in the calico trade, the manufacturers subscribed cheques which covered the losses.*

Garnett himself had originally been apprenticed as a printer in Barnsley, but he also did much of the reporting and editorial writing himself. By the mid-1840s, as a partner in the company, he earned nearly £2,000 a year in dividends – almost as much as Delane of *The Times* in London. A photograph taken later in life shows the epitome of a Victorian self-made man – handsome and open-faced, with a churchwarden beard clinging around his chin, well dressed and with a watch-chain dangling across his waistcoat. When he died in 1870, a former journalist, writing in the *Sphinx*, would recall:

---

* Then as now, winning libel cases could be as expensive as losing them, and truth was not then an absolute defence.

he was as fine an old cock as any village squire in a modern novel... He was occasionally as hard to draw as a reluctant badger, but it was never because he was afraid of the dogs... when properly roused – which was precious seldom – he would have grimly defied the stark naked opinion of a world in arms against him.[42]

Despite their membership of the League, Garnett and Taylor were not uncritical of it and caused ructions when the paper supported Peel editorially because of his Corn Law reform plans. Just like the Labour party a century later, the League had thought the paper ought to be in its pocket without any nonsense about editorial independence. Garnett and Taylor were, said Archibald Prentice of the League, 'Tories who are pleased to call themselves reformers, [men] with a horror of a too rapid march of improvement'. John Bright and Garnett increasingly fell out in coming years. Nevertheless, the two needed each other. The paper's circulation rose exponentially when it reported on League affairs: it went up 315 per cent in January 1840 when it devoted twenty-three columns to a League meeting.

In London, Peel's government had most trouble with *The Times*, which maintained a wry detachment and caused a convulsion in the administration when it revealed the plans to repeal the laws in December 1845, at a time when the move was still only under discussion. The story came from a leak by Lord Aberdeen, the foreign secretary, who was apparently trying to be helpful. *The Times*'s owner, John Walter II, who was a Tory MP, had an awkward relationship with Peel. His young editor, 27-year-old John Thaddeus Delane, was compromised after engaging in private correspondence with the prime minister to wangle a promotion for his civil servant brother. Disraeli, too, courted the editor with obsequious flattery. 'Did you like it?' Delane was asked about the politician's approaches. 'No, but I like to think that Disraeli thought I was of sufficient importance to make it worth his while.'[43] It was said that *The Times* chuckled and sneered at both sides. John Morley, Gladstone's friend and official biographer, wrote that it was 'dealing out blows at protectionist and Free Trader alike from that loftiest moral vantage-ground of one who waits for the final leap of a cat'. But in the end it supported repeal.

How far the press had influenced the process of repeal remained an unresolved matter, though both sides liked to think they had. In such circumstances a contributor to the 1846 edition of *Mitchell's Newspaper Press Directory* thought an elevation of tone was required:

The press has now so great and extensive an influence on public opinion... that... its conductors should be GENTLEMEN in the true sense of the word. They should be equally above corruption and intimidation; incapable of being warped by personal considerations from the broad path of truth and honour and superior to all attempts at misrepresenting or mystifying public events.

Some things never change.

On the day repeal finally gained the royal assent, Jeremiah Garnett sat down in his office in Manchester and gave himself an understandable – and unusually assertive – pat on the back in his paper's editorial column:

The editor of the *Guardian* has witnessed and recorded the completion of that category of reforms which, at the commencement of his labours, he considered absolutely essential to the good government and well-being of his fellow countrymen and from the pursuit of which he has never deviated. They... have all been effected, almost precisely in the form in which they had been advocated in the columns of this journal.[44]

6

The Whole World Railway Mad

'Men who but a few years since scarcely crossed the
precincts of the county in which they were born, and
knew as little of the general features of the land of
their birth as they did the topography of the moon,
now unhesitatingly avail themselves of the means of
communication that are afforded.'

F. S. WILLIAMS, *Our Iron Roads* (1852)[1]

Nothing demonstrates the changing nature of British society
in the 1840s better than the rapid spread of the railways
across the country and the speculative boom that accompanied it. The first suburban railway line in the capital – the
four miles from London Bridge to Greenwich – had only been
opened in 1836. In 1838 there were just 250 miles of railway
tracks in Britain, but five years later there were 1,800 miles
and by 1850 there would be nearly 5,000, creating the most
comprehensive network in the world and establishing most of
the major rail routes that still survive 160 years later. They
snaked across the country, being built at astonishing speed
considering the tools available and the obstacles to be overcome: the first twenty-two-mile stretch of the Great Western
Railway out of London was opened in June 1838 and within
three years the line had reached Bridgwater in Somerset, 152
miles from the terminus at Paddington.

The railway was what enabled Peel (and Russell) to speed

down to Windsor and back in a couple of hours to see the queen on the Saturday before Christmas 1845. It was what brought London within a six-hour journey of the Midlands, enabling travellers to get to the capital and back in a day if necessary, at speeds greater than had ever been considered possible: 'swifter than a bird flies', as the actress Fanny Kemble wrote following her first journey on the line from Liverpool to Manchester.[2] Trains could chug along at thirty or even forty miles an hour, admittedly with regular stops to replenish the water for the engine and to allow passengers off to stretch their legs and buy refreshments, but the journey was smoother than a horse and carriage could manage on the roads of the day. It was also so much faster than any previous mode of transport that people wondered whether their bodies would be able to stand the pressure without exploding. In London, both Paddington and Euston stations were already open and their great, triumphant architectural monuments to the steam age were being erected. Waterloo station would follow in a couple of years and the first railway bridge over the Thames would be completed in 1848.

The novelty of this new mode of travelling was exhilarating where it was not frightening: almost a sense of flying through town and country, faster than men and women had ever gone before. Dickens catches it as Mr Dombey journeys by rail following the death of his son:

Away with a shriek and a roar and a rattle, from the town, burrowing among the dwellings of men and making the streets hum, flashing out into the meadows for a moment, mining in through the damp earth, booming on in darkness and heavy air, bursting out again into the sunny day so bright and wide; away, with a shriek and a roar and a rattle, through the fields, through the woods, through the corn... ever flying... breasting the wind and light, the shower and sunshine, away and still away it rolls and roars, fierce and rapid, smooth and certain.[3]

Across the country more than 200,000 navvies were carving out routes, by brute force, almost entirely with picks and shovels. And in Parliament, since every new line required separate legislation, 225 separate railway bills had been introduced in 1845 and a further 270 would be brought in the following year. Some of the lines, and the companies promoting them, were tiny (the Gravesend and Rochester, built in 1844–5, was just seven miles long)[4] and others would never materialize at all, but the speculative private capital being raised was enormous: £100 million, nearly twice the government's total expenditure, in 1845.

The engineers and entrepreneurs who were building the lines – men like George Stephenson and his son Robert, Joseph Locke and Isambard Kingdom Brunel – were technicians and craftsmen, not the sons of privilege or wealth, and they were put in charge of great projects at extraordinarily young ages. Robert Stephenson, admittedly his father's son, was designing the *Rocket* steam-engine at the age of 27 and was made chief engineer on the London and Birmingham Railway aged 30; Brunel (another engineer's son) was appointed engineer of the Great Western Railway at 29. When they died, such men were honoured and commemorated – Robert Stephenson, by then a Tory MP, was buried at Westminster Abbey. These were inventors and innovators, meeting formidable technical difficulties with élan, surveying the flattest routes and overcoming obstacles with imagination. In Brunel's case, that included spanning the Thames at Maidenhead with the widest and flattest arched brick bridge that had then been built. It has spans of 128 feet with an arch only 24 feet high – in defiance of contemporary critics who claimed that it must collapse under the weight of the first locomotive – and is still carrying trains 175 years later.[5] It is the bridge depicted in J.M.W. Turner's great painting *Rain, Steam and Speed*, first exhibited at the Royal Academy in 1844. Then – also accomplished in the late 1830s as part of the Great Western Railway – there was the tunnel nearly two miles long carved through the limestone rock of Box Hill near Bath. Most of the earliest trains had to be pulled up the slope out of Euston and could not manage gradients, so Brunel's survey for the line of the Great Western Railway across southern England produced a route that was level, or of no greater gradient than 1 in 1,000, for 71 of its 118 miles to Bristol, and was no steeper than 1 in 660 for most of the rest.[6]

Along the routes the engineers selected, new towns sprang up, such as Swindon in Wiltshire and Crewe in Cheshire, both previously villages. So too did stately stations decorated with towers and crenellated battlements, soaring, iron-ribbed roofs, and – in Euston's case – a Doric arch. By the end of the 1840s most towns of consequence had stations and those that did not tended to stagnate economically.

The men who built these lines – the navigators, or navvies as they became known (in the 1840s it was still common to call them 'navies') – were feared and reviled in almost equal measure, for their strength, recklessness, ungovernability and frequent drunkenness. Their arrival along the route, throwing up tents and sod-huts for shelter, was often greeted by local people – especially property owners – with consternation, and magistrates and militias would be placed on heightened alert, as if they represented the invasion of an alien race. 'These banditti… are generally the terror of the surrounding country; they are as completely a class by themselves as the gypsies,' wrote Peter Lecount, one of Robert Stephenson's assistants on the London and Birmingham route:

> Possessed of all the daring recklessness of the smuggler without any of his redeeming qualities, their ferocious behaviour can only be equalled by the brutality of their language. It may truly be said, their hand is against every man and before they have been long located, every man's hand is against them; and woe befall any woman with the slightest share of modesty, whose ears they can assail.[7]

Lecount reckoned that building the line was a greater engineering feat than constructing the Great Pyramid at Giza and believed it was accomplished in a quarter of the time.

The men also saw themselves as a breed apart, not merely as labourers, for their strength, their endurance and the dangers they faced. They even wore distinctive clothing: moleskin trousers, strong canvas shirts, velveteen square-tailed coats, brightly coloured waistcoats, hobnail boots and white felt hats with turned-up brims. Many of them were from Scotland, Yorkshire and Lancashire, or Ireland – another reason for fearfulness as they descended on the South and Midlands. They were also comparatively well paid, at two pounds a week – twice the normal industrial wage, four times that of many farm labourers – though that came with considerable strings attached. Payment by the subcontractors who hired them, the gangmasters and 'butty' men,* was often irregular, or distributed monthly, with a requirement that it be spent at company tommy shops,† where prices were inflated and goods inferior. Out in the wilds of the Yorkshire moors or crossing the bogs of Chat Moss between Manchester and Liverpool there might be nowhere else to buy food and drink, and it was said that a sovereign was worth only fifteen shillings (three-quarters of its value) in the company stores, where the meat might be rancid and other food adulterated. Beer and whisky were easily available – a navvy might take two pounds of beef and eight pints of beer a day to sustain him: 'A man has a right to bring a gallon with him if he likes in the morning,' said the great contractor Sir Morton Peto. When his wages ran out, he could get a ticket for credit until the following pay-day: another incentive to keep him on the job and permanently in hock to his employers. If all else ran short, men would pawn their shovels for whisky. The payment of wages invariably took place in pubs. One engineer said: 'They appeared to me when they got half drunk, the same as a dog that has been tied for a week. They ran about and did not know what to do with themselves.' Understandably, disputes would arise: with the butty man in charge of a gang distributing shares unfairly or keeping too much for himself, or with the tommy shops, cheating on the tickets. Then fights would break out and sometimes men would die – navvies, after all, had the strength and the blunt instruments available, shovels

---

* 'butty' is a North Country dialect word, originally meaning a subcontractor who organizes a small team of mates to work for a gangmaster.

† The tommy shops – after 'tommy', a type of bread-roll the navvies took to work to snack on – were company-owned shops where the men were paid and expected to spend their wages.

and spikes, to do serious damage to each other. In the mid-1840s two men were hanged beside the railway line being built between Edinburgh and Glasgow in front of their work-mates for killing their gangmaster.

Often the men would go to work drunk. It was a highly dangerous thing to do in the circumstances. Three were killed, one after another, when they plunged down a large ventilation shaft above the Kilsby Tunnel, south of Rugby, as they vied with each other to jump across it. The tunnel, on the West Coast main line, nearly a mile and a half long, was beset with engineering difficulties, including having to negotiate quick-sand, and took 12,000 men four years to excavate. Thirty million bricks had to be used to shore up and line the tunnel. As the village's website says:

> The labourers worked until the blood ran from their eyes and when not working their only recreations were drinking, petty theft, pitting dogs and cocks in illegal battle and fighting among themselves. Trouble between the navvies and the villagers was inevitable and frequent and on at least one occasion the military had to be called in to restore order.[8]

One of the authorities' chief fears was political disturbance among such a volatile group of men. In the autumn of 1846, 12,000 of them, building the new Bury line, attended a Chartist meeting at Rochdale to hear subversive speeches from one of the movement's leaders, Ernest Jones, who demanded to know why the royal family spent £70,000 a year on Prince Albert's horses, while the working class was reduced to slavery.[9]

There were fights between the national groups too: at Penrith in February 1846 there were pitched battles between

English and Irish navvies – 500 a side – started, it was said, when an Irishman refused to use a shovel instead of a pick when ordered to do so by an Englishman. The Westmoreland Yeomanry had to be called out with loaded carbines to save the town from being ransacked. 'Pitch into the bugger,' an Englishman called John Hobday was heard shouting to his mates as he kicked an unconscious Irishman. 'He has life enough in him yet.' Three months later at Penmaenmawr in North Wales, Welsh navvies fought the Irish and drove them away, despite the arrest and detention of a ringleader by the local police. 'The conflict became so violent that it was deemed necessary for the magistrates to read the Riot Act... During these proceedings a party of the Welsh went behind the prison and threw a rope over the wall by means of which the prisoner managed to effect his escape,' wrote a resident. 'A body of soldiers was expected to arrive on Monday and then the police would apprehend a number of the rioters whom they knew but dare not take until backed by a strong force.'[10]

Even at the best of times, it was very hard work. Farm labourers forsaking the plough to get a job with the rail gangs found they were exhausted by early afternoon. It was said it took a man a year to build up the strength to do a full day's work. Often jobs were paid by piecework, by so much per foot or cubic yard of earth and rubble shifted. A navvy would be expected to fill seven wagon-loads a day with mud, debris or rock: up to eighteen cubic yards, or twenty tons, day after day, for work did not stop at weekends. There were instances of men working into old age – one, called James 'Daddy' Hayes, died, still at work, at the age of 86 in 1882 – but if they survived alcoholism, accidents, riots and fights or disease, most were worn out by their forties. Deaths were frequent:

thirty-two died during the excavation of the first Woodhead tunnel on the route through the Pennines between Sheffield and Manchester in the mid-1840s; and there were at least 140 serious injuries, including burns, contusions, lacerations and dislocations, but excluding fractures, which presumably were not considered serious. When a second tunnel was bored there in 1849, twenty-eight navvies died during a cholera outbreak. Doctors were often far away and the injuries and accidents could be terrible.

There was a supreme callousness about the men and their welfare. Often their proper names were not known. If they died a long way from a churchyard, they might be buried near the railway track, and if there were injuries, these were regarded as a hindrance to the job rather than a source of concern. One of the engineers, Wellington Purdon, was asked by a parliamentary committee looking into the conditions of railway labourers in 1846 whether it would not be safer to use patent fuses for blasting at the Woodhead tunnel rather than the iron 'stemmers', used to ram in the powder, which could shoot back out through a man's head. 'Perhaps it [would],' he replied insouciantly, 'but it is attended with such a loss of time and the difference is so very small, I would not recommend the loss of time for the sake of all the extra lives it would save.'[11]

What really concerned many Victorians, of course, was the men's immorality – the fact that they might marry their girl-friends or camp-followers, by the ancient irreligious practice of jumping over a broomstick, rather than in church, or that they might die alone and unshriven. Some missionaries would ride along the tracks and try to stop the work on Sundays and religious navvies might conduct prayer services and hymn-singing, but other clergymen would not stir themselves to visit the dying, even when given a horse to help them do so. The Rev. William St George Sargent, a chaplain to the Lancaster and Carlisle line, who was paid £150 a year by a philanthropic family to minister to the men, told the same parliamentary committee:

I think they are the most neglected and spiritually destitute people I ever met. Yes, most vile and immoral characters... they are ignorant of Bible religion and gospel truth and are infected with infidelity and very often with revolutionary principles.[12]

With so many Irishmen at work, when Sargent spoke of ignorance and infidelity, he probably meant popery as well as immorality. The Irish were given a particularly bad name, but they were probably no worse than the rest. As Thomas Carlyle wrote in a letter to the Irish nationalist politician and editor Charles Gavan Duffy from Scotland on 29 August 1846:

The country is greatly in a state of defacement, the harvest with its black potato fields and all roads and lanes overrun with drunken navvies... all the world here, as elsewhere, calculates on getting to heaven by steam. I have not in my travels seen anything uglier than that disorganic mass of labourers, sunk threefold deeper in brutality by the three-fold wages they are getting. The Yorkshire and Lancashire men, I hear, are reckoned the worst; and not without glad surprise I find the Irish are best in point of behaviour. The postman tells me that several of the poor Irish do regularly apply to him for money drafts and send their earnings home. The English who eat twice as much beef, consume the residue in whisky and do not trouble the postman.[13]

It was possible to rise above the squalor, but rare to do so. One who did was Joseph Firbank, who went to work in a mine in County Durham at the age of six and by the age of 22 was a subcontractor on the Woodhead tunnel. He then worked as a contractor on the York and Scarborough line, lost everything, started again, and ended in the 1870s as the contractor on the Settle and Carlisle route, a justice of the peace and deputy lord lieutenant. He was rich and honoured – and one of the few to offer the men working for him water and oatmeal instead of beer and rotten meat. 'And they liked him in spite of it,' as the historian Terry Coleman says.[14]

So the great work of the railways quickened pace through the 1840s, with huge enterprise, verve and brutality. Not all the innovations worked. The Stephensons favoured a standard width of four feet eight-and-a-half inches between the tracks – based, as it happened, on the width of the coal wagons on Tyneside – whereas Brunel was convinced that a seven-foot span would give his trains a smoother, more power-efficient journey. For a time both gauges were being built and passengers on routes where the different tracks crossed each other, as at Gloucester, had to change trains to complete their journeys. The Stephensons' track prevailed – more of it had been laid than the broader gauge – following a royal commission of inquiry in 1846, and their narrower width still prevails today.

Brunel's idea for trains pulled by an air vacuum did not work ultimately either, but his ambitions did not end at Bristol, or Plymouth. Before the railway line was even built, in 1835, he was suggesting that it might connect to transatlantic shipping: 'Why not make it longer and have a steamboat go from Bristol to New York and call it the Great Western?' the young man is said to have asked at an early meeting of the GWR's directors.[15] By the mid-1840s he had designed and built the *Great Britain*, a cast-iron, propeller-driven steamship with a funnel, then the biggest and longest vessel ever built to cross the ocean. It was a wonder of the age, too big initially to be launched from the dock in which it was built: 3,675 tons and 322 feet long. No wonder crowds turned out to gasp at her and cheer a miracle of British engineering. The cost – £117,000 – all but bankrupted Brunel's backers, and when the ship ran aground off the coast of Northern Ireland as a result of navigational errors one night in September 1846, after setting off from Liverpool for New York, its reputation was undermined. 'Oh what a fearful night!' one passenger told the *Illustrated London News*, as she spoke of the anguish and fear on board, 'the cries of children, the groans of women, the signal guns, even the tears of men and amidst all, the Voice of Prayer and this for long, dark hours!' But, as Brunel's biographer L.T.C. Rolt points out,[16] the ship was so well designed and strongly built that it did not break up and none of the 180 passengers was lost.* They were able to spend the night in their cabins instead. By the early 1850s, Brunel's ambitions would stretch even further, as he designed the *Great Eastern* for the Australia run: it was more than twice the length and had ten times the displacement weight.

---

* The SS *Great Britain* later carried immigrants to Australia and was used as a warehouse at the Falkland Islands for nearly a century, before being left a derelict hulk for decades, then brought back to Bristol in 1970 and renovated. It is now a museum.

The Duke of Wellington and Sir Robert Peel pose stiffly for the fashionable German court painter Franz Xaver Winterhalter, 1844.

PEEL'S CHEAP BREAD SHOP.
OPENED JANUARY 22. 1846.

A more irreverent view of Peel and Wellington from *Punch*, January 1846, portrays Peel as a baker, while Wellington carries a placard advertising cheap bread as the promise of Corn Law repeal beckons.

A baleful Lord George Bentinck plots his next move, either on the racecourse or in the Corn Laws debates.

Richard Cobden, Liberal politician and chief spokesman of the Anti-Corn Law League, photographed c. 1850. To his opponents he was a dangerous radical.

The House of Commons in 1849, as portrayed by the *Punch* illustrator 'Dicky' Doyle. Doyle's cartoon catches the chaos of the Commons while imagining a future sitting. It depicts Robert Peel in characteristic pose, hand clutching coat-tails, fingers pounding the despatch box, still dominant even in opposition, and – an unlikely prospect – an impish Disraeli perching beside him. Palmerston slouches third from left opposite, next to little John Russell.

The first news photograph? A panoramic view by William Kilburn of the great – and orderly – Chartist demonstration in Kennington in April 1848: the movement's last hurrah.

Sir John Franklin, old, exhausted, and unfit, wears his admiral's uniform for a daguerreotype at Greenwich, May 1845. The photograph was taken shortly before his expedition set off in a vain attempt to find the North-West passage. Franklin and his crew would never be seen again.

Portrait of a successful novelist: Charles Dickens aged 38 in 1850, the year of the publication in novel form of *David Copperfield*.

Whitehall seen from Trafalgar Square, 1839. This daguerreotype picture,
by de St Croix, may be the earliest photograph ever taken in London.
The equestrian statue of Charles I in the foreground, dating from the 1630s,
stands on the same spot today.

A calotype photograph, by William Henry Fox Talbot in April 1844,
taken from almost the same place as de St Croix's daguerreotype – but
pointing in the opposite direction – shows Nelson's Column under
construction. Work on the structure had halted temporarily while
the government took over the project from the building committee
whose funds had run out.

A view of Field Lane, Clerkenwell, in 1840. The area was the setting for Charles Dickens's *Oliver Twist*. Shop signs in the image are suggestive of its influence.

A Manchester cotton mill operating at full steam.

'A Court for King Cholera': *Punch*'s even less sanitized version of the backstreets of London.

J. M. W. Turner's last great painting *Rain, Steam and Speed – The Great Western Railway*, 1844, depicting a locomotive crossing the River Thames on Brunel's recently completed Maidenhead Railway Bridge. Turner stuck his head out of a carriage window to experience the precise effect he wished to portray. Now trains were powering ahead: off the canvas and headlong into the future.

The Railway King: George Hudson, champion entrepreneur and embezzler – he kept everything except accounts – in his prime.

Farmworkers gathering the harvest pause from their work to pose for the photographic pioneer William Henry Fox Talbot, 1845. For these rural workers harvest would have been the best-paid time of year.

If we want to see what middle-class Victorians looked like in the 1840s, the Edinburgh photographers David Octavius Hill and Robert Adamson provide some of the most vibrant portraits. Here, in the era before photobooths or selfies, a teenaged Miss Munro poses with her friends, the Misses Graham Binney.

Sandy Linton of Newhaven (a fishing village on the Firth of Forth, near Edinburgh), accompanied by his young, shoeless, assistants seems content enough in this famous Hill and Adamson calotype. Still plenty of fish in the sea for him.

'Edinburgh ale': David Octavius Hill, the photographer, on the right, enjoys a drink and a joke with his friends James Ballantyne and George Bell, c. 1844. Hill gave up photography after 1848 when his colleague Robert Adamson, the man who presumably took this picture, died aged 26.

EJECTMENT OF IRISH TENANTRY.

An Irish eviction pictured by the *Illustrated London News* in 1848. The thatched roof of the house is being removed to prevent it being re-tenanted.

Prince Albert's and Queen Victoria's repeated requests to Robert Peel in 1845–6 to provide funds from the public purse to rebuild Buckingham Palace – at the height of the Irish famine and Corn Laws crises – left *Punch* unimpressed: this cartoon was ironically captioned 'A Case of Real Distress'.

A single-wicket match at Lord's cricket grou in June 1846: the bowling is underarm and the fielders do no seem terribly active.

Alongside the engineers and surveyors came the money men, businessmen and crooks, setting up the railway companies and organizing the financing of the lines. None was greater than George Hudson, 'the railway king', a man who was said to have become rich by keeping everything but his accounts. He was the son of a farmer and now the MP for Sunderland, hustling for advantage, elbowing out competitors, and striding through the Commons seeking to lobby MPs to support his latest bills to build yet more lines – sixteen different pieces of legislation at one time. At one stage he and his companies controlled nearly a quarter of the entire rail network. Not that he had to try too hard to drum up support: 157 MPs, a quarter of the membership of the House, had railway interests in 1846 and many had invested large sums – one as much as £291,000. There was cut-throat competition between rival companies to get their bills before Parliament before the arbitrary annual deadline each year, rather like the modern soccer transfer market, and dirty tricks were rife. Six companies competed in Manchester alone. Hudson himself kept ahead of the game by fraud, share manipulation and false accounting, including what would later be called a Ponzi scheme, in which existing investors were paid dividends from the investments of new recruits. He would eventually flee to France.

The cost of the new railways was not only in constructing the track – £31,000 a mile, the equivalent of maybe £2 million today – but in buying out the landowners along the route, who quickly overcame their objections to losing narrow strips of land by demanding and obtaining exorbitant sums for selling it: what the novelist R.S. Surtees termed 'a strong application of the golden ointment – ten thousand pounds for two thousand pounds'.[17] To start with, canal owners fought rearguard actions against the rival railways, but they could not hold out against a transport system that carried heavier loads faster and further than they did. Some, such as the Kennet and Avon Canal, were bought out by the rail companies and thereafter allowed to decline.

Occasionally, people stood out against the tide, but not many. The dons of Oxford did not want the line to encroach too close to their colleges, so it was built on the edge of the city, far from the dreaming spires. The shoemakers of Northampton thought the smoke would stain their leather, so the main line to the Midlands has bypassed the town ever since.[18] James Watt, son of the inventor of the steam-engine, refused to allow the line north of Birmingham to cross his estate at Aston Hall, and John Keate, Eton's flogging headmaster, opposed the railway on the grounds that it would bring Londoners down to ruin the college and tempt his pupils up to town to engage in degrading dissipation.[19] The developers usually found a way round such obstacles. Instead of Eton, the railway went to Windsor, where Queen Victoria was thrilled by its arrival: after her first journey in 1842 she noted that she had got up to London in half an hour 'free from the dust and crowd and heat and I am quite charmed with it,' – free, that is, from the uncertainties and dangers of coach travel and the risk of being attacked in the streets by the public. With the queen's approval, the railways had achieved respectability.

Nor was there any lack of investors. They could purchase shares on margin: £40 worth of shares in the Bolton, Wigan and Liverpool line could be bought in 1844 for just £4 down and the returns seemed to be immediate. Interest rates to borrow were low and returns projected at 10 per cent a year.

Companies were springing up to build railway lines every-where: offering shares, pushing incredible schemes, some utterly impracticable and known to be so. The Manchester and Leeds company's £100 shares were worth £126 in January 1844 and were selling by August for £215. Trading was fren-zied – the same shares were traded in different cities at different prices and, as ever, banks were only too willing to lend exorbitant amounts to those who could not afford to buy them.[20] Everyone was making money. Newspapers were raking in £12,000 a week from advertisements for rail prospectuses. *Herepath's Railway Journal*, one of a crop of specialist magazines that had suddenly sprung up, carried sixty pages of advertisements in its issue of 27 September 1845 and the same week the *Railway Times* had eighty-eight. Lithographers, cartographers, stationers, upholsterers, promoters, engineers and, inevitably, lawyers all cashed in:

> Men were pointed out in the streets who had made their tens of thousands. [Sober citizens] saw the whole world railway mad... they entered the whirlpool and were carried away by the vortex... their infant daughters were large subscribers, their youthful sons were down for thousands. Like drunken men they lost their caution and gave their signatures for everything that was offered.[21]

A *Punch* cartoon of the period, 'The Railway Juggernaut of 1845', shows members of the public bowing down before a railway engine, offering it bags of money. The engine's name-plate reads 'Speculation' and behind its funnel lurks a leering little devil. In a nearby swamp bask crocodiles wearing barristers' wigs.[22]

There were other, graver warnings. The Governor of the Bank of England murmured to the diarist Charles Greville that he 'never remembered in all his experience anything like the present speculation... and that there could not fail to be a fearful reaction', and the *Bankers' Magazine* noted that many of the proposals were fraudulent:

The real object of the concocters of railway schemes has not been to devise desirable and good lines of railway but to start a scheme... in plain language, to rob and delude the public, by squandering and embezzling the deposit money. Pettifogging attorneys and rejected engineers are the true authors 'for a consideration' of three-fourths of the railway schemes before the world at this moment.

The House of Commons published a list of all subscribers who had invested up to £2,000 in the lines that had been authorized in 1845 alone. It ran to 540 pages:

Amongst those names are to be recognised the leading nobility, the largest manufacturing firms and representatives of every branch of commerce, art, science and literature... peers and printers, vicars and vice-admirals, professors and cotton spinners, gentlemen's cooks and Queen's counsel, college scouts, barristers and butchers, Catholic priests and coachmen, bankers and butlers... the lawyer madly risking his client's money; the chemist forsaking his laboratory in search of a new form of the philosopher's stone, the Jew, the Quaker, the saint and the sinner.[23]

In the list, sixty-three names had subscribed £100,000 each, six above £500,000 and three more than £600,000. Some got out in time and made large fortunes, most did not; and when the crash came in May 1847, it took banks, businesses and many families with it:

> No panic was so fatal to the great middle class... Hundreds of families were entirely ruined and thousands were seriously involved in difficulties and were thereby much reduced. There was scarcely an important town in England but beheld the fall of local magnates. Unfortunate and deluded persons found themselves saddled with enormous liabilities in the form of calls on shares for which they had applied in the hope of selling at a profit. Thousands of writs were issued to cajole or compel them into payment.

The stock market fell 40 per cent in a few days and interest rates trebled in less than a year: 'daughters delicately nurtured went out to seek their bread. Sons were recalled from academies.'[24] Among those who lost money were Emily and Anne Brontë, seduced against their sister Charlotte's advice into investing in George Hudson's York and North Midland Railway. The railways had done what had seemed impossible: they had outstripped demand. Building costs rose steeply and passenger numbers could not keep up.

And yet, despite the frauds and the financial crashes, the railways still got built: two-thirds of all the schemes put before Parliament were eventually constructed, even in the most unpromising areas. They provided employment: by the 1850s, 50,000 people were working on the railways, as drivers, stokers, guards, signalmen, station-masters, porters, engineers and labourers. Caterers staffed the station buffets and stationers manned Mr W. H. Smith's book-stalls, selling cheap and improving editions and religious tracts to while away slow and tedious journeys.

The railways were generally safer, usually quicker and often more reliable than the roads, and they changed the face of the countryside and the nature of society. It was not only Queen Victoria and Prince Albert who were charmed: railways could whisk people up to town for work or shopping. The shopkeepers of Stockport complained they were losing business to Manchester. The cattle-drovers and horse-dealers who for centuries had gathered to trade on Hounslow Heath saw their businesses gone. Wet fish could reach the shops in Birmingham within a day of being landed at Brixham or Lowestoft. Cheshire farmers could now deliver their milk direct to Manchester and cattle could be sent down to Smithfield market by train instead of taking a fortnight to be herded there slowly by road, losing weight and value all the way.

At holiday times, families would now head for the newly flourishing seaside resorts – Margate and Scarborough, Eastbourne and Blackpool – by train. It was no coincidence that William Powell Frith, the hugely popular painter of Victorian genre scenes, should have his first popular triumph with *Life at the Seaside*, showing the trippers in the sun at Ramsgate in 1851 (a picture bought by the queen herself for a thousand guineas); or that he would have even greater success later, in 1862, with *The Railway Station*, all human life tumbling across a huge canvas depicting Paddington Station. Such was the fascination that 21,000 people paid to see it when the painting was first exhibited at the Haymarket.[25]

Now, too, everyone needed to know the times of trains.

Clocks across the country had to be standardized and set right. Services had to be regulated as well – the rich could not just flag down a passing express, or delay a departure for their own convenience – so rules of conduct and regulations for travel had to be laid down.

To start with, only the wealthy could travel: a single ticket from Birmingham to London might cost £1.10s, slightly more expensive than the equivalent £79 second-class fare today. Initially the really wealthy could have their carriages loaded onto the wagons so they could travel in their own vehicles, but that was too time-consuming and cumbersome. From the start there were also different classes of railway car and all who could afford a particular ticket would be expected to shift together, mingling with strangers, enduring their conversation, breathing in the smoke from their pipes and the smell from their halitotic breath, and picking up their colds and infections. First-class passengers were advised not to sit too close to the engine, just in case it exploded, and with their backs to the direction of travel so they did not get soot and sparks in their eyes.

Punch had its own advice in 1844: 'The existing railway arrangements render it imperative that you should provide yourself with a large stock of philosophy to enable you to put up with certain inconveniences.' For those in first class: 'your fare will be about twice as much as you ought in fairness to pay. You run perhaps rather less risk... of having your neck broken; but you must not be unprepared for such a contingency'; in second class: 'you will do well to wear a respirator unless you wish to be choked with dust and ashes... also, put on a diving dress because if it should rain much, you will have to ride in a pool of water'; as for third class: 'make up your mind for unmitigated hail, rain, sleet, snow, thunder and light-ning... do not expect the luxury of a seat. As an individual and a traveller, you are one of the lower classes; a poor beggarly, contemptible person and your comfort and conveni-ence are not to be attended to'. And for all:

> Regard starting or arriving at your destination only half an hour too late as luck. You pay nothing extra to attendants for civility, so you must not hope for it. Remember you are at the mercy of the company as to where you may stop for refreshments for which, accordingly, be not surprised if you have to pay through the nose. Beware if you quit the train for an instant, lest it move on; you have paid your money, the rest is your own look-out... and if at the end of your journey you find yourself in a whole skin – thank your stars.[26]

And where could they get to? Eton's Dr Keate was not the only one to be affronted by the prospect of arriving hordes. 'There was a rocky valley between Buxton and Bakewell, once upon a time,' rhapsodized John Ruskin:

> Divine as the Vale of Tempe; you might have seen the Gods there morning and evening – Apollo and all the sweet muses of the light – walking in fair procession on the lawns of it, to and fro among the pinnacles of its crags... You enterprised a railroad through the valley – you blasted its rocks away, heaped thousands of tons of shale upon its lovely stream. The valley is gone and the Gods with it and now every fool in Buxton can be in Bakewell in half an hour and every fool in Bakewell in Buxton.[27]

Presumably that did not hinder Ruskin from taking the train up to the Lake District and the Trossachs whenever he needed to commune with his particular gods, or nature.

The hoi polloi could not be kept away, however, and Peel's government made it easier for them to travel. In 1844 there was the Railway Regulation Act, introduced by William Gladstone, then president of the Board of Trade, requiring each line to run at least one cheap train a day: a remarkable piece of social engineering from a government supposedly committed to laissez-faire. So-called parliamentary trains might be inconveniently timed and slow, but they did at least allow the less well-off to travel at fares of a penny a mile. Now they too could go up to London to see the sights, or take excursions organized by Mr Thomas Cook to temperance meetings, or hear great preachers, visit the races, or watch public executions. When William Palmer, the Rugeley poisoner, was hanged outside Stafford jail in front of 30,000 people in 1856, special trains were laid on from across the Midlands so that people could go and watch him swing. Six months earlier Palmer had been using the train himself to visit London for the day to meet his creditors and pay off some of his debts; part of the evidence at his trial related to whether he could have arrived back in Staffordshire in time to buy strychnine at the local chemist's shop. Eleven years earlier, in 1845, John Tawell, a supposedly pious Quaker, had been the first murderer to be tracked by train. He had been seen leaving his mistress's house in Slough in his distinctive Quaker clothes; when she was found dead on the kitchen floor shortly afterwards, his path was followed to the local railway station, a telegram was sent along the wires and he was arrested as he got off the train at Paddington.[28] 'Them's the cords that hanged Tawell,' it was said.

The implications of this democratization of the means of travel were not lost on the Victorians. 'Feudality has gone for ever,' exclaimed Thomas Arnold, the headmaster of Rugby, after he had seen the first train go past. Thomas Carlyle was inclined to agree: steam power would 'overturn the whole old system of society', clearing the way for 'industrialism and the government of the wisest'. As T. J. Green, chairman of the Bedford, London and North Western Railway, said at the opening of the line in 1846:

> As members of a vast commercial empire we know the great advantages arising from the cheap and rapid interchange of agricultural produce, the minerals and the manufactures of this country and the prosperity and happiness that result from it. And, as members of this enlightened community, we must feel how the cause of morality is advanced, how science is promoted and how society is improved by the quick and easy communication this afforded between all its neighbours.[29]

Or, less prosaically, the portly epicurean the Rev. Sydney Smith:

> Before this invention man, richly endowed with many gifts of mind and body, was deficient in locomotive powers; he could walk four miles an hour while a wild goose could fly eighty in the same time; I can run now much faster than a fox or a hare and beat a carrier pigeon or an eagle for a hundred miles.[30]

In the words of William Thackeray: 'We who have lived before railways were made, belong to another world.'[31]

✍

Rain, Steam and Speed – The Great Western Railway, J.M.W. Turner's painting of a steam-engine pulling a train of open carriages full of people across Maidenhead Bridge in a hazy miasma, was the great artist's last major work: appropriately enough since its symbolism was all concerned with the headlong onwards rush of modernity and industrialization, coming on at a speed and with a clatter that man had never before achieved. Turner had apparently got the idea during a train journey from Bristol to London in 1843 and astonished his fellow passengers who watched as the elderly gentleman stuck his head out of the window into a drenching maelstrom of rain and smoke. The canvas is thick with swathes of blue, grey and white paint, daubed on in thick chunks with a palette knife, so that the only sure outline in the painting is the black engine with its tall chimney and its red tongue of flame, bearing down fast out of the picture. All the rest is faint and dreamlike, dissolving in the mist of steam and damp. In the haze far below there is a tiny man fishing on a boat under an umbrella, on the distant bank a crowd waves, and to the right, again far off, a ploughman appears to be pushing his old technology backwards: all images so indistinct as to be easily missed. Similarly, on the bridge in front of the train, a rabbit or hare seems to be running to escape, though it is scarcely more than a smudge of brown paint. It is a painting of the future, decades ahead of its time, and when it was exhibited at the Royal Academy in 1844, it left the critics awed, but baffled. 'Whether Turner's pictures are dazzling unrealities or whether they are realities seized upon at a moment's glance, we leave his detractors and admirers to settle between them,' wrote *The Times*.[32]

By now the old artist was into his seventies. In 1845 he made his last trip to the Continent and was sufficiently eminent to be invited to dine with the French king Louis Philippe, but in the autumn of 1846 he would make his final home near the Thames in Chelsea with his last mistress Sophia Booth, who also kept the boarding house where he stayed at Margate every year. In Davis Place, overlooking the river just off Cheyne Row, a stone's throw from where the Carlyles and other literary folk lived, the couple were known as Mr and Mrs Booth, though the paint in Turner's hair and on his fingers probably gave his identity away when he visited the local pubs for a sherry or a bottle of gin, or had his hair cut at the local barber's. Sophia also gave the game away with her insistence that the elderly gent was a great man. Descriptions of him in those days, on his appearances at the Royal Academy on varnishing days before the summer exhibition, speak of him with awe as a great, little man with penetrating grey eyes, 'dressed in a long tail coat, thread gloves, big shoes and a hat of most miserable description made doubly melancholy by the addition of a piece of broad, shabby, dingy crape encircling two-thirds at least'. He would go down to Margate and he was still painting: a small platform was erected on his roof in Chelsea so he could watch the river. However, he seldom visited his other devoted mistress Hannah Danby, who lived in Queen Anne Street, across town in Marylebone, in a house he had had since the 1820s and where many of his pictures were stored. When the painter William Leighton Leitch visited in 1842, he had found the rain coming in and cats squatting around the canvasses, one of which was being used as a flap to cover a broken window. Turner was fascinated by daguerreotypes and may have had his portrait taken around this time, but if so, it does not seem to have survived. The photographer J.J.E. Mayall, who had a studio in London, recorded several visits by 'an inquisitive old man' who he later realized was Turner, and said he took 'several admirable daguerreotype portraits of him, one in the act of reading'. He said Turner stayed for three hours on one occasion, talking about light and its curious effects on films of prepared silver.[33]

7

An Agreeable Sight to a Merciful Creator

'What has taken place on the banks of the Sutlej will
have its influence on the banks of the Oregon.'

SIR ROBERT PEEL, 1846

On the December evening following Peel's return from seeing
the queen at Windsor, at about the time that he was meeting
his cabinet, British troops were squaring up to a Sikh army on
the borders of the Punjab near the village of Ferozeshah in
northern India – though the government in London would
not get to hear about it for another two months. In the middle
of the domestic political turmoil, Peel's government in 1846
also faced two foreign crises: the First Sikh War and a confrontation with the United States over the line of the border with
western Canada. Both conflicts, stretching right across the
world, were a sign of the global reach of empire.

In India, the British were realizing slowly how far their
reach exceeded both their grasp and the Treasury's resources.
The government had taken office in 1841 shortly before the
British forces in Afghanistan – trying to install their own
choice of ruler in Kabul and extend British interests in the
region – had suffered a calamitous humiliation, defeat and
massacre. In January 1842 its army was forced to retreat from
Kabul through the snowy mountain passes to Jelalabad; of
the 700 British troops who started the eighty-mile journey
back, only one, the assistant surgeon William Brydon, reached

183

safety.[1] The rest died of exposure, were hacked to death by the Afghans or imprisoned by them. Peel, landed with the occupation by the outgoing Whig administration and its bellicose foreign secretary Palmerston, described the Afghan adventure bitterly as 'the most absurd and insane project that was ever undertaken in the wantonness of power'.[2] He disliked the disdain with which the British in India regarded the Indian princes.

The prime minister largely took charge of foreign policy, though as communications with outlying parts of the empire generally took months to get through, the task could not be a controlling one and sometimes, it seems, was confined to complaints about the ambassadors' standards of written English. You get the sense of the prime minister sitting up late at night in Downing Street, or across the road at his home in Whitehall Gardens, reading endless ill-formed dispatches from the empire with increasing exasperation at the incompetence of its British officials: 'I wish you would require your foreign ministers and ambassadors to write English,' he wrote to Lord Aberdeen, his foreign secretary. 'I read some dispatches yesterday from Lord Stuart and I think Mr Mandeville or Mr Hamilton or I believe both which are too slovenly for endurance.'[3] So much for the virtues of their classical educations! Of H.S. Fox, Britain's man in Washington, appointed by Palmerston in 1836, it was said that he did not mix in American society, knew little of American opinion and spent the greater part of the day in bed. Aberdeen, later to be prime minister himself during the Crimean War debacle, was a much more emollient character than Palmerston, but, as he was convinced that his head was submerged in water, he was scarcely a dynamic force.* When he complained to Peel of 'the noise, confusion and distressing sensations in the head', he was told to get a grip and carry on.

In 1843, against the wishes of the government in London, but with the encouragement of the governor-general Lord Ellenborough, a British force seized control of Sind province, whose capital is Karachi. Presented to him as a fait accompli, this infuriated Peel when he finally heard about it. Then in the autumn of 1845, the British administration found itself embroiled in a power struggle within the Sikh-controlled Punjab, one of the remaining independently governed states in the subcontinent. The roots of the conflict are obscure and contested between British and Indian historians, and both sides had reasons for seeking a confrontation, or at least not avoiding one. The government in London, trying to influence events thousands of miles away, had installed Sir Henry Hardinge, an old soldier and close political ally and friend of Peel, in 1844 to be a more cautious and emollient governor-general of India in place of the belligerent and widely disliked Ellenborough. But within months the internal politics of the Sikh regime had spilled over into an invasion across the Sutlej river border and into British-administered India. They did not get far, having been beaten back by a British and sepoy force at Mudki in mid-December,† an encounter followed a few days later by the vicious two-day stand-off around

---

* Aberdeen suffered from bouts of depression and ill-health, not assisted by the deaths of two wives, four daughters and a son. He wrote regularly to Peel asking to be allowed to resign. In September 1842 he said he was like 'a gentleman walking about with his head under water'; a month later 'my head is completely *submerged*'. He would become prime minister in 1852.

† Sepoys were Indian soldiers fighting for and trained by the British.

Ferozeshah. The outcome of the second battle was highly fortuitous because the British side was on the defensive and on the verge of retreating when the Sikh generals Lal Singh and Tej Singh decided not to renew their attack but retreated themselves.* Hardinge, who had been at the battle and had already ordered his state papers to be burned, believed that the fate of India trembled in the balance.[4]

Ferozeshah was followed a few weeks later, on 10 February 1846, by a more decisive and even more desperate battle at Sobraon, on the banks of a bend in the Sutlej. The Sikh army, which was double the size of the British and entrenched in a strong defensive position, was thrown back after a bayonet charge and some hand-to-hand fighting in the Sikh lines. General Harry Smith, who had fought in the Peninsular War more than thirty years earlier and on many battlefields since, wrote home in a letter that they had 'laid on like devils. This last was a brutal bulldog fight.'[5] 'We drove the enemy into the river where thousands of them were killed by our file-firing and by the grape and canister of four troops of Horse Artillery and a great number must have drowned,' wrote an officer of the 63rd Native Infantry. Robert Cust, serving on Hardinge's staff, observed:

The stream was choked with dead and dying – the sandbags were covered with bodies floating leisurely down. It was an awful scene, fearful carnage... Our loss was heavy and the ground was here and there strewn with the slain, among

---

* Their decision has always been a puzzle and has been controversial among Sikhs ever since. It may have been due to treachery, cowardice or bribery or, charitably, because the retreat of the British artillery, which had run out of ammunition, was mistaken for an imminent counterattack.

whom I recognised a fine and handsome lad whom I had well known, young Hamilton... There he lay, his auburn hair weltering in his blood, his forehead fearfully gashed, fingers cut off. Still warm, but quite dead.[6]

Gunner Nathaniel Bancroft of the Bengal Horse Artillery – who had watched his commanding officer, standing nearby, have his head knocked clean off by round shot at Ferozeshah – recalled that the Sutlej became a bloody foam 'amid which heads and uplifted hands were seen to vanish by hundreds'.[7] The battle ended the war, though the conflict would resume a couple of years later.

These are now largely forgotten battles – unremembered, at least, by most of the British, who have overlooked them even as they remember other colonial battles of the nineteenth century (though the fights are still commemorated annually on their anniversaries by the successor regiments of those that took part). They were achieved at considerable cost by soldiers whose treatment was little better than they would have received in civilian life at home. To reach a pension after twenty or thirty years' service, they would have spent many years abroad at tedious duties in heavy, uncomfortable, impractical and ill-fitting woollen uniforms on remote and dusty frontiers. They would have been boiling in summer and freezing in winter and would have had to survive diseases such as cholera or wounds in battle. Just occasionally, if they won a battle, such as Sobraon, they would have been awarded with prize money and extra pay (sometimes as much as a year's worth).

But for men in the ranks there was always the threat of savage treatment too. In England that summer, John White, a 27-year-old private with the 7th Queen's Own Hussars, stationed at Hounslow barracks, was sentenced to 150 lashes after being convicted at court martial of striking his sergeant with an iron bar during a drunken fight. The punishment, inflicted on 15 June 1846 by regimental farriers working in relays in the presence of the regiment, its commanding officer and a surgeon, resulted in White's death a month later. The brutality of the flogging – ten troopers had fainted just watching it – and the regiment's callousness in attempting to cover up what had happened (the skin from White's flayed back was removed and it was blandly stated he had died from natural causes) resulted in a national outcry after the local vicar refused to bury the soldier until the cause of his death had been established. An inquest, which the War Office tried to obstruct, found that the soldier had died from 'the mortal effects of a severe and cruel flogging' and there was a petition demanding the end of the punishment and a parliamentary debate. It would take another thirty-five years for the army to end floggings – and the punishment would only be formally abolished in 1939 – but White's death shook liberal consciences.[8]

In India, Gunner Bancroft, who was born in the country, was the son of a soldier. He was 22 at the time of the Sikh war, but had already been enlisted for thirteen years. He was proud of his uniform, as he wrote in his memoirs forty years later: 'leather breeches and long boots, brass helmets with red horse-hair manes and jackets with ninety buttons... when shaven chins and upper lips and mutton-chop whiskers (according to regulation) were the order of the day'. Even so, when he was wounded in the arm by the same bouncing shot that had decapitated his officer at Ferozeshah, Bancroft was lucky to survive, for the army had neglected to provide any medical care for the wounded. Those with abdominal or head wounds and many who lost limbs had no chance of recovery. Bancroft wrote:

> The sights were most harrowing. Most of my comrades… who were taken out of the carts had died on the field from loss of blood and scarcity of water and some of them were at the door of death, gasping their last. They were all placed side by side on the ground; several of them had their limbs shattered with round shot and grape; and after the moribund had breathed their last, they were again put into carts and taken outside the fort to be buried in a pit dug for the purpose.[9]

The British suffered 694 killed and 2,415 wounded at Ferozeshah and a further 320 killed and 2,383 wounded at Sobraon; the Sikhs somewhere between 6,000 and 10,000 at both battles combined. These were two smallish battles on a far-off frontier, both with more casualties in a few weeks than British forces have recently suffered in ten years in Afghanistan, and the dead were thrown anonymously and unceremoniously into mass graves.

Afterwards, the British did not seize the Punjab – Hardinge said his purpose was to 'clip' the state, 'which has shown itself too strong, punish and disband the army and give the Hindoos another chance'. Its rulers agreed to pay the British an indemnity, and to accept a garrison stationed in the capital Lahore ('the dirtiest place I ever saw,' wrote one disgusted British officer) for a year. The young Duleep Singh, eight years old and the last maharaja of the Punjab – 'a brave little fellow', according to Hardinge – was taken into British care, converted to Christianity, probably under duress, and eventually removed to Britain where for the rest of his days he lived the life of a country squire, first in Perthshire, then in Norfolk, only twice – briefly – seeing his homeland ever again. Meanwhile, when the British realized the Sikhs were unable to pay the indemnity, they found a Hindu ruler – Maharaja Gulab Singh of Jammu – who could, and gave him the Muslim province of Kashmir as a reward, creating a conflict that remains active to this day. Following the next outbreak of hostilities between the British and the Sikhs in 1850 – after which the British really would annexe the Punjab – the Koh-i-Noor diamond, which now graces the British crown, was confiscated from the maharaja of Lahore by the East India Company and presented to Queen Victoria. Meanwhile, General Harry Smith received a baronetcy and was given the governorship of Cape Colony in South Africa, where his Spanish wife Juana, who had accompanied him on every campaign since they met during the Peninsular War, gave her name to a local township: Ladysmith. For his part, Hardinge was rewarded with a viscountcy for his efforts in 1848 and retired to Tunbridge Wells.

Back in London, when the news of victory came through six weeks later, Peel received the increasingly rare plaudits of his party in the midst of the Corn Law struggle and thoroughly approved of Hardinge's decision not to try to annexe the Punjab. He even toned down the words of the proposed victory proclamation, which he said had made it appear as if God had intervened to destroy the Sikh army:

Considering the sanguinary nature of great battles and that (however just the cause) many thousands forfeit their lives through no fault of their own, too direct a reference to the special intervention of Almighty God is not very seemly... They almost make it appear... that the fire of artillery on the confused mass of Sikhs after they had been driven into the Sutlej had been directed by Divine Providence and was an agreeable sight to a merciful Creator.

As his biographer Douglas Hurd, foreign secretary in the last Thatcher government, remarks about Peel's rewording of the speech: 'It is impossible to imagine Palmerston, or indeed Disraeli or Margaret Thatcher making this change.'[10]

Peel's Tory government was trying to reduce expenditure on the military while this was going on, but at the same time a squabble was brewing with the United States, bringing the two nations, which had already gone to war twice in the previous seventy years, to the brink of a new conflict over the border with Canada. The final line of the eastern border, between Maine and Quebec, was settled by negotiation in 1842, but two years later a new American administration came in making belligerent noises about the line in the west, through what was known as the Oregon Territory. The Democrat party's successful presidential candidate, James Knox Polk, a small-town lawyer and party hack from rural Tennessee, a humourless and uncharismatic Presbyterian known for his self-righteousness and obstinacy but with no knowledge of foreign affairs, had campaigned on the satisfactorily anti-British slogan '54:40 or Fight'.[11] This was a reference to the border area the US was now claiming, which would have encompassed most of what is now British Columbia, all the way up to the south-ernmost tip of modern-day Alaska, hundreds of miles north of the 49th parallel that marks today's border. By a long-standing agreement the territory had been jointly administered while it was largely unpopulated by white settlers, but by the mid-1840s wagon trains of American farmers, many of them with Irish ancestry and no love of the British, were heading west to the rich farm lands that they had been told awaited them in the Oregon valley. Among them, in the summer of 1846, was the ill-fated Donner party. Setting off in May from Missouri, the group would be delayed getting to the Sierra Nevada and forced by snow to winter high in the mountains, where their food ran out and eventually the survivors resorted to cannibalism before they could be rescued.

It was the era of 'Manifest Destiny', a recently coined newspaper slogan which claimed the North American landmass for the United States as of right. In the next few years the US would annex both Texas and California from Mexico. Settlers, including the Mormons, were heading west in increasing numbers, and Polk saw the Oregon Territory as a natural extension further north (it would become the thirty-third state in 1859). If you visit Polk's modest brick home in the town of Columbia, Tennessee, these days, the guide cheerily tells you that the US's largest ever expansion of territory occurred during the now largely forgotten eleventh president's four years in office. Possession of the territory was, Polk announced in his inaugural address in Washington in March 1845, 'a clear and unquestionable right', and the president brusquely rejected the British government's compromise proposal for the border, giving Britain's Canadian territory access to the Pacific through the Columbia River and ownership of Vancouver Island. He seemed happy to override his cautious Secretary of State James Buchanan in blustering for simultaneous war on both the country's northern and southern borders, with both Britain and Mexico. 'We should do our duty towards both... and firmly maintain our rights and leave the rest to God and the country,' he said; to which Buchanan replied: 'God would not have much to do in justifying us in a war for the country north of 49.'[12] It was a good populist wave for the new president to ride, though: 'the only way to treat John Bull is to look him straight in the eye... if Congress faultered [sic] or hesitated, John Bull would immediately become more arrogant and grasping in his demands.'

It was, as Peel had earlier predicted, 'a good deal of preliminary bluster on the part of the Americans', and fortunately cooler diplomacy prevailed. Even Polk realized that the US could not fight on two fronts at once and there was a fear that powerful Britain might ally with Mexico. Negotiations resumed along the lines the British had previously suggested. In May 1846 the US declared war on Mexico – a much weaker target – and, after the British proposals arrived a few days later, Congress ratified them in mid-June. To many, including perhaps Polk, who recorded the compromise curtly in his diary, it seemed like a humiliation. As one Kentucky congressman insisted:

> Whilst we bluster and boast over imbecile Mexico we present the ridiculous attitude of yielding to England what we have asserted to be our just right, 'clear and indispensable', and find ourselves in the humiliating position of a whipped hound, sneaking to the kennel at the roar of the British lion.[13]

Nevertheless, it was a settlement that has lasted ever since.

At the same time as this spikiness was evident in political relations between the two countries, there was a great deal of
interaction between them. A succession of British authors,
including Dickens, had already visited America, usually
recording their impressions in sneering, superior terms, but
American writers were also coming to England: Fenimore
Cooper and Washington Irving had already been, Longfellow
and Nathaniel Hawthorne would follow shortly. The
Mormons were having greater success in the 1840s converting
the cotton-spinners of the Lancashire mills than they were the
farm labourers of the Midwest, and there would be many
northern English accents on Brigham Young's great trek from
the Midwest to Utah in the early months of 1847.

In theatres on both sides of the Atlantic, actors from each
country were being cheerfully heckled from the stage. Edwin
Forrest, the great American actor, had started a second tour of
Britain in 1845, to find his Shakespearean performances
panned. His Othello, according to the *Spectator*, was 'varied
by the Yankee nasal twang... his passion is a violent effort of
physical vehemence... his tenderness affected and his smile
like the grin of a wolf showing his fangs'; his King Lear was
'a roaring pantaloon with a vigorous totter'.[14] Four years later,
in 1849, Forrest would obtain redress of sorts, when his
British rival and bitter foe William Macready performed in
New York. Forrest paid Irish toughs to close down Macready's
shows with rioting outside the theatre, which got out of hand
and left thirty people dead. Macready, the foremost British
actor and greatest tragedian of his day, was a difficult man,
prone to quarrels and grudges: 'very fascinating... of the most

polished and delightful manners and with no fault but of jealousy and unreasonableness which seems to me the natural growth of the greenroom,' said the writer Mary Russell Mitford perceptively, so perhaps he brought it on himself, though scarcely to the point of a lethal riot.

Reciprocal cultural cringes, mutual patronizing and internecine rivalries are nothing new in the 'special relationship'. In the 1840s that relationship was certainly at its most fraught since the war of 1812, with belligerence on both sides: a haughty disdain from the British, fuelled by a genuine and widespread moral repugnance for slavery in the American South; a chippy resentfulness on the part of the Americans, which would soon be exacerbated by the wave of Irish immigration following the famine and all the resentments they brought with them. As contacts between the two nations increased – more visits by Britons to America, more frequent tourism by Americans to the old country – there was a growing realization of the distinctions: of manners, ways of speaking, attitudes and even vocabulary. *Our American Cousin*, the hugely successful comedy that Abraham Lincoln was watching when he was shot, precisely satirized such differences.

Lord Palmerston wrote in 1841: 'It never answers to give way to the Americans because they always keep pushing on their own encroachments as far as they are permitted to do so and what we dignify by the names of moderation and conciliation, they naturally enough call fear.' An American journalist considered: 'Why does America hate England? Americans believe that England dreads their growing power and is envious of their prosperity. They detest and hate England accordingly. They have "licked" her twice and can "lick" her again.' Yet the links were indissoluble, not only of history and heritage but also of trade. In the 1840s the Lancashire cotton mills flourished on exports from the Deep South: another factor in the Manchester manufacturers' campaign for free trade. Britons despised slavery and they lapped up *Uncle Tom's Cabin* – which sold more copies in England in its first year than in the United States – but they appreciated the commerce with the country across the Atlantic. The United States was expanding fast: a 35 per cent population increase, from 17 million to 23 million during the 1840s, with many of those immigrants coming from the British Isles.[15]

Three months after Congress voted on the Canadian border compromise, it also accepted – with varying degrees of grace – perhaps the most generous philanthropic bequest ever bestowed from one country on another. It was the legacy of an Englishman named James Smithson who had never crossed the Atlantic but nevertheless had left the equivalent of $500,000 in his will to establish an institution in Washington for the 'increase and diffusion of knowledge among men'. No one knows quite why he did it. It had taken the American politicians more than a decade to accept the bequest, grudgingly. If they did so, said the South Carolina senator William C. Preston, 'every whippersnapper vagabond that had been traducing our country might think proper to have his name distinguished in the same way. It is not consistent with the dignity of the country.'[16] Smithson, the illegitimate son of the 1st Duke of Northumberland, had died without direct heirs in 1829, and after his unmarried nephew died in 1835, the estate passed as Smithson had intended to the US government. The money had arrived in gold bullion in 1838 and was handed over to Congress because the Anglophobic president Andrew Jackson pronounced that he had no authority to supervise it.

Congress had, however, invested it speculatively and negligently in defaulting bonds in Arkansas and Michigan. There was prolonged wrangling over whether the money should be returned (the senators decided that would be a bad idea), passed straight to the government after all, or used to set up a university, or a library, or, finally, an institution to which the public would be admitted. It was not until the last day of the congressional session, 10 August 1846, that the measure was finally passed and the gift horse was no longer looked in the mouth: 'the most gratifying act of the whole of the session was the unexpected passage of the Smithsonian Institution bill,' said the *New York Evening Post*. Anything else, according to the *New York Post*'s man in Washington, would have been 'a blasting, burning shame upon the country... a national disgrace, as utterly dishonourable as an open, barefaced swindle'.

8

Lead Thou Me On

'Those clergymen: they are always poking themselves
into everything.'

LORD MELBOURNE TO QUEEN VICTORIA[1]

Our image of what the Victorians were like is largely an evangelical one: stern, God-fearing fathers, prudish mothers,
hypocrisy and pompousness, humourlessness and self-
righteousness, a little comic and quite a bit scary. It is a picture
coloured by novels and memoirs. We meet Mr Chadband and
Mrs Jellyby in *Bleak House* (Dickens did not like evangelicals
much), Mr Slope in *Barchester Towers*, Philip Henry Gosse in
Father and Son and perhaps, above all, Mr Brocklehurst in
Jane Eyre: 'a black pillar... the straight, narrow, sable-clad
shape standing erect on the rug, the grim face... like a carved
mask... Presently he addressed me: "Well, Jane Eyre, and are
you a good child?"'[2]

Brocklehurst was based on a real person, William Carus
Wilson, who ran the school for clergy daughters at Cowan
Bridge in north Lancashire to which Charlotte Brontë and her
sisters had been sent unhappily as children in the 1820s. Such
forbidding figures did indeed exist and they played a role in
shaping many Victorians' lives and infusing them with a sense
of seriousness and moral purpose. But they were far from
being the only Victorian religionists, nor was their reach
universal. In a modern, secular age, it is sometimes hard to

understand the effect of religion on earlier generations (though a similar fervour can still be seen in many parts of the world today), but many Victorians took their beliefs very seriously, devoutly and often unquestioningly. The vigour and rancour of the period's religious disputes are difficult to replicate, and modern undercurrents – over gay clergy or women's ordination – are pale imitations of the fury of the nineteenth-century polemics. To their participants those arguments were matters of life, death and eternal salvation, not only of individuals but of the whole of society. They were accordingly fought passionately and even viciously.

So when a survey of those attending religious services across the country was taken for the first time on Sunday, 30 March 1851, religious Victorians were shocked to discover that less than half the population had been to church or chapel that day. The seven million people recorded were nevertheless perhaps three times as many as attend Christian services today, out of a population a third the size than it is now. The 1851 survey is by no means exact: it depended largely on the local clergymen totting up the numbers and took no account of those who were unable to attend on that particular day through employment, age or illness, but it is enough to give a general snapshot picture. Attendance was higher in small towns and rural areas than in the large cities; the Church of England was also strongest in the countryside and in market towns, especially where the squire had some say over village life. Nonconformism was strongest in the north of England and in the industrial cities, Methodism in areas which had seen industrial growth during the Wesleys' time in the late eighteenth century,* and Catholicism was most vibrant in Lancashire and areas with large immigrant Irish populations.

If it was an uncomfortable picture in terms of numbers, it came at the end of a decade of religious turmoil and upheaval in the Church of England. The position of the established church was being challenged and, many felt, undermined by an assertive conservative High Church movement, centred largely on Oxford University, and by the earnest evangelicals at the other end of the doctrinal scale. Nonconformity was vibrant and Roman Catholics had been emancipated:† free to hold secular office and become MPs, for the first time since the Reformation, though they were still regarded with suspicion and distaste. This all meant that the Church of England no longer had a monopoly over positions of authority and influence. And, to add to the sense of insecurity, the age-old biblical doctrines were being intellectually challenged for the first time. Darwin had not yet publicized his theory of evolution, but there were German academics whose works were beginning to question the inerrancy of the Bible's stories and point out inconsistencies in the Gospels' accounts of the life of Christ. No wonder Lord Melbourne told the queen that he was afraid to go to church 'for fear of hearing something very extraordinary'.

---

* John (1703–91) and Charles Wesley (1707–88) were the great evangelical founders of Methodism.

† The Roman Catholic Relief Act of 1829 removed many of the post-Reformation bars (such as the Test Acts of the 1670s) to Roman Catholics from holding public office. It was enacted following Irish agitation led by Daniel O'Connell that had caused Home Secretary Peel to change his mind. He decided that civil strife was a greater evil than emancipation. Tory Ultras regarded this U-turn as his first great betrayal of the party's principles.

William Howley, the archbishop of Canterbury, was himself a courtly, conservative Anglican, who had been deeply opposed both to Roman Catholic emancipation and to the 1832 Reform Act – his carriage had been pelted with stones on the first occasion he visited his cathedral following the passing of the Act. He was one of those who had broken the news to Victoria that she was queen following the death of William IV in 1837, but by 1846 he seemed a figure from another age: touching 80 and a bishop for thirty years, he was the last senior churchman still to wear an eighteenth-century wig during his daily duties as well as at services. He was a timid, gentle man, a poor preacher and public speaker. Although he cut back on the expenditure of his office – no longer would there be thirty liveried flunkeys serving dinner at Lambeth Palace with a further fifteen waiting outside to light the way to the gatehouse – and agreed to participate in an ecclesiastical commission looking into the reform of church practices, he was not the man to re-energize a church that had been in genteel decline for nearly a century – an institution ready, as one churchman put it, to be 'folding its robes to die with what dignity it could'.[3]

There were still plenty of conservative churchmen, abiding by the old formularies and dutifully fulfilling their offices, especially if they had been appointed by the patron of the living – usually the local landowner, aristocrat, City livery company or Oxbridge college – to provide the sort of services that had been traditionally expected. But huge disparities of wealth had developed across the Church of England by the 1830s. Many parishes had absentee ministers and curates. Rich cathedrals and colleges received large tithes from which they paid clergy administering their parishes mere pittances. The bishop of Durham notoriously received a stipend of £19,000 a year, while curates in the diocese struggled to retain their social standing and authority in the parishes on an average annual stipend of just £86.[4] Howley reduced the archbishop's income from the see of Canterbury from about £19,000 to £15,000 (and his successors would not be paid £19,000 again until the 1980s); but redistribution was slow and much opposed by powerful vested church and political interests.

The disparities hollowing out the institution had started to be tackled during Peel's brief administration in the mid-1830s, when the ecclesiastical commission was first set up, but its work drifted on for years through the 1840s and eventually the 1850s. Although the practice of absentee clergy was addressed – in future they would have to live, if not in their parishes, at least close by – redistribution of diocesan wealth was more fiercely contested. Peel pointed out to High Church Tories that opposing reform of the established church's practices would only hasten its decline:

> you will have left hundreds of thousands to become Dissenters, or more likely infidels, because you would not divert one farthing of ecclesiastical revenue from this deanery or that great sinecure... Is this right, that in a parish of 10,000 acres overrun with dissent, the whole tithes go to an ecclesiastical corporation to the amount of £2,000 a year; that there is only one service in the church and cannot be two because the said corporation will only allow £24 a year as a stipend to the vicar?[5]

Peel himself was a practising Anglican, though without the fervour or surplus energy to engage in theological debates within the church that his young colleague Gladstone showed. The prime minister saw his religious belief as a private matter: a guide to practical and pragmatic conduct rather than a reason to engage in dialectics, which was why he had been able to change his mind on Catholic emancipation. Peel certainly did not challenge or dissent from the Church of England, or its establishment status. He walked to services each Sunday when he was at home in Staffordshire, across the estate to Drayton's sandstone parish church, or into nearby Tamworth, or, if he was in London, to one of a number of High Anglican chapels. There were daily prayers at home, he gave privately to charities and he would be buried, like other Peels, in the village church. Presented with Gladstone's polemical 1838 book on relations between church and state, which was to cause the young minister such intellectual turmoil about the Maynooth grant a few years later, Peel remarked drily: 'That young man will ruin a fine career if he writes such books as this.' And so it nearly came to pass.[6]

Insurgent in the church for the last decade had been the Tractarians – or the Oxford Movement – of young dons, seeking to wrest the Church of England back towards a more ascetic and Roman Catholic character, as if the Reformation had never happened. The Tractarians saw this renewal of what they believed to be older, more rigorous traditions as a way to bolster the Anglican church's established status. Indeed, with measures such as the Whig government's decision to reduce the number of Anglican bishops in Ireland in the 1830s, they believed the state was betraying its obligations to support the church. They got themselves extremely het up about such matters. Some members of the group, such as John Henry Newman, the vicar of the Oxford University church, were charismatic preachers, and he and others, including John Keble and Edward Pusey, were skilled polemicists. These were men brought up as evangelicals who were on a pilgrimage to something much more conservative and authoritarian, though their polemics against the state of the Church of England meant they were regarded as dangerous radicals. They certainly had a huge influence within Oxford, the High Tory hub of church and state. 'The undergraduates first went to Newman because he was disreputable among their elders, because his name was exciting, because he banged the regius professor, because the chaplain of New College placarded Oxford against his popery,' writes Owen Chadwick, the historian of the Victorian church:

> From the pulpit of St Mary's they learnt obedience, holiness, devotion, sacrament, fasting, mortification, in language of a beauty rarely heard in English oratory... The undergraduates paid him the compliment of crowding his sermons, of imitating his gliding gait, of holding their heads on one side and pausing long between sentences, of reading in hurried impersonal monotony, of kneeling down with a bump as he knelt, of arguing endlessly over his teaching.[7]

It was a fractious, self-righteous, contrarian movement, in the words of Diarmaid MacCulloch, 'with a good many opinions, as well as a good opinion of itself – perhaps not surprisingly, given the large number of young and single Oxford dons among its leadership'.[8] To clergy outside the city, however, such men and their affectations verged on the heretical: they were seen as purveyors of popish idolatry. What Newman and the others would do with their tender consciences was a matter of some fascination and, for much of the 1840s, they were constantly predicted to be about to convert to Roman Catholicism, however much they protested to the contrary. Newman himself even wrote a notorious pamphlet – *Tract 90*, the last in a series of High Anglican essays – in which he claimed laboriously and sinuously that Catholic doctrine was somehow not incompatible with the Church of England's foundational Thirty-nine Articles – a specious argument that caused outrage. But eventually the polemics had to stop. In the autumn of 1845 Newman, the former evangelical, became a Roman Catholic, on a day of heavy rain and apocalyptic thunder: a monitory symbol to churchmen, but more prosaically an indication of that year's wet weather which had already ruined the potato crop across Europe. Such a conversion was so drastic that it cut him off from the society in which he had previously moved. He was followed by a number of the others, including Henry Manning who, like Newman, would end up a cardinal.

Defections such as this, to an alien and heretical faith, the religion of rebellious Irishmen, whose adherents were still in thrall to a foreign potentate, caused huge ructions at a time when religion – the *right* religion – still mattered, especially in a place like Oxford where dons were expected to take holy orders and remain bachelors.* In 1845, when the Peel government decided to increase its grant to the Maynooth seminary

---

* In the 1840s Oxford undergraduates were classed as noblemen, scholars, gentlemen commoners and commoners – each with a different variety of gown – and only a minority read for an honours degree as opposed to a pass. Such social distinctions would be abolished, against the wishes of many at the university, in 1854 with the passage of the Oxford University Act.

from £9,000 to £25,000, to counteract the political subversiveness of Irish priests – it was 'sending out annually fifty spiritual firebrands, prepared for mischief to convulse the country', in Peel's words – there was a lively sense, certainly among Tories, that the established church was being undermined by Romanists abetted by the government. Each celebrity conversion, or relaxation of restrictions against Roman Catholics, was accompanied by strident proclamations of outrage and hostility, among many of the clergy and in the press. *Punch*'s cartoons, for instance, show sly and devious papist priests – or Oxford undergraduates wearing papal tiaras – burrowing their way into society. One cartoon entitled 'The Thin End of the Wedge', from 1850, depicted the pope, in full regalia, accompanied by a suspiciously foreign-looking priest, attempting to prise open the doors of an Anglican church.[9]

This depiction came at the time of the restoration of Roman Catholic bishops to England, 300 years after the Reformation, during which the first of them, Cardinal Wiseman, scarcely eased Anglican sensitivities by gleefully anticipating the rapid reconversion of the country to its old allegiance. Wiseman ordered the letter to be read aloud in every Catholic church in his diocese of London, though *The Times* called it 'one of the grossest acts of folly and impertinence which the court of Rome has ventured to commit since the crown and people of England threw off its yoke', which gives a fair flavour of the tenor of the period.[10] Other Tractarians, such as Keble and Pusey, stayed with the Church of England and in the coming decades became active participants in the polemical and occasionally arcane internecine disputes within the university and church over practice and belief. It was a time when passionate battles could be fought in the university over the religious orthodoxy and hence suitability of candidates for the professorship of poetry. Even in the city of Exeter a riot would break out over a local curate's decision to wear a surplice while preaching.

You could certainly tell – then as now – the High and Low Church parties by their dress and manner. Each was contemptuous of the other and they rarely mixed. Accusations of heresy flew about. A sense of the loathing is clear in this assault on the Tractarians:

> Who does not recognise, when he meets them in the railway
> or on the street, the clipped shirt collar, the stiff and tie-less
> neckcloth, the MB coat and cassock waistcoat, the cropped
> hair and unwhiskered cheek? Who does not know that the
> wearer of this costume will talk of 'the Holy Altar' and the
> 'Blessed Virgin', 'Saint Ignatius Loyola'... and that he will
> date his letters on 'the eve of St Chad' or the 'Morrow of
> St Martin'?

This was by one W. J. Conybeare, writing about what he considered their Satanic church parties in the *Edinburgh Review* in 1853 (the clipped shirt collar is what we now call a dog collar and MB stands for 'Mark of the Beast').[11] By contrast evangelicals wore cut-away tail-coats, white shirts, clerical bands and high collars. Such things mattered. High Church Anglicanism fed into and drew support from some of the wider, more secular interests of the period: medieval gothic architecture (or at least a pastiche of it) and the Middle Ages' supposed chivalric modes and manners. It also drew on Roman Catholic ritualism and even the new so-called Pre-Raphaelite school of painting: all a sort of antiquarian fascination with an imagined, purer and simpler past. With all this came their absorption with the correct ritual at services, the precise vestments and the appropriate decoration of their churches.

Nor were these divisions just south of the border, though the walkouts in Scotland were by conservative evangelicals rather than High Church Anglicans. In May 1843 the General Assembly of the Church of Scotland split when a third of its ministers left to set up their own free church, independent of patronage and free of pressure to conform or submit to doctrinal rulings of which they did not approve. They did, however, bow to having their calotype photographs taken by the young Edinburgh pioneers Hill and Adamson in preparation for a huge painted group portrait.

In England, the evangelicals were also relentless in debate: serious young men trying to wrest the Church of England in their direction. By the 1840s, this revivalist movement was well established (if otherwise considered wrong-headed, or even Satanic) among both laity and clergy. It was beginning to penetrate the bench of bishops and Howley's successor after the old man died in 1848, John Bird Sumner, would be the first archbishop to have evangelical tendencies (and also the last Old Etonian archbishop of Canterbury until Justin Welby 160 years later). Evangelicals were characterized by their seriousness of purpose and energy, their sense of public duty, their moral righteousness and ardour for conversions. To them, salvation through Christ's good offices was the ultimate goal: an awakening to faith and a conversion experience from which there could be no backsliding, nor the slightest hint of a surrender to temptation. Not a day was to be wasted in spreading the Lord's word before the terrible day of judgement and warning people what awaited them unless they saw the light. As the evangelical Sir Thomas Dyke Acland, for forty-five years MP for Devon, told his son, they faced 'the awful decision of an all-wise, unerring judge who will require a strict account of every talent, every trust that he has at any time committed to your care – our time, health, strength, abilities and possessions are all included'.[12] For some of them frivolous things – playing cricket, reading novels, going to the theatre or letting children play with toys – had no place in God's scheme for their lives. The positive side was that their beliefs bred self-discipline and earnestness. These admirable traits could – and sometimes still do – shade into pomposity, humourless-ness and self-righteousness and a sense that those who did not share their credo were either in error, or even inferior. Here is the social reformer Lord Ashley, a Tory who described himself as 'from deep-rooted conviction, an Evangelical of the Evangelicals', primly describing the shortcomings of his party leader in 1841: 'Where is Peel's heart now? Is it set at the foot of God's throne... praying that he might become an humble instrument of His providence, laying aside all private interests, prejudices and carnal affections? I do not know.' A few weeks later he added that there was an 'awful probability that it may not please God to render Peel an instrument of good to this nation... He has an abundance of human honesty and not much of divine faith.' This was because the prime minister did not share his priorities for factory reform. If he would only turn to Ashley's vision of God: 'the world lies before us and we shall march under God's banner, through the length and breadth of all lands... as the moral sovereigns of [his] power.'[13] Thoughts like this inevitably rendered such folk relentless and tiresome, and Ashley could be both.

By the 1840s, evangelicals were advancing in the church: using their wealth to build new churches, or buying up advowsons (the right to present candidates to a particular living) by which they could change the character of a parish. They were contemptuous both of the laxness of other, more old-fashioned clergy and of the error they taught their congregations and (rather like the Scientologists a century later) they encouraged their flocks not to mingle with those of different Christian, including Anglican, persuasions – even members of their own families. (Some conservative evangelical Anglicans are like this even today.) Their preaching was often powerful, their hymns moving and inspirational. The men of seriousness could reach congregations of a size that others could only imagine: hundreds would flock to hear their sermons. They sent young clergy out into new parishes almost like missionaries, and they had particular success in the middle-class suburbs and expanding towns. One such was Edward Hoare, vicar of Holy Trinity, Tunbridge Wells, for more than forty years, who was appointed to his living by Charles Hardinge, brother of the governor-general of India, Henry Hardinge. Hoare, a member of the banking family, was known to some as 'the Grand Amen' for the vigour of his prayers at church congresses. He devoted his considerable energies and his own money to establishing a string of evangelical parishes around the town and, almost equally, to attempting to prevent the setting up of a High Church Anglican parish and persecuting the sole local representative of the secular society.[14]

Now the evangelicals were starting to get bishoprics too. In the 1820s, an eighth of the Church of England's clergy were thought to be evangelicals; in 1844 *The Times* surveyed ninety-three senior clerics in London and found forty-six were evangelicals, twenty-five high churchmen and twenty-three 'moderates'. By the time Sumner became archbishop there was a phalanx of senior evangelical bishops, where twenty years before there had only been two.[15]

It was the evangelicals' energy that was phenomenal, in political campaigning and in the setting up of societies for the relief of poverty and other social ills. 'Ours is the age of societies,' wrote Sir James Stephen in 1849, and it was true. Evangelicals had been in the vanguard of the fight against slavery and they would be instrumental in setting up ragged schools, to teach Christianity and morals to the children of the poor. They were indefatigable organizers: of Sunday schools, of proselytizing church missions seeking converts, the Foreign Bible Society, the Religious Tract Society, the Jew Society, the Vice Society, the Society for the Reception of Penitent Prostitutes, the Friendly Female Society for the Relief of Single Women of Good Character, even the City of London Truss Society. The Lord's Day Observance Society is still limping on, as are, much more successfully, the Royal Society for the Prevention of Cruelty to Animals (RSPCA), the Young Men's Christian Association (YMCA), founded in 1844, and its counterpart the YWCA, started in 1855, and Dr Barnardo's Homes, first launched in 1870. All these bodies had the purpose of moral improvement and some were motivated by the desire to stop others doing things of which evangelicals disapproved: the Vice Society, for instance, campaigned against theatres, fairs and horse racing. It was a scatter-gun approach which could be inspiring and radical – the prevention of children being sent up chimneys, the ending of transportation for criminals – but also undiscriminating, disproportionate and even ludicrous in its reasoning. The Rev.

Josiah Pratt, for instance, argued that 'a sermon is the essence of dullness after a play: this shows the evil of the play'. Or then there was Ashley, agonizing when invited to Ascot races by the Queen. He decided he had to go, but prayed that his visit 'may not be productive of any mischief to the slight influence I may have in the world for carrying forward measures and designs of good to mankind'.[16]

The zeal of the evangelical Anglicans came as the dissenting groups – Methodists, Baptists, Congregationalists and Unitarians – were becoming more 'respectable' and middle-class too. These sects, originally proselytizing among the working classes, had long felt excluded from mainstream society, but their activism – first against the slave trade, then more widely in other campaigns, such as for political reform – had seen their members become more influential. The repeal of the Test Acts in 1829 had enabled them to enter public life and become MPs or to be active in local affairs. Some of them had grown rich through industrial enterprise and were now harnessing their religious beliefs to their political campaigning. For Quakers such as John Bright and Birmingham's Joseph Sturge, campaigns for free trade were an offshoot of their religious convictions: they believed that the free exchange of goods would facilitate international trade and promote peace. With secular success, however, came doctrinal divisions and internal jealousies: by mid-century there were Wesleyan Methodists, Calvinistic Methodists, New Connexion Methodists, Primitive Methodists, Protestant Methodists and Wesleyan Reformers, all guarding their separate identities. Some followers inevitably splintered off into other sects, or even joined the Anglicans.

Many evangelicals, such as Charles Trevelyan, took their particular calls to seriousness into the civil service, or into

professions such as banking, where their probity was appreciated. The Barings and Deacons had evangelical roots.
Tunbridge Wells's Canon Hoare married a Gurney, of the
eponymous banking family, both Hoares and Gurneys having
originally been Quaker families. Some became soldiers, for
there was no disapproval of militarism among most of the
sects (though not, of course, the pacifist Quakers). Others had
a moral mission: Charles Mudie's circulating library contained
only improving works, as did W.H. Smith's first book-stalls at
railway stations. They certainly knew who they were aiming
at, and it was usually the working class. For it did not pass
unnoticed that campaigners were more interested in stopping
the pastimes of the poor than those of the wealthy. They
targeted dog-fighting and bear-baiting, but not hunting and
shooting. As the Rev. Sydney Smith, no evangelical, noted:

> Is there one single instance where they have directed the
> attention... to this higher species of suppression and sacri-
> ficed men of consideration to that zeal for virtue which
> watches so acutely over the vices of the poor? They should
> denominate themselves a Society for Suppressing the Vices
> of Persons whose income does not exceed £500 per annum.[17]

By the 1840s, though, the strictness of some evangelicals
was proving counterproductive. Some were peeling away to
less oppressive sects; others such as Gladstone were becoming
mainstream Anglicans; a few, including Gladstone's sister
Helen, three of William Wilberforce's children and his son-in-
law Henry Manning, were gliding right across the spectrum
and converting to Roman Catholicism. Others still were
becoming agnostics or atheists, losing their faith altogether.

There were indeed new threats to religious certainties: a German school of theology was beginning to suggest that the Bible's inerrancy could be challenged and that Christ's miracles, even the facts of his life, should be reinterpreted. In 1846 a 26-year-old woman living in Warwickshire, called Mary Anne Evans, later to be better known as George Eliot, was finishing the first English translation of the German theologian David Strauss's *Life of Jesus*. The book's heresy – that much of the Gospel accounts was mythical and symbolic rather than factual – would cause a sensation and lead to it being described by Lord Ashley as 'the most pestilential book ever vomited out of the jaws of Hell'. In the words of the church historian Owen Chadwick: 'the name of Strauss became a ghostly whip, a bogey, a talisman... he seemed to free Christian truth from the shackles of history and so the mind from the torment of doubt... the ship of faith rocked gently at its moorings.'[18] And in doing so, the new, questioning climate affected the faith of men such as the headmaster Thomas Arnold, his son Matthew, and Arnold's pupil and Matthew's friend, the poet Arthur Hugh Clough.

The translation of 1,500 pages of dense, philosophical German, interspersed with snatches of Hebrew, Latin and Greek, had taken Evans two years, working at a steady six pages a day. It largely finished off her own evangelical religious belief and also gave her headaches: 'I am only inclined to vow that I will never translate again if I live to correct the sheets for Strauss,' she wrote to a friend. When the work was published in three volumes in June 1846, she received £20 for her efforts.[19]

In her literacy, Evans was far from unique as a young woman, though perhaps she was in her dedication and command of foreign languages (all the more commendable as her German was not fluent, at least when she started the book). Education was a developing feature of British society, sponsored largely by the churches, though it was by no means universal. In 1851 it was estimated that about 30 per cent of the male population and 45 per cent of women were unable to sign their names, the most basic test of literacy, but there were some opportunities for learning available even to the poorest members of society. There had long been dame schools (usually run by elderly, untrained and little-educated women) and many towns had ancient grammar schools in varying states of decrepitude, but in 1844 evangelicals gathered to form the Ragged Schools Union, to coordinate a movement already underway in setting up free classes for the poor in the city slums, and teaching those whose clothes were too ragged to be admitted anywhere else how to read and write, the better to study their Bibles. Ashley, inevitably, was the society's first president and Dickens too was a supporter. Horrified by the conditions of children in London, he had depicted them in *A Christmas Carol* in 1843, cowering under the cloak of the Ghost of Christmas Present. The Sunday school movement also taught not only Bible stories, but reading, writing and arithmetic: more than two million were enrolled by 1851, one in eight of the population, including adults and three-quarters of working-class children. For those who could afford it there were also endowed schools – charging a farthing a week – industrial and workhouse schools, schools run by trade associations and livery companies, and systems of apprenticeships.[20] If a child was really unlucky, it might end up at an establishment like Carus Wilson's where two of Charlotte Brontë's sisters, Elizabeth and Maria, both died during a typhoid epidemic; or at the Bowes Academy in Greta Bridge, run by William Shaw, on whom Dickens modelled Wackford Squeers; or at a baby farm, such as Bartholomew Drouet's in Tooting, where eighty small children sent from the Holborn workhouse died in a cholera epidemic in 1848, probably caused by a nearby stagnant ditch where Drouet kept human excrement he had collected from the Surrey lunatic asylum, planning to resell it as manure.[21]

In 1848 Nathaniel Woodard, a curate in Shoreham, near Brighton, struck by the poor quality of education among his middle-class parishioners, founded the first of what would become a network of fee-paying schools at Lancing, on the hill behind his parish. The guiding principle behind them was the inculcation of sound knowledge firmly grounded in the Christian faith. Unsurprisingly, Woodard had started as an evangelical before being attracted to Tractarianism while a student at Oxford.

The old public schools themselves were changing their character, distancing themselves from the dens of mayhem, savagery and riot that they had been earlier in the century. Headmaster Keate of Eton had flogged all 100 boys of the lower fifth in June 1810, even as they pelted him with eggs. They were grim places, where boys sometimes found themselves sharing their bed with six others, where food was foul, the Latin-based curriculum narrow and tedious, and the punishments severe. When Charles Vaughan arrived to become headmaster of Harrow in 1844, his shocked friends advised him not to throw himself away on the school, and Steuart Adolphus Pears, the new head of Repton, was discovered head in hands on taking over, 'overwhelmed by the desolate prospect... in the attitude of a man appalled'.[22] But by the 1840s a new generation of headmasters was infiltrating the schools, instilling Christian beliefs, sometimes with the swish of a birch, imposing discipline, filling the timetable, broadening the curriculum and encouraging the release of surplus energy by the organization of games. The most famous of these was Thomas Arnold of Rugby, who was not an evangelical (he deplored their narrow cliquishness) but shared many of their principles: 'it is not necessary that this should be a school of 300 or 100, or fifty boys; but it is necessary that it should be a school of Christian gentlemen.'[23] Arnold raised teachers' pay and banned pupils from having dogs and guns in school. Increasing pupil numbers was imperative if schools were to survive and prosper. Many of them were in decline in the 1830s: Eton dropped from 627 to 444 pupils in a year, Rugby from 300 pupils in 1821 to 123 in 1827. This was partly due to impoverishment caused by the post-Napoleonic War economic slump, but partly also to parental fears about the schools' reputations: many wealthy evangelical parents educated their sons at home rather than allowing them to mix in such stews of iniquity. Public schools were not then necessarily regarded as the passports to social advancement that they later became. Many eminent Victorians, even from wealthy families, were not sent to them: Macaulay, Tennyson, Newman and Disraeli among them.

Arnold was not alone in acting to raise the tone and character of his school and its pupils, though it was his example – which other headmasters, several of them his acolytes, followed – that allowed public schools to gain the reputation and social standing that they had earlier lacked. Vaughan of Harrow, for instance, had been one of Arnold's pupils at Rugby, 'able and willing to carry out the Arnold system of education'. Arnold, of course, had the huge posthumous advantage of having his reputation (and that of Rugby) burnished in the public mind by the publication in 1857 of *Tom Brown's Schooldays* by his former pupil Thomas Hughes, who became a radical MP but was a champion of the education afforded by his old school: 'the object of all schools is not to ram Latin and Greek into boys, but to make them good English boys, good future citizens.'[24] As Tom's father, the Squire, reflects:

> Shall I tell him to mind his work and say he's a good scholar? Well, but he isn't sent to school for that – at any rate, not for that mainly. I don't care a straw for Greek particles... no more does his mother... If he'll only turn out a brave, helpful, truth-telling Englishman and a gentleman and a Christian, that's all I want.

The book remains one of the most popular of school stories and was a huge and influential success when it first came out. According to the novelist, historian, social reformer and clergyman Charles Kingsley: 'From everyone, from the fine lady on the throne, to the redcoat on his cock horse and the school boy on his form... I have heard but one word and that is that it is the jolliest book they ever read.'[25] If he had not died of a heart attack in 1842 (thanking God for the affliction: 'I have suffered so little pain in my life that I feel it is very good for me'[26]), Arnold would probably have become a bishop, like so many of his contemporaries. Charles Longley of Harrow even went on to be archbishop of Canterbury.

And then there were the colleges of Oxford and Cambridge, still rejoicing in their medieval statutes and intellectual complacency, their bachelor fellows firmly conservative and indolent in outlook and habits, pining for the return of the eighteenth century. T. E. Kebbel wrote in the *National Review* in 1887, looking back forty years:

> A don in my day was only partially associated with the ideas of education and learning. Each college was a close, powerful and wealthy corporation, doing what it liked with its own, repelling interference from without... the members, as long as they remained unmarried and unbeneficed held their fellowships for life and were practically irremovable... ancient immemorial nests of life-long leisure, centuries of undisturbed repose and inviolate prescription. The whole body of Oxford men were like one gigantic common room: all members of a highly exclusive society, all members of the Church and, with some very few exceptions, which did not in the slightest degree affect the tone or manners of the place, all gentlemen.[27]

It took New College, Oxford, twenty years to agree that its undergraduates should take university examinations rather than merely claiming degrees as of right, as they had for the previous five centuries (and once it did so, only one member of the college was awarded a first-class degree in the following twenty years). And it would not be until 1852 that the inevitable royal commission, headed by the Bishop of Norwich, investigated reforms.[28] Peel's performances in the public *viva voce* examinations that comprised finals in 1808 had won him the first double first Oxford had ever awarded, in classics (including divinity) and mathematics; but even he had been run out of town as one of the university's MPs after he espoused Catholic emancipation (a door at his old college, Christ Church, still has the words 'No Peel' hammered into it with nails). It was no surprise that many of the dons regarded the commission's inquiry as impertinent at best and treacherous at worst. It was an undermining of God's will, as Edward Pusey reminded them:

> [the task of a university was] not how to advance science, not how to make discoveries, not to form new schools of mental philosophy, nor to invent new modes of analysis... but to form minds religiously, morally, intellectually which shall discharge aright whatever duties God, in His Providence, shall appoint to them.[29]

But change, welcome or not, would come.

9

The Noblest and Wealthiest of the Land

'In the character of a noble, enlightened and truly
good man, there is a power and sublimity so nearly
approaching what we believe to be the nature and
capacity of angels that... no language can describe
the degree of admiration and respect which the
contemplation of such a character must excite.'

MRS SARAH ELLIS, *The Wives of England:
Their Relative Duties, Domestic Influence and
Social Obligations*, 1843[1]

Despite their fears for the future of British agriculture in 1846,
those who had been born into the aristocracy lived a charmed
life. Their wealth and social position remained largely unchal-
lenged, whatever Chartists and radicals might hope, and
would do so for many decades to come. Industrialists and
middle-class professionals might be gaining in prosperity, but
overwhelmingly those who had landed estates remained the
ones with power. Well into the second half of the nineteenth
century, nine out of ten British millionaires still owed their
wealth to land and 180 peers held estates of more than 10,000
acres.[2] Only following the agricultural depression of the 1870s
would they need to seek other sources of wealth in order to
maintain their lifestyles and expectations. These men occupied
seats in the House of Lords as of right and controlled through
patronage many of the constituencies represented in the House

of Commons. The more progressive of them were investing in new agricultural techniques: breeding new strains of cattle and pigs, improving crop yields and draining unproductive land. Peel's government offered grants for such innovations as compensation for repealing the Corn Laws, but to no effect as far as the die-hard protectionists were concerned.

The prime minister himself was among the improving landowners. He treated his tenants more humanely than some of his peers, carried out improvements such as drainage on his Staffordshire estate, and took an active interest in stock breeding, vegetable cultivation and even manure. His letters, including those written from Downing Street to colleagues, attest this. Peel occasionally also invited local farmers to dinner so that they could hear improving and useful talks by scientific and agricultural experts on subjects such as soil preparation and cattle feeding. All these measures helped to quadruple yields on his estate and he probably could not understand why all farmers and landowners did not do the same – as they would have to when the Corn Laws were repealed.[3]

In the Highlands of Scotland, the great landowners and clan chiefs had been busily clearing their land of tenants and clan followers throughout the first half of the nineteenth century, in order to replace their subsistence crofts with vast acreages of open glens for sheep grazing. The tenants, much as their counterparts in Ireland during the famine, were either evicted by force, or sometimes offered compensation to move. Some migrated to Scottish industrial cities such as Dundee and Glasgow, and many emigrated to Canada, Australia or New Zealand. Across the world place names still commemorate the homeland that the emigrants would never see again: Banff and Glengarry, Perth and Kincardine, Dunedin and

Invercargill – a sense of exile made worse by the betrayal of the lairds who had evicted them. They in turn grew rich without any sense of obligation. The 1st Duke of Sutherland, who also owned estates in Staffordshire, Shropshire and Yorkshire, cleared his land in the north of Scotland in the first two decades of the nineteenth century and was described by Greville as a leviathan of wealth, 'the richest individual who ever died'. His wife Elizabeth, who had watched the clearances, wrote to a friend that 'the Scotch people are of a happier constitution and do not fatten like the larger breeds of animal'.

Their son, the second duke, was busy building or buying grand homes for himself in the 1840s. Dunrobin Castle, on the north-east coast of Scotland, described as 'French renaissance meets Scottish baronial' in architectural style, with 189 rooms and its own railway station down the hill, was started in 1845. Trentham Hall in Staffordshire, an Italianate villa in 500 acres on the outskirts of Stoke-on-Trent, was finished in the mid-1840s. Cliveden, on the escarpment just above the Thames near Maidenhead, would be built in the English Palladian style in 1851, and – grandest of all – Stafford House in London, overlooking St James's Park, which was described as the most valuable private house in the capital, was purchased at this time too. When Queen Victoria came to call, she was said to have exclaimed that she had left her house to visit a real palace. It was later renamed Lancaster House. All four properties were designed in their varying ways by Sir Charles Barry, who was also supervising the construction of the new Houses of Parliament in the gothic style at the same time.

The Sutherlands were fantastically wealthy, but they were not alone in employing men like Barry to build, or expand and then expand once more, their mansions across the country. The

3rd Earl of Carnarvon got him in to transform his eighteenth-century Georgian house at his 1,000-acre Highclere estate, in north Hampshire, near Newbury. The old, square building, described as being the epitome of 'flatness and insipidity of bare classicism', was converted and refronted so entirely that it turned into an exotic, be-towered and crenellated edifice in Bath stone, which Barry described as Anglo-Italian and which others have called Jacobethan – a sort of pastiche mix of doge's palace and seventeenth-century English manor house. It took so long to rebuild that both the earl and Barry were dead long before the building, now called Highclere Castle, was completed. It is best known today as the backdrop to the television period soap opera *Downton Abbey*, which is perhaps appropriate for such a theatrical property.[4]

There were many others like it. Shadwell Park in Norfolk was a modest Georgian manor house which was turned first into a mansion with Tudor turrets and chimneys in the early 1840s and then enlarged again a decade later with a new wing and more gothic towers and windows. Harlaxton Manor, outside Grantham, replaced a genuine fourteenth-century building with a grand mock-Elizabethan one in 1837. Eaton Hall in Cheshire, home of the Dukes of Westminster, grew progressively bigger and grander through the nineteenth century as a succession of architects encased a seventeenth-century building with the Victorian concept of what one should really look like.[5]

Such houses required dozens of servants and, whatever their external appearance, the buildings were designed to a plan. Servants' quarters were rigidly segregated between men and women, and the working parts – kitchens and pantries, bakehouses and sculleries, laundries and coal-holes – were kept well away from the main house, along winding corridors (to baffle smells) and up backstairs so that the maids and footmen did not jostle the guests. Those servants who were to appear in public were now dressed in uniforms: knee-breeches and dress-coats for the footmen, flaxen wigs and cocked hats for coachmen, as if they had stepped straight out of the eighteenth century.

Large houses required a good many staff: Petworth in Sussex was estimated to have 135 people working inside the house. Thomas Creevey, visiting in 1828, noted that they were 'very numerous tho' most of them very advanced in years and tottered and comical in their looks'. He was told that there were more there 'of both sexes and in all departments than in any house in England, that they were all very good in their way, but they could not stand being put out of it and were never interfered with, that they were all bred on the spot and all related to each other'.[6] There was a rigid hierarchy for staff. The steward's room was for the so-called 'upper ten' of senior indoor staff: steward, housekeeper, head cook, butlers, valets, ladies' maids and sometimes the head gardener. The servants' hall was for the 'lower five,' the junior staff who might then be allowed into the housekeeper's room for pudding. Outside, the staff was also copious: gardeners, gamekeepers, groundsmen, kennelmen, ostlers and grooms, who might only be allowed inside the main house for grand occasions such as the annual servants' ball. Englefield Park in Berkshire, west of Reading, the home of the Benyon family since the eighteenth century, employed twenty gardeners in the 1850s. Beyond the grounds would be a spreading web of retainers, tenant farmers and local shopkeepers. The vicar of the parish would likely have been appointed to his living by the squire or landowner, as might a schoolmaster too.

Such an army would not be particularly well paid, but together they did not come cheap: a good cook might command £120 a year, housemaids £8 each – and there would be lots of them. Samuel Adams, author of *The Complete Servant* in 1825, gave a table of wages for twenty-seven servants, ranging from a cook at eighty guineas (in modern terms, approximately £5,000 per annum) and a butler at fifty guineas, down to the assistant gardener on twelve shillings a week, comparable to a farm labourer's wage. Adams thought 'a respectable country gentleman with a young family and a net income of £16,000 to £18,000' might expect expenses not exceeding £7,000.[7] New modes of living and dining were coming in at fashionable households in the 1840s: afternoon tea with cake, to fill the long, hungry gap between luncheon at one o'clock and dinner at eight; and service *à la russe*, whereby guests were helped individually to dishes carried around the table by footmen, rather than *à la française*, where they each had a servant to help them from dishes placed in the centre of the table. The new system economized on servants and theoretically allowed for smaller dining rooms.

At New Year 1838, the diarist Charles Greville embarked on a tour of the great families of the East Midlands, noting twenty-two guests to dinner at Burghley House near Stamford on 2 January. There were the Duke of Wellington and the Earl of Aberdeen and various Salisburys and Wiltons, 'a mob of fine people; very miserable representatives of old Burleigh [sic], the two insignificant looking marquesses who are his lineal descendants and who display no more of brains than they do of his beard'. Then they all moved on en masse the following day to Belvoir Castle in Leicestershire, another

Tudor castle built in the nineteenth century – 'nearly 40 at dinner, but it is no use enumerating the people' – to celebrate the Duke of Rutland's birthday. Down in the servants' hall, it did Greville's heart good to see nearly a hundred retainers loyally raising their glasses to drink their master's health at a dinner with beer, roast beef and music. Then the party doubled the next day as the local tenant farmers and villagers came up to the big house for the annual birthday ball.[8]

This feudal society of long-serving retainers was usually deeply conservative and deferential. They did not last long in employment if they were not. If their employer was a staunch churchman, they would be expected to attend Sunday services. If they got married – especially if, as was likely, it was to another member of staff – they would be served notice for it would be assumed their loyalties were divided. In return they expected a certain duty of care from their employers. 'The Duke of Rutland is as selfish a man as any of his class,' Greville noted:

> That is, he never does what he does not like and spends his life in a round of such pleasures as suit his taste, but he is neither a foolish nor a bad man and partly from a sense of duty and partly from inclination, he devotes time and labour to the interest and welfare of the people who live and labour on his estate. He is a guardian of a very large union [Poor Law workhouse] and he not only attends regularly... every week or fortnight and takes an active part in their proceedings, but he visits those paupers who receive outdoor relief, sits and converses with them, invites them to complain if they have anything to complain of and tells them that he is not only their friend but their representative

at the assembly of guardians and that it is his duty to see that they are nourished and protected.[9]

How sincerely the duke said that and how seriously he took any complaints from the destitute of the villages around Belvoir may be a matter for conjecture, but he and other aristocrats at least purported to have the locals' interests at heart. The 5th Duke of Grafton visited the cottagers on his Suffolk estate regularly, asking after their needs and distributing gifts such as blankets. Such men knew what was best for the lower orders and some became patrons of worthy, or patronizing, charities: the 8th Duke of Argyll was president of the Society for the Encouragement of Purity in Literature.[10]

Others were not so philanthropic. The third Lord Crewe reputedly dismissed female servants if they were spotted by visitors: he 'hates women and thinks all his guests must detest them too'. Then there was the reclusive 5th Duke of Portland (the older brother of Lord George Bentinck), who created a network of tunnels under his house, Welbeck Abbey in Nottinghamshire, one a mile long and wide enough for two carriages to pass, so that he could move around the place without being seen. He ordered his servants to treat him as if he were invisible and not look at him if they saw him. A valet said of his lordly employer in Wiltshire that he 'never spoke to an indoor servant except to give an order and all the ten years I was with him never, except on Christmas and New Years' days, gave me any kind of greeting'.[11]

The days of the old eighteenth-century and Regency roués were, however, waning. They were epitomized by men such as Lord Hertford, whose passing was recorded by Greville in March 1842:

There has been no such example of undisguised debauchery exhibited to the world... Between sixty and seventy years old, broken with various infirmities and almost unintelligible from a paralysis of the tongue, he had been in the habit of travelling about with a company of prostitutes... generally picking them up from the dregs of that class. He got up and posted with his seraglio down to Richmond. No room was ready, no fire lit, nevertheless he chose to dine there amidst damp and cold, drank a quantity of champagne, came back chilled and exhausted, took to his bed, grew gradually worse and in ten days he died. And what a life, terminating in what a death! Faculties far beyond mediocrity wasted and degraded, immersed in pride without dignity, in avarice and sensuality.[12]

He really sounds quite Dickensian, if Greville is to be believed, and it is said that Sir Mulberry Hawk, who made his malign appearance in *Nicholas Nickleby* four years earlier, was modelled on him. Hertford was also allegedly the prototype for the Marquess of Monmouth in Disraeli's *Coningsby* and the Marquess of Steyne in Thackeray's *Vanity Fair* – quite a distinguished gallery of characters. But he was also a knight of the garter and a noted art collector, whose paintings formed the core of the original Wallace Collection.

For such men taxation might have been a concern, but little cause for worry. They were only lightly taxed, though they naturally resented what they had to pay after income tax was reintroduced by Peel at seven pence in the pound in his 1842 budget. That gave them another reason to despise and distrust him, but they were still able to pay their servants low wages and to spend their resources conspicuously. The 3rd

Marquess of Conyngham, drawing £50,000 a year from his Irish estates, admitted to twice losing £500 a night at the gaming tables when he was a 24-year-old Life Guards officer. Lord George Bentinck was said to have won £100,000 from gambling (£10,000 on a single race), and in the 1820s the Goodwood foxhounds pack was already costing the Duke of Richmond – the man who claimed free trade would ruin British agriculture – £19,000 a year.[13]

Alternatively, those with sufficient wealth could buy them-selves into regimental commands in the army – a system the old Duke of Wellington saw nothing wrong with: 'It is promo-tion by purchase, which brings into the service... men who have some connection with the interests and fortunes of the country.' It also brought in Lord Cardigan, the fortuitous hero of the Charge of the Light Brigade at Balaclava in 1854, who paid £35,000 for the lieutenant-colonelcy of the 15th Hussars in 1832 and a further £40,000 when he took charge of the 11th Hussars in 1836, having been ignominiously dismissed from his first regiment. His hated brother-in-law Lord Lucan had earlier bought himself a colonelcy in the 17th Lancers for £25,000, five times the official price.[14] The 1844 edition of the *Queen's Regulations* listed the prices for commissions, ranging for the Foot Guards from £1,200 for a subaltern to £9,000 for a lieutenant-colonelcy. Evidently there were those who were prepared to pay well over the odds for a fashionable regiment, although the rules suggested that anyone who did would be cashiered. Both Lucan and Cardigan spent annual fortunes kitting out their regiments with dress uniforms. These were men, as they repeatedly proved, who were quite unfitted to command troops and yet were permitted to do so because they could afford to buy their commissions. The system, discredited by the failings of the army's leadership in the Crimean War, would finally be reformed in 1871.

Something of a behavioural change took place in the Victorian era, in reaction to the perceived moral licentiousness of the Regency period; a change that mirrored the way in which the royal family now conducted itself more respectably. Victorian gentlemen were expected to behave rather better than their predecessors and their houses were intended to reflect this. As the architect Gilbert Scott wrote: 'he has been placed by providence in a position of authority and dignity; and no false modesty should deter him from expressing this, quietly and gravely, in the character of his house.'[15] And the character of that house was, increasingly, gothic.

The taste for gothic architecture was just part of the fascination many Victorians and their predecessors in the late Georgian period had for what they saw as a nobler, more chivalrous, and simpler age of virtue. It was a romantic, fairytale, nostalgic view of a world that had never really existed, weaving in knights in armour, Arthurian legends and occasionally fancy dress. It showed itself in church ritual and vestments, in literature, art and poetry, and, most substantially, in buildings, from quaint estate cottages to the towering railway terminus at St Pancras Station. It even had a reflection in Young England, a group of aristocratic young Tory politicians of the mid-1840s, who hankered after a fantasy feudal age before factories and the modern theories of utilitarianism were ever thought of, imagining a romantic idyll in which the landowning classes condescended to the peasantry and the peasantry were duly grateful. Its members included Lord John Manners, the heir to Belvoir Castle, and George Smythe, the son of Lord Strangford. The disaffected Disraeli was part of the coterie too, and he danced attendance on them, flattered them and portrayed them in his novels. Manners was Lord Henry Sydney and Smythe was Coningsby in the eponymous novel, and the two nations, famously referred to in *Sybil*, 'formed by different breeding, fed by a different food, ordered by different manners and not governed by the same laws... THE RICH AND THE POOR',[16] represented the divide which the Young Englanders hoped paternalistically to bridge. The movement, said Disraeli's biographer Robert Blake, 'has all the charm and nostalgia which attend tales of forlorn hopes and lost causes, like Jacobitism'.[17] Blake sees it as a political counterpart to the Oxford Movement and for a short time its members periodically rebelled against Peel, supporting the reduction in factory hours and opposing the Maynooth grant. But the movement faded away, leaving Disraeli to nurse his grievances alone.

By the 1840s the gothic revival in architecture had already been going for three-quarters of a century (Horace Walpole had built Strawberry Hill, his gothic-revival house in Twickenham, as early as the 1750s), but it was now in full swing. Its high priest of the moment was the young architect Augustus Welby Pugin, whose contempt for the cod classicism of Georgian architecture was fervent and extreme. 'We have Swiss cottages in a flat country,' he wrote in his 1836 manifesto. 'Italian villas in the coldest situations; a Turkish kremlin for a royal residence; Greek temples in crowded lanes; Egyptian auction rooms... It is hardly possible to conceive that a person who had made the art of Architecture the least part of their study, could have committed such enormities.' The title of the work, *Contrasts, or a parallel between the noble edifices of the fourteenth and fifteenth centuries and similar buildings of the present day, shewing the present decay of taste*, says it all.[18]

Pugin's ardour for the simple, devout and serviceable buildings of the Middle Ages was prompted by his Catholicism, which he thought echoed that of the medieval builders: 'Such effects as these can only be produced on the mind by buildings, the composition of which has emanated from men who were thoroughly embued with devotion for and faith in the religion for whose worship they were erected.' Buildings should not have the artifice of the Regency period, but their functions should be clearly visible: 'not masked or concealed under one monotonous front, but by their variety in form and outline increasing the effects of the building.'[19] Not everyone, even among his patrons, shared his vision, or welcomed the expense it entailed, but by the mid-1840s he was working manically, obsessively hard, on his way to a breakdown and an early death in 1852. There were new rectories and chapels for the Church of England and the newly emancipated Catholics across the country, though only two country houses of any size were commissioned from him: Alton Towers and Scarisbrick Hall in Lancashire, together with the design of practically all the internal fittings of the new Houses of Parliament.

Pugin was not the only architect at work: others, such as Barry, took a less dogmatic, more eclectic approach. Decimus Burton, a pupil of John Nash, for example, designed the Athenaeum Club in a classical style, then Italianate villas and a gothic church in Tunbridge Wells. It was gothic that captured the imagination of architects such as G.E. Street and William Butterfield, the designers of the major building projects of mid-century Britain.

The taste for the gothic took many forms. Its supposed code of chivalry was adopted in the formulation of the rules of games, imbued on the rugby and cricket fields of the public schools where team sports were being taken seriously for the first time as character-building exercises. Medieval soldiers in uniform adorned public monuments and stained-glass memorial windows. Facsimiles of the era's costumes were worn to fancy-dress balls and even to a full-scale re-creation of a medieval tournament. This extravaganza, at Eglinton Castle in Ayrshire, took place in August 1839 and nearly bankrupted its organizer, the thirteenth earl of Eglinton, who may have spent as much as £500,000 on the event. He and his friends took the occasion immensely seriously, had their armour specially made, and followed what they thought were the rules of jousting, though they took them from Sir Walter Scott's 1820 novel *Ivanhoe* rather than original source material. On the day of the tournament, the road from Glasgow thirty miles away was completely blocked by spectators and 100,000 people were said to have attended. Unfortunately, it rained torrentially, leaving the participants sheltering under un-medieval umbrellas. That did not stop the publication of eight books about the tournament, together with souvenirs ranging from jigsaws to scent bottles with little knights' helmets for stoppers.[20] The whole affair was a sort of prototype fancy-dress Glastonbury festival – and, in a way, the distant forerunner of today's historical re-enactment events.

The queen herself was fascinated by the tournament, though censorious when it turned into a fiasco: 'I said it served them all right for their folly in having such a thing.' But she too would take part in a medieval-style fancy-dress ball at Buckingham Palace on 11 May 1842. She attended in costume as Queen Philippa and Prince Albert went as Edward III. The whole court attended eclectically as assorted twelfth-century

Albanian knights, characters from Scott's Waverley novels, merry Muscovites and, in Sir Robert Peel's case, probably rather stiffly and uncomfortably, as a character from a seventeenth-century Van Dyck painting. 'Nothing could have gone better,' wrote the queen. 'It was a truly splendid spectacle... I danced a quadrille – I own with some difficulty, on account of my heels.' Later, she would have a portrait painted of Albert dressed in a suit of armour.

It was very hard to escape the iconography of the Middle Ages as the Industrial Revolution powered Britain forward into the modern world. Suburban villas for the middle classes would soon abandon the attempt to resemble Venetian palazzos and become gothic palaces instead, with high-pitched gables, pointed windows, tiled floors, stained-glass motifs and even the occasional turret. The daring young painters of the Pre-Raphaelite brotherhood – Holman Hunt, Millais, Rossetti and Ford Madox Brown – would exhibit their first efforts at recreating polychromatic murals in the supposed style of the early Italian masters at the Royal Academy in 1849. They chose suitably medieval subjects, mounted within inscribed gilt frames: *Rienzi Vowing to Obtain Justice for the Death of His Young Brother, Slain in a Skirmish between the Colonna and Orsini Factions*, in Hunt's case, and *Isabella* by the 20-year-old Millais.[21] Such ardent and melodramatic works contrasted radically with the anthropomorphic pets and grim scenes of animal carnage painted by Sir Edwin Landseer, who was already drinking heavily in his manic depression, and the stiff, gorgeous court portraits of the German artist Franz Xaver Winterhalter. But even Landseer had been required to paint the queen and her consort in their fancy-dress costumes from their famous Bal Costumé.

Such fancies must have passed over the heads of most servants, who were required to keep houses clean and their occupants serviced. It was a hard life with long hours and little reward. The 1851 census would estimate that there were about 1.5 million domestic servants in the country; one in three young women between the ages of 15 and 24 in London were in service and about one in six of any age.[22] Even the urban middle classes could afford servants, though perhaps only a cook or a skivvy. If you hired an orphan child from a workhouse to do the work, she might only cost you £5 a year, including board and lodging – though you could allow her to sleep on the kitchen floor, or in the basement, which was probably damp and airless. It was generally male servants who slept there, as William Tayler, a footman in Great Cumberland Street, reported in a diary he kept in 1837:[*] 'In London men servants has to sleep downstairs underground, which is generally damp.'[23] It would probably also be positively unhealthy and foetid. A skivvy from the workhouse might not be much good, having had no training, but she would be considerably cheaper than experienced, mature servants with references who would demand ten times as much. Such children routinely had desperate lives. Liza Picard recounts the story of one girl from Bethnal Green in east London who began at the age of ten by looking after a shopkeeper's baby for one shilling and sixpence a week, twelve hours a day, and by her early teens was looking after four children and a baby in another household and being paid three shillings a week. At a house in

---

[*]   William Tayler worked for a rich widow and decided to keep a diary for the year 1837 as a means of improving his education. His observations of servant life form a colourful and insightful picture of the period.

Hampstead, she said: 'I was fairly happy, but had to sleep in a basement kitchen which swarmed with blackbeetles and this made me very wretched at nights... I was often so tired... that I fell asleep on the stairs on my way to bed.'[24]

The best-known account of such a life is that written by Hannah Cullwick, who eventually became the mistress of Arthur Munby, a barrister who worked for the Ecclesiastical Commissioners and seems to have had a thing for grubby servant women in their work clothes. They married but kept their liaison secret. Hannah described her work as a nursery-maid in Shropshire when she was about 10 years of age, in the mid-1840s:

> I stopp'd here through the winter & had a deal of hard work to do, for there was eight children. I'd all their boots to clean & the large nurseries on my hands and knees & a long passage & stairs, all their meals to get & our own – the nurse only dress'd the baby & look'd over me. I'd all the water to carry up and down for their baths & coal for the fire, put all the children to bed & wash and dress of a morning by eight & I wasn't in bed after 5.

By the age of 17, in 1850, she was working for Lady Boughy elsewhere in Shropshire, but she lost her job as an under-housemaid after eight months when she was caught larking about with another maidservant while cleaning some kettles. 'She gave us both warning... I ax'd Lady Boughy if she would please forgive me & let me stop. But she said "NO," very loudly.'[25] Hannah (and certainly Lady Boughy) would probably be surprised to learn that her diaries ended up among Munby's papers at Trinity College, Cambridge.

There were few labour-saving devices available to servants in the kitchen or the scullery in the 1840s. Gas stoves, though patented, would not be widely used for decades: cooking was carried out on cast-iron coal-burning stoves. Prams were not patented until 1850 and vacuum cleaners not until the following century. A housemaid's day would therefore be spent in arduous and back-breaking tasks, scouring and rubbing clean, hauling hot water upstairs, preparing meals and laboriously washing clothes by hand. The laundry alone might take several days to wash, dry, air and iron each week: the first washing-machine was patented in the US in 1846 but would not be widely available until much later, detergent was a twentieth-century invention, and even a mangle was new-fangled.

Such a housemaid would have little time to herself during a twelve-, fourteen- or even sixteen-hour working day – maybe not even time to eat properly or sit down (sewing or darning was regarded as downtime) – and very few days off. The food that her mistress would buy for her would probably be inferior to the food she was preparing for the family and a check would be made by her mistress to make sure she had not eaten more than her allowance, or, worse still, eaten up the family's left-overs unless specifically allowed to do so. An employer would feel free to dictate that she must go to church and what clothes she should wear even in her own time and, being dissatisfied with her real name, might call her by another, generic name such as Mary or Susan. Henry and Augustus Mayhew, in a book called *The Greatest Plague of Life* published in 1847, spoke of a servant 'whose godfathers and godmothers (stupid people) had christened Rosetta as if she had been a duchess. As of course I wasn't going to have any of my menials answering to a stuck-up name like that, I gave her to understand that I should allow no such thing in my house but would take the liberty of altering pretty Rosetta into plain Susan.' When the girl appeared with her hair in ringlets and in her own best clothes on May Day, including patent leather shoes, she was made to go and change so that 'the girl… was no longer dressed out as showily as if she was the mistress instead of the maid'. There clearly could be nothing more degrading than to be mistaken for a servant – usually the calibre and quality of their clothes distinguished them – and Judith Flanders, the historian of the Victorian house, adds: 'It was only in the 1850s and 60s with the arrival of new manufacturing methods and cheap cotton cloth imports from India that uniforms had to be created so that servants could continue to be differentiated from their mistresses on sight.'[26]

No wonder staff turnover was high and the alternative attractions of working in shops or factories exercised an increasing pull. Jane Carlyle, wife of Thomas, sounds as if she was an exacting mistress in their house in Cheyne Row. She objected to maids who read novels and she got through thirty-four servants in the thirty-two years the couple lived there (this at a time when the average length of a domestic servant's employment was three years). On 29 December 1846, she was writing to her friend Mary Russell about the latest crisis, caused by a disastrous Scottish maid:

> The girl had come out of a family where eight servants were kept – fancied it would be nice to get to London – and was willing to undertake anything until she got there and then she satisfied herself within the first 12 hours that

it was 'too lonely' to be a single servant – that all work 'spoiled her hands' and having no more sense of duty than a cat she threw up her engagement for 6 months at the end of 6 days (!) and declared that if she was not allowed to depart she would 'take fits'... Carlyle bade her go then in the Devil's name, rather glad to be rid of such a 'lump of selfish, dishonest fatuity' on any terms – so she walked off with her two guineas as happy as a pig on a Sunday morning (!) leaving me very ill in bed, my cousin Helen here on a visit and no servant in the house! So much for the whim of bringing a servant from Scotland.[27]

It was one of those occasions when it would have been interesting to have been a fly on the wall to hear the Sage of Chelsea's anathema falling on the poor girl's head – or at least to have listened to the Scottish maid's side of the story.

It might be difficult to find good, loyal servants, but there was a pool of labour around. The footman Tayler said: 'It is surprising to see the number of servants walking about the streets out of place... servants are so plentiful that gentlefolk will only have those that are tall, upright, respectable-looking young people and must bear the very best character.'

There was understandably a tension in relationships between employers and servants, a nervousness that came from living in close proximity, overhearing secrets, a fear of over-familiarity: one reason for keeping them in the basement to be summoned upstairs by bells. And of course there were bad servants. Polite society shuddered at the example of the Swiss valet Benjamin-François Courvoisier, who lost patience with his 'fussy' master, Lord William Russell, in May 1840 and slit his throat – though that did not stop polite society from besieging the house in Norfolk Street, Mayfair, where the murder had occurred in the hope of catching a look at the murder scene. Russell, who was the elderly brother of the Duke of Bedford and an uncle of Lord John Russell, was clearly a difficult employer. Courvoisier admitted to losing patience with the old man after being sent upstairs and down-stairs several times to fetch a warming pan; possibly more likely was that his employer had accused him of stealing the silver. 'My God!' he exclaimed when Russell's body was found. 'What shall I do? I will never get a place again!' A large mob turned out to see him hanged outside Newgate after his trial two months later, including Dickens and Thackeray.[28]

There was more public sympathy a few years later for Sarah Thomas, a 17-year-old serving maid in Bristol who lost patience with her brutal mistress Elizabeth Jefferies and beat her to death with a stone. Despite the jury's plea for mercy, she was executed, having to be dragged screaming and struggling to the scaffold. The *Liverpool Mercury* said: 'Though our reporter has witnessed many public executions, he states that this was the most harrowing and disgusting that he ever saw.' The respectable public's taste for these displays of punishment was waning, and the last public execution in England would take place in 1868.

Courvoisier's justified fear of losing his place was a common one for servants who had committed far less serious indiscretions than his: without a character (for morals were the first thing prospective employers checked) it was easy to slip into destitution. Servant women and shop-girls had to do what no respectable woman would be expected to: go out at night on their own, for chores and errands. There was a thin line between respectability and prostitution, almost the only alternative occupation open to the desperate or the indigent who had lost their job or their good name. In 1841 the Society for the Suppression of Vice estimated that there were 80,000 prostitutes in London – nearly ten times more than the Metropolitan Police's figure, but perhaps more accurate since the police covered only the central area and had other priorities, unless the prostitutes were causing a public nuisance. In an era when methods of birth control were limited (though abortions common) husbands may well have sought an outlet elsewhere. They were expected as a rule to abstain from intercourse with their wives unless the couple were seeking more children: no more than 'once a month for preference, once a week if the situation was desperate and never during menstrual periods or pregnancy'.[29] Since the average middle-class family in mid-Victorian Britain had six children and nearly a fifth of such families had ten or more, there must have been quite prolonged periods of imposed celibacy, which was probably a relief to the wives. In such circumstances the idea that married men might seek sexual relief elsewhere was not necessarily viewed with disapproval, except by stern moralists, so long as it was not accompanied by 'unregulated excitement' – and provided that it was carried out without the extravagant expenditure of emotion and accordingly with less derangement than if a man forced himself on his wife.

In London and other cities men knew where prostitutes were to be found. In Norton Street, Marylebone, they even sat naked in the windows or ran after passing men in their underclothes, and they also haunted the theatres around Leicester Square and down the Strand. Many of them were little more than children. *The Times* in June 1848 estimated that nine out of ten females leaving London workhouses at the age of 14 to go into service later ended up on the streets, while the London Society for the Protection of Young Females claimed in the mid-1830s that there were 400 pimps in the capital procuring girls exclusively between the ages of 11 and 15.[30]

For the working classes, sex was often even more casual. Dr Peter Gaskell, a Manchester surgeon, wrote in a study called *The Manufacturing Population of England* in 1833: 'The chastity of marriage is but little known or exercised; husband and wife sin equally and an habitual indifference to sexual rights is generated, which adds one other stem to assist in the destruction of domestic habits.' The Rev. J.W. Trevor, chaplain to the bishop of Bangor, noted: 'Fornication was not regarded as vice, scarcely as a frailty by the common people in Wales.' And a Dr John Mitchell Strachan, who was a doctor in Stirlingshire for thirty-eight years, claimed that nine-tenths of the women getting married in his area were pregnant or had had children by their bridegrooms: 'Courting in bed at late hours leads to familiarities and that leads to fornication.' Bundling was the country name for it. It was not unknown – as in Hardy's *The Mayor of Casterbridge* – for husbands to sell their wives. In Nottingham it was said that a working man had sold his wife in the market for a shilling, 'including the price of the rope around her neck'.[31]

Very few servants escaped their class. One who did, Joseph Paxton, the head gardener at Chatsworth, would become the man who sketched out the design for the Crystal Palace – used for the Great Exhibition in 1851 – and ended up knighted and an MP. Another was the dairymaid Mary Ann Bullock, whose singing as she worked so entranced her elderly employer, Sir Harry Fetherstonhaugh of Uppark, that he married her. She cared for him for nearly another twenty years until he died, and then inherited the house.[32] But it was much more likely that a girl would lose her character if she entered a relationship and find difficulty securing a position as a maid anywhere else.

∽

How different from these lives was that of their own dear queen who, in 1845 and 1846, was much concerned with the royal family's living arrangements and badgered Sir Robert Peel regularly about them even during the Irish famine and Corn Laws crises.[33] Buckingham Palace was much too small for her growing family, cold, pokey and inconvenient. In this, she was probably correct: at this stage the palace still lacked the east frontage for which it is best known today. Instead, it had an open courtyard, built by John Nash, facing the Mall with the Marble Arch in front obscuring the view. 'Most parts of the palace are in a sad state and will ere long require further outlay to render them decent for the occupation of the Royal Family or any visitors the Queen may have to receive,' she wrote to Peel in February 1845, adding that the palace needed a ballroom, additional apartments, offices and servants' quarters:

> It will be for Sir Robert to consider whether it would not be best to remedy all these deficiencies at once and to make use of this opportunity to remedy the exterior of the palace such as no longer to be a disgrace to the country which it certainly now is. The Queen thinks the country would be better pleased to have the question of the Sovereign's residence in London finally disposed of, than to have it so repeatedly brought before it.

Such complaints are familiar to royal correspondents 170 years on, listening to the Keeper of the Privy Purse complaining about the dilapidation of the palace under government budgetary economies.

Peel fobbed off the queen and Prince Albert for a year, blaming the financial situation and murmuring about how unfortunate it would be if the government's reintroduction of income tax should become somehow tangled in the public mind with the rebuilding of the palace. In May 1846, at the height of the Corn Laws crisis, the prince was now badgering the prime minister: 'You know that the execution is absolutely necessary... you admit the justice and urgency of the demand and there will be no difficulty in carrying the measure through the House of Commons. What do you intend to do now?' Finally, it was the first item on the agenda of Peel's meeting with his successor Lord John Russell after his government fell. Peel offered to give Russell an excuse, so that he could say the work had been agreed by the previous government. Even so there was a row when the architect Edward Blore's estimate for filling in the east front of the palace and moving the Marble Arch was presented: £150,000 for the new frontage, at a time – as William Williams, the Radical MP for Coventry complained – that two-and-a-half million Irish fellow subjects were in a state of starvation such as was unknown in any other part of the world. There were also complaints – and these have been voiced ever since, too – that Blore's plan was dull and mediocre, but the money was approved and the work carried out by Thomas Cubitt, the property speculator and builder of nearby Pimlico. In return, the government sold off the Prince Regent's Brighton Pavilion, which Victoria and Albert did not like and which Cubitt promptly offered to buy and knock down for housing. The furniture there was mostly carted off to Windsor or Buckingham Palace, or sold at auction, but fortunately the building itself was saved.

The queen, though, had decided she needed a place by the sea and not one where she might be mobbed by shop-boys as she had been during her last visit to Brighton in 1845. At Peel's suggestion, she and Albert bought Osborne House on the Isle of Wight for £26,000 as a holiday home and the prince settled down to designing – with Cubitt's help – a rather grander building than had been there before: an Italianate palazzo to go with the Mediterranean blue that the royal couple thought they detected in the Solent. 'The sea was so blue and calm that the Prince said it was like Naples,' the queen wrote to Lord Melbourne. 'And then we can walk about anywhere by ourselves without fear of being followed and mobbed, which, Lord Melbourne will easily understand, is delightful.' They were able to move in fully in September 1846. Lady Lyttelton wrote:

Nobody caught cold or smelt paint... After dinner we all rose to drink the Queen and Prince's health as a house-warming and after it the Prince said, very naturally and simply but sincerely: 'We have a hymn in Germany for such occasions'... It was dry and quaint being Luther's; but we all perceived that he was feeling it.[34]

Unfortunately, the royal renovations did not include the drains at Windsor Castle where, as the Lord Chamberlain reported:

The noxious effluvia which escapes from the old drains and numerous cesspools still remaining, is frequently so exceedingly offensive as to render many parts of the castle almost uninhabitable and scarcely any portion can be said to be entirely free from the effects of imperfect drainage.[35]

Fifteen years later it was these that were said to have given the Prince Consort his fatal attack of typhoid.

10

The Silver Bullet

'I would not allow this blackguard combination
to break up the Government.'

DUKE OF WELLINGTON TO SIR ROBERT PEEL,
8 JUNE 1846

During a private conversation with Lord John Russell in April
1846, the foreign secretary Lord Aberdeen warned him that if
the government fell, Russell would require the Peelites'
support to establish an administration of his own, so he
should be careful not to antagonize the government's Tory
loyalists in the meantime. Russell laughed and replied that it
would take a silver bullet to kill Peel and he did not think that
the one that could do it had yet been cast.[1] Perhaps Russell
was being unduly sanguine. He must have known that the
government was rocking, uncertain now of the support of a
majority of its backbenchers over the Corn Laws, and that, if
an issue could be found on which the Whigs and the protectionists could consistently unite, Peel must fall.

Both men probably knew too that the Ultras had found
one: the Protection of Life (Ireland) measure, which came to
be known as the Irish coercion bill, introduced in the Commons
on 30 March in response to a request from the Lord Lieutenant in Dublin. The bill was a revival of previous legislation
which had lapsed and it was intended to deal with rising
political violence and intimidation in Ireland. It would give

the authorities the power to proclaim disturbed districts, impose curfews and deploy additional police and troops. As such it was not an extension of previous restrictions, nor was it the imposition of national martial law. Under normal circumstances the measure would have gained cross-party support and many protectionists, including Bentinck, initially voted for it.

But these were not normal circumstances. The government was probably ill advised to introduce the measure before the Corn Laws had been repealed as the coercion bill gave its opponents another issue to unite against; but the calculation was that the situation in Ireland was an emergency and the opposition would not be so captious as to combine against a security matter. What happened was that the Radicals and Irish MPs fought the measure in the Commons and, in the days before the parliamentary guillotine had been added to a government's procedural armoury to cut short the proceedings, the debates dragged on through April. That gave the protectionists the opportunity to devise a strategy which would defeat the government. It was Disraeli who suggested a pretext to oppose the bill: if the Irish bill was so important, should not the Corn Laws repeal be delayed until after it had passed? If so, there would not be time in the session, before the summer with luck, for repeal to go through and it would have to wait until the following year. On the Whig side, too, from the opposite perspective, the argument was growing that the Corn Laws repeal was so urgent that it should take precedence over the Irish measure.

But it was now clear that the Corn Law legislation would pass in the Commons if given enough time: the second reading had a majority of eighty-eight at the end of March, though the number of Tories supporting the government measure had sunk to 102. The second-reading debate showed that the protectionist MPs were growing increasingly disdainful of the prime minister. On the last night of debate, running again early into a Saturday morning, Peel even had to sit through a vituperative maiden speech from John Stuart, the man who had replaced Gladstone as the member for Newark and was determined, remarkably and perhaps uniquely, to use the occasion to denounce the front bench of his own party. Peel's speech which followed was defiant and delivered through heckling; his statement – 'I have abandoned no duty and betrayed no trust' – was met with derision. He was not used to it, and his speech was peppered with appeals to hear him out – unheard-of pleas for a prime minister then to have to make:

> Listen with patience to the answers I have to give you...
> I have not quarrelled with any man for offering his oppo-
> sition... I have listened to the attacks on me with sorrow
> but not with anger... Really these interruptions are very
> unpleasant... What possible interest can I have to injure the
> agricultural interest? I attach the utmost importance to it.[2]

Hansard records gasps, ironical cheers and shouts of 'no'. You can almost hear the rising inflexion and bafflement in Peel's voice. He ploughed on as the shouting grew louder. They clearly were not listening to the force of his argument. Peel tried reasoning. Labourers were spending more than half their meagre weekly wages on bread; in Yorkshire, where their pay was better than in some other agricultural areas, eight shillings out of fourteen a week was spent buying flour. The protectionists' contention that wages rose as the price of wheat rose, so that workers were better able to afford bread, was just not true. Peel doggedly spelled it out: over the last ten years, as the price of wheat had fluctuated from fifty shillings to seventy shillings a quarter, labourers' wages had varied scarcely at all – in Dorset from seven shillings to eight shillings a week, in Cornwall from eight shillings to nine shillings. 'The rise in price of wheat is almost immediately in favour of the agricultural interest. I put this to you in perfect good faith and sincerity, do you think that you can maintain this system of protection much longer?' At one point Colonel Sibthorp, the Tory MP for Lincolnshire and an arch die-hard opponent of all reform under all circumstances, got up to insist that agricultural labourers were happy with their lot. 'The gallant colonel says yes. I say no,' retorted Peel.

There was even a note that has contemporary resonance:

Taxation falls much heavier on [the labourers'] class than upon us. The poor cannot resort to other countries where the scale of taxation is less than here. They are fixed, as it were, to the soil. Undoubtedly taxation falls more heavily upon them than upon us.

It was the speech in which Peel asked ('Good God!') how much diarrhoea the Irish were expected to bear before they were provided with food (see page 74) and then, more generally, pointed to the effect cheap food would have on the working classes of Britain: 'You may talk of improving the habits of the working classes, introducing education amongst them, purifying their dwellings, improving their cottages; but believe me the first step towards improvement of their social condition is an abundance of food.' He was introducing the bill 'for the true interests of every class... not for the purpose of prolonging my ministerial existence but for the purpose of averting a great national calamity and... sustaining a great public interest'.

Practically the only positive news for the government at that time was the arrival of a letter from Hardinge in India with the first news about the victories against the Sikhs nearly two months earlier. Peel went to see the queen at Buckingham Palace that Saturday afternoon, a day of thick fog, to tell her about the further reduced majority. 'Disappointed very much as we had reckoned on a majority of at least 100,' she wrote in her journal. 'The protectionists were, of course, exulting. It will be impossible now to get the bill through before Easter... We then talked for some time about India and looked over the map which shows the enormous size of our empire.'[3]

The two bills were indeed bogged down in the Commons through April, with tempers fraying further: 'everything here is in a disturbed, doubtful and uneasy state, people angry, perplexed and dissatisfied,' wrote Greville in his diary.[4] At one point Peel's brother Jonathan, also an MP, strode up to Disraeli in the chamber and challenged him to a duel, which was only headed off with a written apology brokered by Bentinck. The endless debate was wearing everyone down, not least Peel, whose headaches and gout were worsening. He knew his government would fall and was becoming fatalistic about it, but he was determined to get repeal through first. Then, on 15 May, the end of the Commons third-reading debate loomed and with it the final arguments before the bill moved to the Lords.

That night – another late sitting into the early hours – saw scenes of extraordinary tension, with Peel all but howled down and, some thought, in tears. It was sparked by another slashing speech by Disraeli, a verbal assault that lasted three hours and culminated in his most contemptuous and vitupera- tive attack yet on the prime minister. As midnight approached, in a crowded, seething, overheated House with the protection- ists roaring him on, Disraeli concluded with a peroration, the more powerful because his tone was so dry and ironic, not blustering, and addressed as is still customary – supposedly to deflect such personal attacks – to the Speaker of the Commons. Peel was a betrayer and a mediocrity and the people of England would see through him; he was not even an original thinker and had not been during his whole career:

> His life has been a great appropriation clause. He is a burglar of others' intellect... there is no statesman who has committed political petty larceny on so great a scale... I know, Sir, that we appeal to a people debauched by public gambling, stimulated by an inefficient and short- sighted Minister. I know that the public mind is polluted by economic fancies – a depraved desire that the rich may become richer without the interference of industry and toil. I know, Sir, that all confidence in public men is lost. But, Sir, I have faith in the primitive and enduring elements of the English character. It may be vain now in the midnight of their intoxication to tell them that there will be an awakening of bitterness... But the dark and inevitable hour will arrive.[5]

As with many such speeches, the final meaning, unless it was a call to insurrection, was obscure, but its effect was elec- tric. It was a sweeping personal indictment, not a detailed rebuttal of the case for repeal. Disraeli's repeated trope – he made it again years later in his biography of Bentinck, after Peel's death – was that the prime minister, the first Oxford double first, was not an original or imaginative thinker, which sat strangely with the contention that he had acted impetuously and rashly in deciding to repeal the Corn Laws. Greville recorded later:

> A speech of D'Israeli's, very clever, in which he hacked and mangled Peel with the most unsparing severity and positively tortured his victim. It was a miserable and degrading spectacle. The whole mass of the protectionists cheered him with vociferous delight, making the roof ring again and when Peel spoke, they screamed and hooted at him in the most brutal manner. When he... talked of honour and conscience they assailed him with shouts of derision and gestures of contempt. Such treatment in a House of Commons, where for years he had been an object of deference and respect, nearly overcame him... they hunt him like a fox and they are eager to run him down and kill him in the open and they are all full of exultation at thinking they have nearly accomplished the object.[6]

Peel rose to speak an hour or so after Disraeli and for a while could not be heard above the screams. He was forced to stop and then tried to start again, defending his honour once more against the personal attacks. No one present would have seen any previous prime minister being so humiliatingly assailed. Russell and the Whig front bench, sitting a few feet away, saw his eyes fill with tears and the Speaker thought he would have to sit down. But then, jaw jutting, he gathered himself, turned to Disraeli, sitting high on the benches behind him, and said contemptuously: 'I foresaw... that I must forfeit friendships which I most highly valued. But the smallest of all the penalties which I anticipated were the continued venomous attacks of the Member for Shrewsbury.' Probably Peel snapped. He then added, devastatingly, that if Disraeli held such views about his whole career, it was strange that he had ever wanted to be a minister in his government: 'It is still more surprising that he should have been ready – as I think he was – to unite his fortunes with mine in office, thus implying the strongest proof which any public man can give of confidence in the honour and integrity of a Minister of the Crown.'

It was true. Disraeli had written obsequiously to Peel in September 1841 asking for a government position in view of the support he had given the party in the general election six weeks earlier. He had been waiting all through that August while ministers had been appointed and had heard nothing. Then he had written, in a letter Peel still possessed: 'I confess, to be unrecognised at this moment by you appears to me to be overwhelming and I appeal to your own heart, to that justice and magnanimity which I feel are your characteristics to save me from an intolerable humiliation...'[7] Not only that, but Disraeli had in 1843 also unsuccessfully solicited both the ministers Lord Stanley and Sir James Graham to appoint his brother James to a government post.[8] Peel's allusion to hypocrisy and bad faith could have broken his career, but when his speech ended, Disraeli was immediately on his feet to deny the charge. It was a false insinuation, he blustered, to assume that his opposition had been caused by being disappointed in office. It would not have been dishonourable if he had applied for a position, but nothing of the kind had ever occurred:

'I never shall – it is totally foreign to my nature – make an application for any place.' He had had an amicable conversation with a minister, that was all, but their discussion had not been originated by him.

Peel merely retorted that the honourable gentleman had not correctly stated what he had said: he had never implied disappointment as a motive for his opposition. But neither did the prime minister withdraw the charge that he had sought office. There has been controversy ever since about why Peel did not read out Disraeli's letter and suggestions that he had had it with him among his papers that night and could have done so to discredit him. It would probably have destroyed Disraeli's political career and ultimately therefore his later premierships, and so altered the whole shape of late Victorian Britain and the new character of the Conservative party that emerged under his leadership in the following decades. But it seems unlikely that Peel would have had the five-year-old letter with him, since he could not have anticipated the precise terms of Disraeli's verbal assault. In any event, he disdained to humiliate the man who had just excoriated him. Probably he was just contemptuous of him. It was, however, extraordinarily reckless of Disraeli to mislead the House in front of hundreds of other members – or maybe to gamble on Peel's integrity. Even in the fevered atmosphere of the debate, he surely could not have forgotten his earlier pleas for patronage. Nor could he have been sure that the letter would not be leaked by Peel's friends. It was, says Disraeli's biographer Robert Blake, reckless mendacity: 'The most likely explanation is panic... He may well have been flustered and he probably blurted out his unconvincing denial without fully considering the risk.'⁹ This may well be true, but Disraeli had certainly had more than an hour while Peel's speech progressed to consider what to do. Perhaps he was egged on. He was lucky to get away with it.

And so the moment passed. Peel had pushed on against the hecklers, yet again defending his honour and integrity and arguing ponderously with more copious statistics that free trade would benefit agriculture and elevate the social condition of all the people, including those who did not have a vote. This repeatedly stated concern for the living conditions of the poor was not something previous prime ministers had ever felt the need to express. Like his predecessors, Peel knew all about suppressing dissent and transporting ring-leaders and troublemakers to Botany Bay. But his insistence that there were legitimate and real discontents that had to be addressed to improve the lives of the poor, for the well-being of all society, was new from a prime minister. It contrasted, too, with the protectionists' sectarian assertions that the labouring population was content, except when they were stirred up by agitators – a stance they had to maintain if they contended there was nothing wrong with the price of bread. And it contrasted, too, with the Anti-Corn Law Leaguers' insistence that manufacturers should be untrammelled in their quest for prosperity and that their workforces should accept what they were offered for they had perfect liberty to choose their employment. In his paternalistic insistence that the condition of England was a legitimate concern and responsibility of its government and that it must find national solutions to help people who had no vote and, as far as he was concerned, would never have a voice in future elections, Peel was breaking new ground. 'Is this to be the statesmanship for the future?' asked the conservative *Morning Post* – no friend of Peel – a few days later, foreseeing politicians bowing to extra-parliamentary pressure. To which the answer was yes.[10]

Peel saw such a position as an absolutely legitimate one for a conservative to take. In doing so, he believed, he was not undermining but protecting the institutions of the state. He spelled it out in the speech:

> If I look to the prerogative of the Crown, if I look to the position of the Church, if I look to the influence of the aristocracy, I cannot charge myself with any course inconsistent with conservative principles, [or] calculated to endanger the privileges of any branch of the legislature, or of any institutions of the country... Deprive me of power to-morrow, you can never deprive me of the consciousness that I have exercised the powers committed to me from no corrupt or interested motives – from no desire to gratify ambition, or attain any personal object.[11]

It was his self-righteousness which undoubtedly aggravated his critics and increased the ferocity of their attacks on his character, but minds were already made up. At four o'clock in the morning the House divided for a government majority of ninety-eight – a slight improvement on the second reading – and the bill was through the Commons. There was one final defiant outburst: Mr Eliot Yorke, the member for Cambridgeshire, demanded that, as the bill would 'displace the labour of our hardworking countrymen in order to give employment to foreign serfs', it should be retitled the Foreign Lands Improvement bill – an authentic touch of little Englandism. Then MPs made their way home through the looming dawn.

After that, the bill went through the Lords with surprising ease, considering how many Tory peers were opposed to it. The Duke of Wellington conceded that he did not really understand the details of the measure, but nevertheless held firm and insisted that it must be passed if a damaging rift with the Commons was to be averted. Passage of the measure was assured when Russell warned a meeting of Whig peers that he would resign as leader if the bill was not passed unamended. Given his public opposition to the Corn Laws, he could hardly do anything else and they fell into line.

By now the protectionists had lost hope of defeating repeal. What they wanted was revenge: to bring down the arch-traitor Peel. The Irish coercion bill would help them do it, in an unholy alliance with the Whigs, Radicals and Irish, with whom otherwise they had little in common. There was no secret about this: their blood was up and everyone knew what was in store. Peel was resigned to defeat and clearly exhausted, battered by the incessant personal attacks, but defiant. He refused calls from colleagues, including the Iron Duke, to defeat the 'blackguard combination' by calling a general election: 'this bold step will certainly carry for you the Corn Bill and probably the Assassination bill,' the old man had written – the latter being the derogatory title bestowed on the coercion measure.[12] No, replied Peel, it would not solve the issues which any new government, drawn from weak and divided parties, would have to face. And repeal must be passed urgently.

The final stages of the political crisis were acted out during a heatwave, which brought tempers to the boil. June 1846 was one of the hottest months anyone could remember. For the first three weeks the average daily temperature was around 30 degrees in the shade, much hotter in the sun. In Kent, midday temperatures were said to have reached 38 degrees. Boatmen on the Thames that month died of heat-stroke, farm labourers collapsed in the fields. Jane Carlyle complained: 'The great heat of London has made me quite ill again.' There were fears of cholera outbreaks in the north and typhus spread in London. Dogs were ordered to be muzzled for fear of rabies. Fires were frequent in the tinder-dry cities, and the sewers and rivers – including the Thames just outside the walls of the Palace of Westminster – smelled rank in the heat. Even when thunder-storms broke out, they did not clear the atmosphere. 'The heat is terrible for our air is so thick and heavy that, when heated, it is like a casing of hot lead,' wrote Geraldine Jewsbury in Manchester to her friend Mrs Carlyle in Chelsea.[13]

Against this stifling atmosphere, in the building site that was the Houses of Parliament next to the Thames, on 8 June, the Irish bill returned for its second-reading debate. The Commons met in the evenings, but temperatures would not have cooled much in the chamber. During the debate there was another slashing speech, this time by Lord George Bentinck. The noble lord lacked Disraeli's finesse or wit and he clearly exploded with rage. They could no longer have any faith in the government: 'We can no longer entrust them with the charge of so unconstitutional a power as the bill contains,' shouted the noble lord, who had voted for the bill himself only a few weeks earlier. 'The sooner we kick out the bill and Her Majes-ty's ministers together the better.' This was all because the government had not shown sufficient energy in bringing the coercion bill back earlier for debate in the Commons. He was not finished: Peel was depending on the payroll vote of just forty paid janissaries and seventy other renegades – 'He has lost the confidence of every honest man in this House.' It was not a speech calculated to win friends. And then the final insult, quite irrelevantly: 'The Rt. Hon. Baronet chased and hunted an illustrious relative of mine to death... It is time [that] all Europe... that the world should know the treachery that has been committed by those now in power.'[14]

This was an allusion to Peel's refusal to serve under Bentinck's uncle by marriage, George Canning, when he became prime minister nearly twenty years previously in 1827. The details were almost impossibly obscure and, if they had smouldered in Bentinck's remorseless mind all that time, he had not raised them before. Peel had refused to serve in the government Canning had attempted to form because he knew Canning supported Roman Catholic emancipation, which he opposed; but two years later in 1829, when he was a minister in Wellington's administration after Canning's death, he had changed his mind and supported the lifting of restrictions on Catholics. Bentinck's furious point was that Peel had already changed his mind on the issue (a supposition based on a speech he had made in the Commons in 1825, which had been reported in *The Times*), but had still refused to serve under Canning, increasing the stress on his relative in trying to form his ministry. Canning had actually died four months afterwards, having formed his government, from a chill caught at Chiswick House. But Bentinck's allegation tipped over the edge of reason with the accusation that he had personally killed a prime minister. It was a shocking claim to make and members of both parties were stunned by the reckless suddenness of Bentinck's attack.

In the febrile atmosphere of the Commons in June 1846, it threw Peel off balance by reopening a very old sore. He did not answer immediately. Instead that night he asked his friend Lord Lincoln, the chief secretary for Ireland, to wait for him while he wrote a note to the queen about the day's proceedings. The two men paced up and down a deserted Whitehall in the early hours discussing what Peel should do. He was so furious that he was all for calling Bentinck out for a duel – the last prime minister to threaten such a thing: so much for his supposedly passionless demeanour.

His young colleague tried to argue him out of it and apparently even threatened to call the police to restrain the prime minister. At last, as the first workmen appeared on the street in the hazy heat of dawn, Peel promised to sleep on the matter and stumped off home to Whitehall Gardens. It must have been a turbulent few hours' rest for him, because when Lincoln called on Peel later that morning, he was still determined on a duel to defend his honour and was only eventually dissuaded by Lincoln's argument that it would upset the queen to have her prime minister illegally fighting in public.[15] Only in such a feverish political atmosphere could such an old, meaningless row cause such upset: a clear indication of how much stress Peel was now under. Ultimately the situation was defused a few days later after Peel made a long statement to the House in the midst of the ongoing government crisis, proving that he had not dissembled in refusing office under Canning all those years before and that he had never said the words attributed to him in the earlier speech. 'Nineteen years after the fact I am to be called on and condemned upon that report and on what ground? Because there was a deaf reporter for *The Times*. He said I was indistinctly heard in the gallery. Every other reporter reported me correctly...' Peel's long and detailed speech must have taken well over an hour to deliver.[16]

In a scene which will be familiar to any current lobby correspondent, what had happened was that the reporters had got
together afterwards and compared notes to come up with
agreed verbatim quotes, except perhaps for *The Times* man:
the version was four to one.

But Bentinck and Disraeli were not to be appeased. Both
responded with the sort of obsessive tunnel-visioned self-righteousness of the conspiracy theorists of later generations. It
was clear, though, that the House was not listening to them.
Others, including Russell and even the Radical MP John
Roebuck, stood up to say they supported Peel's version and
the issue died on its legs. Neither of the accusers apologized,
however.

The diarist Greville had hobbled down to the Commons to
watch the debate despite having an attack of gout. He knew
Bentinck very well from their mutual enthusiasm for racing.
He wrote the following day:

[Peel's defence] was very triumphant, crushing GB and
D'Israeli and was received with something like enthusiasm
by the House. GB rose in the midst of a storm of cheers at
the end of Peel's speech which lasted some minutes, in a fury
that his well-known expression revealed to me and with the
dogged obstinacy which super-eminently distinguishes him
and a no-less characteristic want of tact and judgement...
Nothing could be more injurious to himself and his party...
Nothing could be more miserable than the figure which the
choice pair, GB and D'Israeli cut... this affair has been of
great service to Peel and sheds something of lustre over his
last days.[17]

The affair certainly did nothing to diminish Peel's sense of integrity and may well have dissolved some of the bile against him among the protectionists. But there was no denying that the battle was entering its final phase and would have only one outcome now, in the defeat of the Irish coercion bill. The Whigs, Irish and enough Tory rebels would vote against it at second reading to bring the government down. The protectionists could have chosen a different measure: John Fielden, a Radical MP (and cotton manufacturer), was trying to get through a bill to bring factory working for adolescents down to ten hours a day in the face of government opposition.[18] Peel (and, of course, the free-traders) had adamantly opposed the reform when the Tory MP Lord Ashley had put it forward as an amendment to a factory act two years earlier. On that occasion the move had narrowly passed in the Commons but the vote had been reversed after Peel threatened to resign. Now Ashley was out of the Commons (he had resigned his Dorset seat to give his constituents the opportunity to express their opinion on Corn Law repeal and they had taken it by voting him out) and so it was left to Fielden to campaign on limiting factory hours. Had the protectionists supported Fielden's bill (which was eventually passed the following year), it would have gone through and their claims to be acting in the interests of the labouring classes in opposing the repeal of the Corn Laws might have gained some traction. In that case their opposition to free trade might even have been viewed more favourably by posterity. But they didn't. Instead, enough of them chose to vote against a measure they supported to ensure that the Irish bill fell.

Before the debate, Peel received an extraordinary letter from Richard Cobden, who joined loyalist Tories in suggesting

Peel should call a general election and campaign on a slogan of free trade. Cobden, the radical Anti-Corn Law Leaguer, had bitterly denounced the prime minister up and down the country in his tirades at public meetings, and had taken umbrage three years before when Peel had accused him of encouraging violence. Belatedly now, as he needed all the support he could get, the prime minister had removed the charge during one of the Commons debates, and Cobden, the Tory protectionists' most hated and reviled bogeyman, reciprocated with the suggestion that Peelites and Leaguers could fight on the same platform. 'Are you aware of the strength of your position in the country?' Cobden wrote to him on 23 June. 'Practical reforms are the order of the day and you are by common consent the practical reformer. The condition of England question – there is your mission. You represent the Idea of the Age and it has no other representative among statesmen.'[19] Peel responded gently that he was weary of office and anyway such an election would be bound to be fought on the Irish question and no popery rather than free trade. He had no appetite for the political horse-trading that would be needed to form a new government or to embark on the reform programme all over again.

Cobden's was not Peel's only letter. He also received a parcel from Thomas Carlyle in the post, containing a copy of the second edition of his biography of Cromwell, which he had dedicated to the prime minister, and an unaccustomedly fulsome letter from the author who had formerly pilloried Peel as Sir Jabez Windbag:

> Let this poor labour of mine be a small testimony... to a late, great and valiant labour of yours. By and by, as I believe,

all England will say what already many a one begins to feel, that whatever were the spoken unveracities of Parliament, and they are many on all hands, lamentable to gods and men, here has a great veracity been *done* in Parliament, considerably our greatest for many years past – a strenuous, courageous and needful thing, to which all of us that so see it are bound to give our loyal recognition and further-ance as we can. Your obliged fellow-citizen and obedient servant...[20]

Such an encomium from a public intellectual must have flattered Peel's sense of self-esteem and he wrote a letter of thanks a few days later.

The final vote was on 25 June. The Irish bill debate had a valedictory tone. Everyone knew what would happen. The final speech was Cobden's and, in saying he would vote with his colleagues against the measure, he added that, in contrast, the Corn Laws repeal was about the most popular that any minister could have introduced: 'Whatever honour-able members opposite might say, the Rt. Hon. Baronet would carry with him out of office the esteem and respect of as large a number of the population as has ever been done by any minister that was ever known.' Early on in the debate the Speaker interrupted to announce that the Lords had agreed the Corn Importation bill without amendment and loud cheering broke out in the Commons. Then a few hours later they proceeded to reject the Irish bill by seventy-three votes. This was a much wider margin than expected, even though more protectionists voted with the government than abstained or joined the Whigs and Irish in opposing it. Only a third of the Tory Ultras took their disdain for Peel to the extent of following Bentinck and Disraeli into a final rebellion: seventy instead of the 242 Tories who had opposed the repeal of the Corn Laws.

In his biography of Bentinck, Disraeli proudly lists the roll-call of famous old aristocratic family names following them into the Noes lobby. With ringing phrases he pictured them marching past Peel through the chamber:

> It was impossible that he could have marked them without emotion: the flower of that great party which had been so proud to follow one who had been so proud to lead them... Right or wrong, they were men of honour, breeding and refinement, high and generous character, great weight and station in the country, which they had ever placed at his disposal... He must have felt something of this, while the Manners, the Somersets, the Bentincks, the Lowthers and the Lennoxes passed before him. And those country gentlemen, 'those gentlemen of England'... they trooped on: all men of metal and large-acred squires.

Disraeli did not mention those who had deserted their cause to support the measure. The scale of the defeat was whispered to Peel as he sat on the front bench. Disraeli was watching him carefully: 'Sir Robert did not reply or even turn his head. He looked very grave and extruded his chin as was his habit when he was annoyed and cared not to speak.'[21] If so, it was a wry rather than angry gesture. 'A much less emphatic hint would have sufficed for me,' Peel wrote ruefully afterwards to Hardinge in India. 'We have fallen in the face of day and with our front to the enemies.' Peel's biographer Norman Gash writes of those famous old family names as a 'hard knot of revengeful Tory members [voting] the Peelite cabinet out of office and the Conservative party out of power for the next thirty years'.[22]

Peel wrote his customary note to the queen immediately after the vote, at 1.30 a.m. on that Friday morning, and it was sent down by special train to the Isle of Wight where the royal family was on holiday, a month after the birth of the queen's latest child. The prime minister himself followed the next day. 'Received very unwelcome news from Sir Robert Peel,' the queen gave vent to her annoyance in her journal:

> The Govt. had been beaten on the unfortunate Coercion Bill, by 73. The same Messenger brought a box for my signature to give the Royal Assent to the Corn & Customs Bill! In one breath, triumph & defeat. These abominable, short-sighted, & unpatriotic Protectionists, — from mere spite & personal feelings & interests, — defeat the Govt. & expose the Country to mismanagement & disquiet, — thereupon to resign. What annoyance & inconvenience! Really one might have hoped & expected a grain of good sense & feeling! Though long pending & to a certain extent foreseen, the reality when it comes, is none the less disagreeable.[23]

The weather was again fine that weekend and Peel stayed on with the queen and Prince Albert, discussing the new government and the issues it would face. Victoria was taking the loss of Peel badly, nearly as badly as she had taken Melbourne's replacement by Peel seven years earlier. They sat outside in the garden in the sunshine and discussed the news.

Felt very low on waking, & my thoughts occupied with all the troubles & annoyances that lie before me, but blessed as I am, with such a beloved excellent husband, who shares all with me, I can bear it. Still to lose friends, or at least to part from esteemed devoted friends, — cannot but be very painful, & I am not feeling strong yet or up to much.

Sir Robert Peel tendered his resignation. He is evidently much relieved at quitting a post, the labours & anxieties of which would seem to have been almost too much for anyone to bear, & which during these last 6 months have been particularly onerous. In fact, he said he would not have been able to stand it much longer. What a terrible loss such a high minded honourable & clever man, will be to us & the country. The others will never be able to stand. To turn out the Minister, who has carried the Corn Law, & in fact done so great a work these last 5 years, is really dreadful. Sir Robert sat next to me at dinner & was very cheerful... He said it appeared to him like a dream, & that he could hardly believe he was to be out of office. To me it appeared like a very bad dream.[24]

On the Monday morning – another brilliant, warm summer's day – Peel left Osborne and took the train, almost certainly alone (a prime minister did not travel with a retinue then), back to London. Later that afternoon, he walked the few hundred yards down Whitehall from his house to the Commons to announce his government's resignation. Cheering crowds lined the route. Samuel Wilberforce, the young bishop of Oxford, who watched him that day, noted he was 'colder, dryer, more introverted than ever; yet to a close gaze showing the fullest working of a smothered volcano of emotions'.[25] It was, said the *Nottingham Review* later that week, 'something more than a mere *temporary huzza*. It was the utterance of emotions in no sense confined to a *London* crowd.'[26] Peel arrived in the chamber breathless from the walk and the emotion and sat on the government front bench for the last time to recover his breath. If the Tory protectionists and their newspaper supporters saw Peel as an arch-traitor, the working classes clearly did not – and that would be echoed in days to come in supportive papers and magazines. *Punch* pictured him as a theatrical impresario – 'Manager Peel taking his Farewell Benefit' – making a self-conscious bow in a packed and enthusiastic theatre with the audience tossing him bouquets, while down in the stalls a 'peeler' – one of the specialist police force he had created – manhandles a solitary figure, looking a lot like Disraeli, who is vainly shaking his fist.[27]

In the Commons that evening Peel had one more announcement to make. Fortuitously a letter from the British ambassador in Washington had arrived at the Foreign Office that morning saying that the American Senate and the administration had agreed to the settlement of the Oregon border dispute, in the terms that London had suggested. It was the line along which the border still runs 160 years later. War, which might have been a real possibility if President Polk's intransigent belligerence had continued, was now averted. Peel paid magnanimous, non-gloating tribute – 'by moderation, by mutual compromise' they had avoided the 'dreadful calamity of a war'.[28]

The speech was not long by Peel's standards. All passion was spent. But there were two remarkable passages at the end. The first was a fulsome tribute to Richard Cobden of all people – the bête noire of the protectionists, but the man, Peel said, who more than any other had achieved repeal. It was almost as if Margaret Thatcher had paid tribute to Arthur Scargill in her resignation speech, and it stunned the Tories almost as much as Cobden listening on the benches opposite. Peel said:

> The name which ought to be, and will be, associated with the success of those measures, is the name of one who, acting, I believe, from pure and disinterested motives, has, with untiring energy, made appeals to our reason, and has enforced those appeals with an eloquence the more to be admired because it was unaffected and unadorned: the name which ought to be chiefly associated with the success of those measures, is the name of Richard Cobden.

As a gesture of defiance it was breath-taking. It was pique, wrote Disraeli.

Then, reverting to the self-righteous tone he had adopted in the debates, Peel added a final passage that many, even of his closest followers, thought was a mistake – a naked and sentimental appeal to the labourers of Britain:

> I shall leave a name, severely censured I fear by many who, on public grounds, deeply regret the severance of party ties... from the firm conviction that fidelity to party engagements – the existence and maintenance of a great party – constitutes a powerful instrument of government: I shall surrender power severely censured also, by others who, from no interested motive, adhere to the principle of protection, considering... it to be essential to the welfare and interests of the country: I shall leave a name execrated by every monopolist who, from less honourable motives, clamours for protection because it conduces to his own

individual benefit; but it may be that I shall leave a name sometimes remembered with expressions of good will in the abodes of those whose lot it is to labour, and to earn their daily bread by the sweat of their brow, when they shall recruit their exhausted strength with abundant and untaxed food, the sweeter because it is no longer leavened by a sense of injustice.

He sat down to prolonged and sentimental cheers from the packed benches, now that he was going, and the House adjourned. Parliament was not dissolved and it would now be up to Lord John Russell to form a new administration, which this time he would be able to do successfully and to win a mandate a year later.

Peel left by a side entrance and walked home, again cheered by a large crowd 'including many well-dressed persons', said *The Times*. He seemed 'much gratified by his reception, notwithstanding the somewhat rude and inconvenient pressure',[29] and the cheers continued for some time after he reached his house and closed the door. The cheering crowd also surged around the Duke of Wellington as he mounted a horse to leave the Palace of Westminster. 'God bless you Duke!' a workman cried. 'For heaven's sake, people, let me get on my horse!' he retorted.

In the days to come there would be testimonials and public addresses, dinners and banquets in honour of repeal and the man who had steered it through. No one else but Peel could have done it, said his friends; he had calmed the markets and the commercial men in the City were so trusting of his judgement and sagacity that their concerns about the measure were put to rest.

His final speech, however, was not universally applauded. Peel's singling out of Cobden was resented by other free-traders, and his paean to the labouring classes denounced as Jacobinism and, in the words of the protectionist *Liverpool Courier*, as 'exquisitely ludicrous were it not so absolutely disgusting'.[30] Charles Greville wrote in his diary that the speech was being very generally condemned: 'his clap-trap about cheap bread in the peroration exasperated to the last degree his former friends and adherents... condemned by all parties indiscriminatingly.' But he added:

> The protectionists don't seem to know what to do... after having contributed to drive Peel out and thereby forced the Government on Lord John they should not feel justi-fied in raising any opposition to his government, so that in fact, for the present there is no Opposition of any sort or kind; everybody seems to be acquiescent and the swords are universally sheathed. So curious a change in so short a time was never seen.[31]

Bishop Wilberforce, who, unlike Greville, had watched the speech, noted instead:

> It was very fine: very effective: really most solemn: to fall at such a moment. He spoke as if it were his last political scene, as if he felt that between alienated friends and unwon foes he could have no party again... there was but one point in the speech that I thought doubtful – the apostrophe to Richard Cobden. I think it was wrong, though there is very much to be said for it.[32]

Even the great William Macready, the actor, was impressed: 'Read the paper, not losing one word of Sir R. Peel's interesting speech... with Sterne one might say: "Oh how I envied him his feelings!"'[33]

One of the many letters Peel received has been widely quoted. It came from a working man in Nottingham, thanking him 'for unfettering the Staf of Life to the poore man... Be assured that you do dwell in the Hearts of Thousands for ever utering those memerable words.'[34]

11

A Few Paltry Pounds

'They rush by thousands to see Thumb. They push,
they fight, they scream, they faint, they cry help and
murder and oh and ah... their eyes are open but their
sense is shut.'

BENJAMIN ROBERT HAYDON, 1846

By the summer of 1846, the painter Benjamin Robert Haydon
was at the end of his tether. As always throughout his life, he
was short of money, his landlord was threatening to evict him
from his home in Burwood Place, just off the Edgware Road
in north London, his paintings were not selling, he was not
winning commissions and, worst of all, he was denied the
public esteem which he thought his genius deserved. A few
years earlier, he had suggested that the new Palace of Westminster should be decorated with large paintings of scenes
from British history – such as those in which he specialized –
but when he submitted his entries, they were rejected. Even
more humiliating, when he had begged and borrowed money
to exhibit his latest huge compositions, *The Banishment of
Aristides* and *Nero at the Burning of Rome*, at the Egyptian
Hall in Piccadilly that April – they had taken him two years
to paint – he was upstaged by the midget next door. The
American showman Phineas T. Barnum had just brought his
latest sensation, the 31-inch-tall, eight-year-old boy Charles
Stratton, known as General Tom Thumb, to London and was

exhibiting him in the hall's largest salon to huge acclaim. The self-possessed little child had been besieged by excited crowds wherever he went and had been invited to the palace by Queen Victoria no less than three times. To make matters even worse, his speciality was a tableau in which he appeared in miniature costume dressed as Napoleon Bonaparte, who just happened to be Haydon's great hero and the subject of one of his best-known paintings: *Napoleon Musing at St Helena*. Haydon's speciality was musing paintings: he had also done Wellington musing at Waterloo and Wordsworth musing on Helvellyn, and he was planning to do Byron musing at Harrow next. And now here, next door, was General Tom Thumb striking a musing pose too and being wildly applauded for doing so. By contrast, almost no one had bothered to look in on Haydon's paintings: he had sent out 400 invitations to the private view and only four people had turned up. It was all too much to bear. 'They rush by thousands to see Thumb. They push, they fight, they scream, they faint, they cry help and murder and oh and ah. They see my bills, my boards, my caravans and don't read them... their eyes are open but their sense is shut. It is an insanity, a rabies, a madness, a furore, a dream. I would not have believed it of the English people!' he confided bitterly in his diary. By the time his exhibition closed on 18 May, he had lost £111 by it – money he did not have.[1]

The truth was that Haydon was not a great painter. He was so short-sighted that he wore three pairs of spectacles at once as he worked and the room where he painted – in a house he could not afford – was itself so small that he could not see his enormous paintings properly by standing back, with the result that his figures often appeared deformed and out of proportion, with large bodies resting on short legs. He had acquaintances in the literary world, he had sold his works to leading figures, he had even taught and lectured to up-and-coming, fashionable artists such as Frith and Landseer, but he was sinking fast. In desperation, he wrote to former patrons, including Sir Robert Peel, begging for money or commissions. In mid-June he sent five paintings and three trunks of papers and sketches to the house of the poet Elizabeth Barrett in Wimpole Street, who had once offered to look after them for him, to safeguard them from the bailiffs. Haydon had been arrested for debt seven times in the previous twenty-five years – he had even gone to prison – and now he owed about £3,000 which he had not a hope of paying.

On 18 June, his diary recorded his desperation: 'Oh God Bless Me through the evils of this day. Amen. Great anxiety… No reply from Brougham, Beaufort, Barry or Hope! – and this Peel is the man who has *no heart.*' In this, he was quite wrong, for in the middle of the political crisis, on the day he was composing his reply to Bentinck's slurs about his relationship with Canning, the prime minister broke off to write Haydon a letter of sympathy and send him a personal cheque for £50. It was not enough, of course, but Peel was the only one to send the artist money. Four days later, Haydon wrote back to him with fulsome, grovelling gratitude: 'Life is insupportable. Accept my gratitude for *always* feeling for me in adversity. I hope I have earned for my dear wife security from want. God bless you.' That morning he walked down to Oxford Street and bought himself a pistol in Riviere's gun shop, then came back and wrote some more begging letters, including one to the Duke of Sutherland. After that he locked himself in his studio, wrote his will and entered a final, punctilious epitaph in his diary: 'God forgive – me – Amen. Finis of B. R. Haydon. "Stretch me no longer on this tough world" – Lear. End – XXVI volume.' A little while later, having thought some more, he added: 'Last Thoughts of B. R. Haydon. ½ past 10. No man should use certain evil for probable good, however great the object. Evil is the prerogative of the Deity. I create good, I create, *I* the Lord do these things.' He set up his portrait of his wife – who, all unknowing, had just left the house on a visit to friends – opposite his last, unfinished canvas, *Alfred and the First British Jury*, laid out his watch next to the last letters, took out the pistol and shot himself in the head. The bullet deflected off his skull and gave him just a glancing wound, so he reloaded, thought better of it, dropped the gun and took out a razor instead, with which he slashed his throat deeply, twice. That did the trick.

When Peel heard the news the following day, he jotted a typically precise addendum on the artist's final thank-you note: 'Last letter from Haydon. It must have been written a few minutes before he deprived himself of life. Observe the word "wife" had been originally written "widow" and been altered by him.' The prime minister sent a cheque for £200 from the Royal Bounty Fund for the immediate relief of Haydon's family and promised to write a personal cheque once a subscription was opened. By contrast, as soon as the Duke of Wellington saw a report of Haydon's death in *The Times*, he promptly sent a servant round to Haydon's house to reclaim a pair of boots and a cloak he had loaned the artist when he had painted a portrait of him musing at Waterloo.

Two days later, the coroner, Dr Thomas Wakley MP – the man who founded *The Lancet* – asked Haydon's daughter at the inquest: 'Had he complained of his head in any way of late?' Mary Haydon replied: 'Yes. It was very unusual for him to do so; but on Sunday night last he did complain and during the last two or three days I recollect to have seen him frequently put his hand up to his head.' The coroner asked whether he had seen a doctor and she said no, he had not thought it necessary. 'Bless me,' said Dr Wakley. 'How extraordinary it is that persons will so neglect themselves. The number of lives annually sacrificed through a neglect of symptoms of this sort is perfectly monstrous.' Peel's generosity was publicized at the inquest, adding further to his popularity.

In the next issue of the *Comic Almanac*, George Cruikshank drew two contrasting cartoons: one called 'Born a Genius', showing a starving artist in a garret; the other 'Born a Dwarf', depicting an overdressed pygmy on a sofa surrounded by bags of money. Haydon was buried in Paddington New Churchyard under a tombstone bearing the inscription: 'He devoted forty two years to the improvement of the taste of the English people in high art and died broken hearted from pecuniary distress.'[2]

∽

On 4 July 1846, Charlotte Brontë received the first reviews for the book of poetry she and her sisters had written. 'It is long since we have enjoyed a volume of such genuine poetry as this,' wrote *The Critic's* anonymous reviewer. 'Amid the heaps of trash and trumpery which lumber the table of the literary journalist, this small book has come like a ray of sunshine.' It was such a good notice that the sisters paid out a further £10 to advertise it in the London periodicals. The publishers, Aylott and Jones, said, however, that they were not interested in seeing the sisters' newly completed manuscripts of *Wuthering Heights*, *Agnes Grey* and *The Professor* as they did not do novels.[3]

Soon, though, Charlotte had other things on her mind. She was taking her father, the Rev. Patrick Brontë, to Manchester to see a specialist doctor about the condition of his eyes. The old man was suffering from cataracts and could no longer see to read or write. The family was concerned that he might lose his living at Haworth and consequently their home at the parsonage if he was too blind to conduct services or preach. They arrived in Manchester in mid-August to see William James Wilson, the surgeon and founder of the Manchester Royal Eye Hospital, and he was able to offer them the good news that he could operate the following week. They established themselves in lodgings at 83 Mount Pleasant in Boundary Street, knowing that they would have to stay for a month, with Mr Brontë lying in a darkened room while his eyesight recovered. The operation on the old man's left eye took a quarter of an hour ('the feeling was of a burning nature – but not intolerable,' he wrote later)[4] and Charlotte remained in the room throughout. Then, she settled down to write *Jane Eyre* to give herself something to do as a nurse tended to her father and applied leeches to his temples to reduce the swelling on his face. Charlotte was suffering from severe toothache – within a few years she would have virtually no teeth left – but she found the writing came in a rush for the next three weeks. She was short-sighted and wrote the text in pencil in small paper books, held close to her face as she worked. When the plot reached Thornfield and the appearance of Mr Rochester, she was so carried away that she could not stop.

It was, of course, partially autobiographical. Carus Wilson and the Cowan Bridge school became Brocklehurst and

Lowood. The tragic child Helen Burns was based on the Brontës' sister Maria, and Charlotte's former Belgian employer Constantin Heger was Rochester. The pace of writing would slow later when she and her father returned to Haworth, but at least his operation had been a success. Now the sisters had to worry about their brother Branwell whose drunkenness was getting worse and whose debts were mounting. In the freezing December of 1846, up on the moors, Charlotte was writing to her friend Ellen Nussey:

> The cold here is dreadful. I do not remember such a series of North Pole-days – England might really have taken a slide up into the Arctic zone – the sky looks like ice – the earth is frozen, the wind is as keen as a two-edged blade... We have all had severe colds and coughs.

Then she added:

> Nothing happens at Haworth – nothing at least of a pleasant kind – one little incident indeed occurred about a week ago to sting us to life... It was merely the arrival of the Sheriff's officer on a visit to Branwell – inviting him either to pay his debts or to take a trip to York.

By 'take a trip to York' Charlotte meant 'go to prison for debt'. She went on:

> Of course his debts had to be paid – it is not agreeable to lose money time after time in this way but it is ten times worse – to witness the shabbiness of his behaviour on such

occasions – But where is the use of dwelling on this subject: it will make him no better.[5]

In 1847, their spirits would rise: in June *Wuthering Heights* and *Agnes Grey* would finally be accepted for publication, and in August William Smith Williams, the reader for Smith, Elder and Co. – the sixth publisher to see the manuscript – would decide that *Jane Eyre* was good enough to publish.

∽

On the day after Patrick Brontë's cataract operation in Manchester, 100 miles away in Birmingham, the composer Felix Mendelssohn conducted the first performance of his new oratorio *Elijah*, on which he had been working on and off for most of the year between recitals in Leipzig, Aachen and Carlsbad. The British were wild for the young German. He was a particular favourite of Queen Victoria and Prince Albert, and he had toured Britain many times. This was his ninth and penultimate visit, at the age of 37, fourteen months before his death. The Birmingham Festival had invited him to perform the year before and he had decided to write the oratorio for its orchestra. He had started the composition in December 1845, worked on it through the spring and finally finished it only a fortnight before the performance, which was scheduled for 26 August. He had arrived in London a few days before the concert and rehearsed the scratch orchestra and singers – 400 musicians altogether – for three days, and then they had all caught the train up to Birmingham together.[6]

The audience at the town hall was ecstatic. *The Times* pronounced the performance an absolute triumph and the

Birmingham Journal's critic was carried away by the composer's personality as much as his music:

> Mendelssohn's manner both in the orchestra and in private
> is exceedingly pleasing. His smile is winning and occasionally, when addressing a friendly correction to the band or
> choir, full of comic expression... He possesses a remarkable
> power over the performers, moulding them to his will...
> and though rigidly strict in exacting the nicest precision,
> he does it in a manner irresistible – actually laughing them
> into perfection.

Mendelssohn himself was thrilled with how it had gone, though he did not rate the soprano soloist: 'so pretty, so pleasing, so elegant, but without soul, so unintelligent, a kind of amiable expression,' he wrote scathingly afterwards. But the orchestra, the audience and the hall had been wonderful, he wrote to his friend the singer Livia Frege:

> The rich full sounds of the orchestra and the huge organ,
> combined with the powerful voices of the chorus who sang
> with sincere enthusiasm, the wonderful resonance in the
> huge grand hall, an admirable English tenor, Staudigl too
> who took all possible pains in his role as Elijah... some
> very good second sopranos and contralto solo singers, all
> executing the music with special zeal and the utmost fire
> and spirit, doing justice not only to the loudest passages
> but also to the softest pianos in a manner I have never
> before heard from such a loud choir and, in addition,
> an impressionable, kindly, hushed and enthusiastic audience – at times quiet as mice, at times exultant – all this

is indeed enough good fortune for a first performance. In fact, I have never in my life heard a better or as good a performance and I almost doubt that I shall ever again hear one equal to it.

The composer was not in a hurry to return to Germany. He lingered in England for a month through September, had four days in Ramsgate 'to breathe sea air and to eat crabs', and then took the boat across the Channel and wended his way slowly home to Leipzig by train. He was exhausted with overwork. His last trip to England the following spring, to conduct *Elijah* in London, Manchester and again in Birmingham, wore him out: six performances of the oratorio, four piano concerts and several organ recitals in twenty-seven days. Seven months later, in early November 1847, he died following a series of strokes.

∽

A few days after Mendelssohn's triumph in Birmingham there was another cultural innovation that would have a lasting impact on English life: William Clarke's All England cricket eleven took the field for the first time, at Hyde Park in Sheffield, against twenty local men. It was the dawn of the professional era in team sports. There had been ad hoc England teams before, playing one-off matches against local sides, but William Clarke, a 48-year-old one-eyed former bricklayer, now the landlord of an inn beside the River Trent in Nottingham, was the first entrepreneur to recruit a national side comprising the best players in the country, drawn from north and south, to play exhibition matches from Truro to Scotland. Clarke, a wily bowler of round-arm spin, had been the leading cricketer in the Midlands for thirty years, but his fame was mostly local and now he had the ambition, drive and financial acumen to take his plans nationwide, with the assistance of the railways that could carry his team all over the country.

In this, 'Old Clarke', as he was known, was catching a rising trend. The young gentlemen coming out of the public schools and universities were also setting up their own clubs, not to play professionally but for fun against their own kind. The previous year a group of them had founded a club whimsically called I Zingari – roughly, Italian for 'gypsies' – for the purpose of playing matches while staying at the country houses of England, with the rule that they would not employ any professional working men to bowl for them, preferring to play the game fully (including carrying out the mundane bowling work) for themselves. Members of the aristocracy, who had formerly bet on games between their own elevens of hired men, were now also starting to found county clubs to play against each other. The Sussex club was founded in 1839, then Nottinghamshire in 1841, Kent in 1842 and, in 1846, Surrey, which would play on the site of a former market garden in Kennington. In a gesture towards the game's rustic roots and, perhaps more pointedly, as a way of ensuring that control of the sport was kept in the hands of the country gentry and away from the industrial metropolises and the sort of manufacturing men who had funded the Anti-Corn Law League, these clubs were based firmly on counties, rather than cities, and they have remained so ever since.[7]

Old Clarke was not like that and his enterprise was strictly professional. His men might play for counties, but he also offered them up to £6 a week to play for All England: a little more than they could get as professional players for the

Marylebone Cricket Club, the premier London club which had taken over control of the laws and conduct of the game. Large crowds attended their matches. Clarke was not excessively generous. He might rake in £70 as a fee for his team's appearance and then also claim most of the money taken at the gate, but the professionals' pay was at least regular, considerably better than a labourer's wage, and many of his stars were short of cash. Alfred Mynn, a giant Kentish farmer, the most feared bowler in England and a mighty hitter – perhaps the Andrew Flintoff of his day, though at 21 stone he was considerably heavier – had spent part of the previous season in prison for debt. He was joined by men like William Lillywhite, who had been employed as a bricklayer – and bowler – on the Duke of Richmond's Goodwood estate before becoming a pub landlord in Brighton; by Nicholas Wanostrocht, who was an impoverished school teacher and so played under the pseudonym of Felix lest he put off his pupils' parents; by Fuller Pilch from Norfolk, the best batsman in England, who now ran a pub in Canterbury; and by young George Parr, another Nottinghamshire man and a mighty hitter. Such men became sufficiently well known to be given portentous nicknames by the promoters and the Victorian press: Mynn, the Lion of Kent; Lillywhite, the Nonpareil; Parr, the Lion of the North.

These and other men moved across the country playing fixtures usually against teams of fifteen, twenty or twenty-two men, mainly in urban centres: Manchester, Liverpool, Leeds, York, Stockton, Sheffield, Birmingham, Newcastle, Stourbridge – wherever a local organizer would pay to have them. They wore team colours at a time when it was unusual to do so: cream flannels and red polka-dot shirts. And they

caroused and drank their way from fixture to fixture, sometimes even being put up by the country squires who would
otherwise not have allowed such working men across the
thresholds of their homes. 'What fun we had in these matches
to be sure,' exclaimed Richard Daft, another Nottinghamshire
batsman years later:

> Arrived early, breakfasted on bread, cheese and bottled ale.
> Tom Foster would leave his umpire's post and come into
> the pavilion for more at the fall of each wicket... Cricketers
> now talk about being hard-worked. But when I began to
> play for All England we used to play six days a week for
> five months and never had a day's rest except on Sundays
> and when it was wet.[8]

Clarke, said one of his players William Caffyn, 'did more
than anyone else to popularise our great national game'.[9] He
was, John Arlott wrote, 'the first man to make a fortune out
of cricket; he was also the first to see that there was a fortune
to be made out of it'.

By the early 1850s All England was playing more than
thirty matches a season and posing a serious challenge to the
gentlemen of the Marylebone Cricket Club in London. The
MCC, then as now, was not really in the vanguard of change:
round-arm bowling was still regarded with suspicion and
Robert Grimston, one of the club's most influential members,
famously paid a group of navvies to smash a new-fangled
mower – 'an infernal machine', in his words – which had been
brought in to cut the grass of the MCC's ground at Lord's. But
he was an old Tory. The All England eleven was popular and
successful, even if its members did occasionally have to scythe

out a wicket themselves before a game could start. As the game's first historian, the Rev. James Pycroft, wrote in 1851: Clarke's travelling circus 'tended to a healthy circulation of the life's blood of cricket, vaccinating and innoculating every wandering rustic with the principles of the game'. It could not last: soon Clarke would face a rebellion over pay and some of his stars left to form their own team – the United England Eleven. A few years after that, there would be the first privately sponsored tours abroad: to the US in 1859 and then to Australia. Soon, too, working men who could never hope to play professionally would be forming their own teams and leagues as factory legislation limiting working hours closed down the mills and the mines on Saturday afternoons, giving them at last a little spare time.

∽

On the morning of 12 September 1846, two women, a lady and her maid, could be seen making slow and furtive progress along Wimpole Street in London. It was the poet Elizabeth Barrett and her maid Elizabeth Wilson walking to St Marylebone parish church for Barrett's clandestine wedding to the poet Robert Browning. Wilson had been sworn to secrecy and Barrett herself had told no one about her plans, except one friend, for fear of what her wealthy father Edward Barrett would do. She was terrified of being found out and stopped. It was a brief journey that sunny morning, but the walk was laborious because the bride, an invalid for most of her adult life, had to keep stopping for a rest and on one occasion to go into a chemist's shop for smelling salts.[10] The marriage had been precipitated because her father had announced two days earlier that he was moving the family out to the country while their house was redecorated. 'We must be married directly and go to Italy,' Browning had written to her. The only hold-up had been the urgent need to recover her pet spaniel Flush from an East End villain named Taylor who had kidnapped the dog twice before and was holding it to ransom again.

At the church, Browning and his cousin James Silverthorne were already waiting, together with a verger and a clergyman. No one else was present and the service was over in a few minutes. Then the bride and groom left in separate cabs. For the following week, they communicated by letter, just as they had for the previous year, and then, the following Saturday, they arranged one of the most famous elopements in history. Barrett with Wilson slipped out of the family home in the afternoon, met Browning outside Hodgson's bookshop on Marylebone High Street and caught a cab to Vauxhall Station, where that evening they took the boat train to Southampton. There they boarded a steamer to carry them across the English Channel to France, before later in the autumn moving on to Italy. On that Saturday afternoon Elizabeth Barrett Browning had posted letters explaining her actions to the rest of the family. She could be confident that they would arrive promptly with the Saturday evening post.

The subterfuge was necessary because Edward Barrett was, if not quite the tyrannical father of legend, at least a controlling and autocratic one who, in due course, would disinherit all his remaining children when they married. He had felt sure of his eldest daughter Elizabeth's loyalty as she hid herself away in her bedroom at the family home, writing poetry to keep her lively mind amused. But she knew that he would never approve of the impecunious young poet, six years her junior, who had been writing to her and semi-secretly visiting once a week for more than a year. Browning was not yet as famous as she was, but, although he had a rising reputation, he had no other occupation and little family money or social status. He had wooed her gently and considerately, and gradually won her trust, affection and love. Elizabeth was lucky to have a small private inheritance, but otherwise her father cut her off without a penny. She was already 40 and had never dreamt that love would come to her, but now she was blissfully happy. She wrote to her sister Arabella from the French capital: 'I am seeing near in him all that I seemed to see afar... thinking with one thought, feeling with one heart.' It was like riding an enchanted horse, they could now 'sit through the dusky evenings watching the stars rise over the high Paris houses and talking childish things'.

Elizabeth Barrett Browning's frustrations were shared by many middle-class Victorian women: their horizons were often limited, their opportunities for education – or a career – strictly curtailed. Once married, their property became their husband's. They were expected to obey their father's, or their husband's, whims. In her book *The Women of England*, published in 1842, Mrs Ellis complained about 'the number of languid, listless and inert young ladies who now recline upon our sofas, murmuring and repining at every claim upon their personal exertions'. It was, she said, 'a truly melancholy spectacle'.[11] Elizabeth was not like that, as it turned out, but even she could tell her husband-to-be: 'I belong to that pitiful order of weak women who cannot command their bodies with their souls at every moment and who sink down in hysterical disorder when they ought to act and resist.' But when she got to France and then to Italy, she found to her and her husband's surprise that she was well enough to be more physically active than she had ever thought possible. She would even bear a child.

❧

Charles Dickens was back in London for a few days before Christmas 1846, leaving his family in Paris, to oversee the publication of his latest seasonal short story, *The Battle of Life*, which, as usual, would be a sell-out despite being one of his feeblest works. Dickens himself had struggled with the plot: 'sick, giddy and capriciously despondent… there may be NO CHRISTMAS BOOK!' he had written to a friend in September. But it sold 23,000 copies on the day of publication, even though it got a critical panning: 'exaggerated, absurd, impossible sentimentality,' said the *Morning Chronicle*'s review on 24 December.[12]

Dickens's latest novel, *Dombey and Son*, whose first monthly part had been issued in October, however, was already a huge critical success: its characters so well embedded in the public consciousness that *Punch* would soon be caricaturing Peel as Mr Dombey instructing his little son, Prime Minister Russell, in the finer arts of economics. By Christmas itself the author was back in Paris with his family, sending greetings to his friend John Forster: 'Many merry Christmases, many happy new years, unbroken friendship, great accumulation of cheerful recollections, affection of earth and heaven at last for all of us…'[13]

He already had his own immense scheme in view. In the next instalment, he was planning to kill off little Paul Dombey. And, in preparation, Dickens spent New Year's Eve visiting the Paris morgue, alone, at dusk, to view the unidentified bodies laid out there.

That Christmas there was a new pantomime at the Theatre Royal, Manchester: *Harlequin Gulliver, or Dwarfs and Giants*. It was a show in the old eighteenth-century style with stock characters such as Pantaloon and Clown, 'a stupid jack-pudding of a servant', joining the lovers Harlequin and Columbine. The *Manchester Guardian* gave it a column and a half, placed ahead of the political and local news. Its anonymous reviewer did not think much of the plot, which he outlined from memory, but was impressed by the spectacle, which was the whole point of such extravaganzas. Clearly, no expense had been spared:

> We think the piece is overcrowded with tricks and trans-formations in the pardonable anxiety to give variety and interest to it so that many of them are hurried over before their meaning can be ascertained... some it must be confessed have no point in them. Great praise is due to the manager for the liberal expenditure which he has bestowed upon the piece – we believe about £400 – and to Mr Wallack for the complete style in which it is produced.[14]

12

A Vote More or Less is Nothing to You

'Freedom from the base servitude to which a minister
must submit who is content to sacrifice the interests
of a great empire to those of a party.'

ROBERT PEEL TO HENRY HARDINGE, FEBRUARY 1847

The fall of the government at the end of June ended the political crisis of 1846. Lord John Russell was left to form a Whig minority government and Sir Robert Peel retreated to spend the rest of the summer on his Staffordshire estate, free for the first time in years from the hard, unending work of office. Within a month he was echoing the sentiments of the newly retired everywhere in a letter to Lord Aberdeen, the former foreign secretary:

I do not know how other men are constituted but I can say with truth that I find the day too short for my present occupations, which chiefly consist in lounging in my library, directing improvements, riding with the boys and my daughter and pitying Lord John and his colleagues.[1]

At the age of 58, after many years in ministerial office and leading a political party, he was still relatively fit and wondering how to spend the rest of his life, beyond enhancing his collection of portraits of his fellow politicians (some of which now hang in the National Portrait Gallery), supervising the drainage and improving the crop yields on his land at Drayton, and fulfilling the role of disinterested elder statesman in the Commons.

What he was absolutely certain he would never do again was seek ministerial office. He would not be a subordinate minister, least of all to Russell, and he was never going to be prime minister again, however popular he was in many parts of the country. Nor would he attempt reconciliation with the protectionists to rebuild the Conservative party. He wrote scornfully to a friend:

> protectionists indeed! to close their eyes to the result of every commercial experiment that has been made... to find everyone of their predictions falsified, to disregard the state of public opinion, to call the Corn Laws a labourer's question and yet listen to the appalling facts as to the condition of the labourers in Dorsetshire for years past... to be willing to encounter the tremendous risks of two bad harvests and the recurrence of such a state of things... as was witnessed in the winters of '41 and '42, not to see that the Corn Laws would... be swept away with dishonour on the demand of a starving population – this is to be a protectionist! Thank God I am relieved for ever from the trammels of such a party.[2]

Old friendships were sundered for ever. In January 1847, Croker, the Tory politician and journalist who had opposed repeal wrote regretfully to Peel that their differences must, after 37 years' friendship 'render any personal intercourse between us awkward and painful... If we should happen to meet, I hope it may be with such civil forms and as much personal kindness as may very well coexist with strong political differences.' He obtained a dusty answer from the former prime minister who had evidently read what Croker had been writing in the *Quarterly Review*:

> I concur entirely in the opinion you express, that any personal intercourse between us would be awkward and painful... personal goodwill cannot co-exist with the spirit in which those articles are written, or with the feelings they must naturally have excited. I trust there is nothing inconsistent with perfect civility in the expression of an earnest wish that the same principle which suggests to you the propriety of closing a written correspondence of seven and thirty years may be extended to every other species of intercourse... Your obedient servant, Robert Peel.

There were still ninety Tory MPs who saw themselves as Peelites and they included most of the ablest members of the party, some of them former ministers, but he made no attempt to lead them. In time most would either retire, or, like Gladstone, join the Liberal party that evolved from the amalgamation of the Whigs and Peelites. The attacks had been too bitter and the wounds too livid, the enmities too raw and life-long for reunification with the Ultras. The Peelites sat in a phalanx on the opposition benches, even though they agreed with much of the Whig government's policies. They and the protectionists were agreed about just one thing: the need to keep Russell in office, at least temporarily – the protectionists to make sure Peel never got back in, the Peelites to ensure that a protectionist government, unlikely as it might seem, would be impossible.

That gave Russell some strength. As Sir John Hobhouse, one of his ministers, wrote to him: 'A vote more or less is nothing to you and you may laugh at the idle menaces of any man or set of men.'[3] But that was the least of Russell's difficulties: he had much more trouble imposing his authority over his fractious and imperious colleagues, several of them more dynamic characters than he was. Russell was not only physically small, he was also small-minded and peevish, convinced that he should have had credit for abolishing the Corn Laws, which had somehow mysteriously been denied him. Little Lord John was always caricatured as a diminutive, childish figure, though he was only four years younger than Peel and had been an MP for thirty-three years and a minister in Melbourne's government: *Punch* pictured him on taking office trying on his predecessor's clothes, which were inevitably much too big for him. He might have been the younger brother of the Duke of Bedford but he was a relatively impoverished one, surrounded by much wealthier, landed members of the great Whig families: Lords Grey, Clarendon, Lansdowne, Minto and Auckland and, not least, Lord Palmerston, who became foreign secretary as of right, despite the reservations of his colleagues about his bumptious personality and belligerent attitudes to foreigners. 'Every great family claims what it considers to be its due,' noted Prince Albert, who was surprised on meeting the new ministers that each of them complained about their differences with each other.[4]

Even more disastrously for Ireland, now in its second year of famine, four of the new ministers had landed estates there and, far from being anxious about the worsening starvation on their doorsteps, they were more concerned with avoiding any additional expenditure on relief than helping to diminish the looming catastrophe. Palmerston had even spent the summer and autumn of 1845, as the famine took hold, on his estates in Sligo, taking picnics with his wife, overlooking the sea, meeting tenants and supervising building works in the nearby harbour. Lady Palmerston thought the Irish untrustworthy but delightful.[5]

But the second year's potato failure was worse than the first – five-sixths of the crop was lost – and when it came to helping the destitute population, the government's actions were disastrous. They cut funding for relief – subsidies were a sixth of what they had been the previous year – and in pursuit of doctrinaire laissez-faire economic policies, they stopped buying emergency food supplies to relieve starvation altogether. It was to be left to the market to supply the wants of the population and to landowners to pay labourers enough to live on while they employed them to improve their estates. The landowners received government loans to enable the work to be done, but many of them did not pay sufficient wages for the workers to buy enough food to live. The policy was guided by Charles Trevelyan, whose political allegiance as a Whig was now undisguised, and by Charles Wood, Russell's choice as chancellor of the exchequer. The best that Russell's biographer John Prest can say in defence of the policy was that the government was conned by Irish corn-dealers into believing that if it intervened by buying grain, it would have to buy the lot: 'Either the government must take over the entire supply of corn to Ireland, or it must supply none and when the merchants demanded a specific undertaking, Wood gave it.'[6] Russell meekly accepted his chancellor's assurance that the merchants had bought up every atom of corn on the market – there was apparently 'no corn now in the world unbought' – and blithely insisted that the government could not convert scarcity into abundance. 'We cannot feed the people. It were a cruel delusion to pretend to do so,' Russell wrote to the Irish Lord Lieutenant Bessborough in October 1846. And so that winter people died in the streets and country lanes from starvation. The scale of distress was recognized even by Queen Victoria. 'Received some heart-rending accounts of the state of Ireland,' she wrote in her journal at the end of 1846:

Really too terrible to think of. In one district alone, 197 people have died from fever produced by want and half as many have died in their cabins and in the lanes and streets of starvation. To save expense they are buried without affairs or the services of any clergy. The scenes of horror, the starving people shivering with cold and devouring raw turnips they say, too dreadful and in the midst of all this the landlords appropriate the people's corn! After all we have done to supply the needy with food. God alone can bring help for no human means seems to be able... the poor people in the North Western isles are equally in a state of starvation, existing only on seaweed and bearing their terrible plight with such exemplary patience. It makes one very sad.[7]

Peel's government had differentiated in sugar import duties between crops produced by free labour and those from slave plantations, the latter taxed at three times the free sugar rate. Now, in a further application of the laissez-faire principle, Russell's government removed that distinction: both sugar from slave estates and that produced with paid labour would have equal duties. Peel himself watched this with wry exasperation, particularly when ministers attempted to introduce a measure to curb violence in Ireland after having voted him out of office over the Irish coercion bill. 'I met Lord John at Windsor Castle and certainly without any feelings of envy at his triumph,' he wrote to Lord Lincoln that October. 'He looked miserable enough. Every Irish murder must give him a twinge – a shooting pain under the left ribs.'[8]

In all this the Tory protectionists were floating off into political irrelevance. Lord George Bentinck showed evidence of future seriousness by selling his horse-racing stud in order to concentrate on politics – and then was aggravated to see his former colt Surplice win the 1848 Derby. Disraeli came across him in the Commons library researching sugar duties shortly afterwards:

> He gave a sort of superb groan: 'All my life I have been trying for this and for what have I sacrificed it!' he murmured. It was in vain to offer solace. 'You do not know what the Derby is,' he moaned out. 'Yes I do; it is the blue ribbon of the turf.' 'It is the blue ribbon of the turf,' he slowly repeated, and, sitting down at the table, he buried himself in a folio of statistics.[9]

But within a few months Bentinck, aged 46, would suffer a fatal heart attack while out for a walk on his Nottinghamshire estate and Lord Stanley in the Lords assumed the Tory leadership. That left Disraeli to lead the rump of MPs in the Commons and wean them gradually away from protectionism as their worst fears about the future of British agriculture failed to be realized. The Duke of Argyll wrote years later in his memoirs: 'By this strange event Disraeli was soon left absolutely alone, the only piece upon the board on that side of politics that was above the level of a pawn… He was like a subaltern in a great battle where every superior officer was killed or wounded.'[10] About this time, Disraeli murmured to Hobhouse that if Peel had only assembled his party in January 1846 'and told them openly his opinions they would have given way and followed him'.[11] That may have been so, but Peel certainly told them often enough why he was taking the course he was. Probably, Disraeli would never have become the party's leader without his role in destroying Peel. At least in the wake of the 1846 debates, his precarious financial situation would be eased. Lord George Bentinck and his brothers bought him Hughenden Manor, outside High Wycombe, that December: 750 acres of prime Buckinghamshire estate which, deep in debt, he could never have afforded himself. He was at last a landed country gentleman. It would take him until 1874, however, to climb to the very top of the greasy pole and become prime minister in charge of a majority Tory government.

Peel last spoke in the Commons on 29 June 1850, the fourth anniversary of the resignation of his government, during the Don Pacifico debate, when Palmerston defended a characteristic piece of gunboat diplomacy following an incident in Athens when a Gibraltar-born Spanish merchant claiming British citizenship had had his house burned down during an anti-Semitic riot.[12] Palmerston had sent a British fleet to blockade Piraeus until the Greek government compensated Pacifico. Peel spoke against the action: diplomacy, he said, should be used by civilized society for maintaining peace, not perverted into a cause of hostility and war.[13]

Later that day Peel attended a meeting of the committee planning the following year's Great Exhibition, then that afternoon took a horse ride past Buckingham Palace towards Hyde Park Corner. Peel was a very experienced rider, but the horse was a new acquisition and of uncertain temper, and when he paused to greet two young ladies riding in the opposite direction, it was suddenly startled and kicked, swerved and threw the portly former prime minister over its head. It then fell on top of him, crushing his back. Peel was carried, conscious but in agony, back to his home in Whitehall Gardens where he lay on an inflatable mattress on a table in the dining room, the furthest he could be moved. There was nothing doctors could do about his internal injuries. A silent crowd of mourners gathered outside waiting for news. It took him three days to die, conscious but in great pain, and after he did so, there was an outpouring of national grief and commemorations. *The Times*, no particular friend, wrote in its obituary of the shock of his sudden demise:

A great age has lost a great man... He has been taken from us, as it were, from his very seat in the Senate, with nothing to prepare us for his departure and everything now to remind us of it, with his powers unabated and his part unfulfilled... they who speculate or dream over the great game of politics have to readjust their thoughts to the loss of the principal actor.[14]

A fund known as the Working Men's Memorial of Gratitude to Sir Robert Peel was set up with 167 local branches to collect penny subscriptions and more than a quarter of a million people donated. 'We are living in an age emphatically of statues and testimonials,' said the *Athenaeum* magazine, and in due course there would indeed be statues across the country, from Parliament Square to many of the great northern cities and towns. An advertisement in the *Leeds Mercury* reverently trilled:

> Mementoes rise on every side,
> Fit tributes of his worth;
> His name's revered – his loss is mourned,
> Throughout the mighty earth!
> Whilst *Yorkshire* nobly has awoke
> Its feelings to reveal,
> And LEEDS devotedly has given
> A *Statue unto Peel!*

The notice, placed by Samuel Hyam, tailor, clothier and outfitter of Briggate, helpfully pointed out that, while Peel had cheapened the price of bread, Hyam's had won its popularity by cheapening the price of clothing.[15]

Peel, shy, chilly in temperament and remote, would probably have been more content with another memorial to free trade. In the decade from the mid-1840s to the mid-1850s, British imports and exports doubled, ushering in the mid-Victorian period's prosperity.

There was one other sort of export now, too: people. The late 1840s would see a great exodus, not only from Ireland, but also from Scotland and the other home countries. In the sixty years from American independence to 1845, it was calculated that only 1.6 million people entered the young republic, but in the following ten years 1.8 million would do so from Britain and Ireland alone. They were mainly fleeing famine and poverty in search of a new life in a better climate, with more wholesome air, more space, jobs, money and, as Benjamin Franklin had said, 'kind neighbours, good laws, a free government and a hearty welcome'.[16] Some of them even found it. None was more successful than Andrew Carnegie, who left Dunfermline for New York at the age of 13 with his parents in May 1848 and later accumulated hitherto unimaginable wealth as the magnate of US Steel.

Nor was it just the impoverished and destitute who left on coffin ships and steamers that took anything from sixteen days to a month or more to cross the Atlantic – if they made it at all (fifty-nine ships were lost on the crossing in the six years from 1847). Members of other classes were going too, as Ford Madox Brown illustrated in his painting *The Last of England*. After he had finished it, he wrote in 1855:

> This picture is in the strictest sense historical. It treats of the great emigration movement... The educated are bound to their country by quite other ties than the illiterate man, whose chief consideration is food and physical comfort. I have therefore in order to present the parting scene in its fullest tragic development, singled out a couple from the middle classes, high enough through education and refinement to appreciate all that they are now giving up and yet depressed enough in means to have to put up with the discomforts and humiliations incident to a vessel 'all one class'.[17]

As models he chose himself, his wife and children and selected another from 'all the red-headed boys in Finchley'.

On the first day of 1847 the queen filled in her journal

about the previous night's party with Albert and guests at Windsor Castle:

> As 12 o'clock struck there was a dead pause, after which when the clock ceased striking there was a flourish of trumpets and we all wished each other a happy New Year. We embraced each other warmly when we got to our room. Full of gratitude for all the blessings and mercies of this past year which I grieve to part with as I do with all those years since our marriage. I offered up my prayers to our Almighty Father in hope and confidence for the future. May he protect and preserve us and our dear children.[18]

The young queen may not yet have realized it but 1846 had been one of the most important years of her reign. It had seen the fall of her admired prime minister, a major and lasting realignment in politics, and the culmination of a free-trade economic system and policy of cheap food that would endure for much of the following century. In addition, it marked the start of a huge humanitarian crisis in Ireland that would have a lasting impact on the character and populations of at least five countries: Ireland itself, Britain, the United States, Canada and Australia. Meanwhile, a lasting and final agreement was reached over the border between Canada and the US and over the absorption of the Punjab into the empire. The map had changed in so many ways, and the country would never be the same again.

Notes

INTRODUCTION

1 Asa Briggs, *Victorian Things* (Penguin 1990), p. 375.
2 Michael Leapman, *The World for a Shilling* (Hodder Headline 2002), p. 124.
3 The quotes are from *The Times* obituary of Sir Robert Peel, 2 July 1850, reprinted in *The Times: Great Victorian Lives* (Times Books 2007).

CHAPTER 1: CHRISTMAS 1845

1 Queen Victoria's journal, 20 December 1845. See http://www.queenvictoriasjournals.org/home.do.
2 Douglas Hurd, *Robert Peel: A Biography* (Phoenix 2007), p. 349.
3 Cathal Poirteir (ed.), *The Great Irish Famine* (Mercier Press 1995), p. 26; A.N. Wilson, *The Victorians* (Hutchinson 2002), p. 78.
4 Wilson, op. cit., p. 79, citing James Anthony Froude's letter of 1841.
5 Hurd, op. cit., p. 338. The duke's phrase was recorded by Charles Greville in his diary entry for 13 January 1846.
6 Cecil Woodham-Smith, *The Great Hunger* (New English Library 1968), pp. 50–1.
7 Norman Gash, *Sir Robert Peel* (Longman 1972), p. 471.
8 Hurd, op. cit., pp. 342–3.
9 Lord John Russell's Edinburgh Letter. See www.victorianweb.org/history/eletter.html.
10 Gash, op. cit., p. 560.
11 Edward Pearce (ed.), *The Diaries of Charles Greville* (Pimlico 2006), p. 240, entry for 21 December 1845.

12 Hurd, op. cit., p. 349.

13 *Observer*, 21 December 1845, p. 3.

14 *Manchester Guardian*, 24 December 1845, p. 4.

15 Richard A. Gaunt, *Sir Robert Peel: The Life and Legacy* (Tauris 2010), p. 95.

16 Hurd, op. cit., p. 348.

17 Hurd, op. cit., p. 355. See also Benjamin Disraeli, *Lord George Bentinck* (1851).

18 Pearce, op. cit., p. 142, entry for 21 February 1835.

19 Robert Blake, *The Conservative Party from Peel to Thatcher* (Fontana 1985), p. 18.

20 *The Times* obituary of Sir Robert Peel, 2 July 1850, reprinted in *The Times: Great Victorian Lives* (Times Books 2007).

21 Donald Read, *Peel and the Victorians* (Blackwell 1987), p. 58.

22 Read, op. cit., p. 61.

23 Paul Schlicke, *Oxford Companion to Charles Dickens* (OUP 2011), p. 128.

24 Claire Tomalin, *Charles Dickens: A Life* (Viking 2011), pp. 174–5.

25 Juliet Barker, *The Brontës* (Phoenix 1995), p. 485.

26 Adrian Desmond and James Moore, *Darwin* (Penguin 1991), pp. 330–3.

27 Owen Beattie and John Geiger, *Frozen in Time: The Fate of the Franklin Expedition* (Bloomsbury 1987), pp. 15–17.

28 Anthony Brandt, *The Man Who Ate His Boots: Sir John Franklin and the Tragic History of the Northwest Passage* (Jonathan Cape 2011).

29 Hurd, op. cit., p. 350.

30 Read, op. cit., p. 167.

31 *The Times*, 23 December 1845.

32 Queen Victoria's journal, 31 December 1845.

CHAPTER 2: THE CONDITION OF ENGLAND

1 Gavin Stamp, *The Changing Metropolis* (Viking 1984), pp. 27–34.

2   See, for instance, Naomi Rosenblum, *A World History of Photography* (Abbeville Press 1984), pp. 57–8, showing portraits of James Linton and a group portrait of the Misses Binny and Miss Monro.

3   Censuses 1841 and 1851. See http://homepage.ntlworld.com/hitch/gendocs/pop.html.

4   Boyd Hilton, *A Mad, Bad and Dangerous People? England 1783–1846* (OUP 2006), pp. 5–7.

5   E.P. Thompson, *The Making of the English Working Class* (Pelican 1968), p. 365.

6   S.E. Finer, *The Life and Times of Sir Edwin Chadwick* (Methuen 1952), p. 213.

7   Barrie Trinder, *The Making of the Industrial Landscape* (J.M. Dent 1982), pp. 176–8.

8   Trinder, op. cit., p. 176.

9   James Stevens Curl, *The Victorian Celebration of Death* (Sutton 2000), pp. 113–16.

10   Friedrich Engels, *The Condition of the Working Class in England* (OUP 1993), pp. 9, 72–3.

11   Liza Picard, *Victorian London* (Weidenfeld and Nicolson 2005), p. 98.

12   Judith Flanders, *The Victorian House* (Harper Perennial 2004), p. xxxix.

13   Thompson, op. cit., p. 356.

14   Edward Pearce (ed.), *The Diaries of Charles Greville* (Pimlico 2006), p. 107, entry for 27 July 1832.

15   'Song of the Shirt' is in *Punch* (1843), vol. v, p. 260.

16   'Advice Gratis to the Poor', cartoon in *Punch* (1846), vol. xi, p. 97.

17   G.F.A. Best, *Shaftesbury* (New English Library 1964), p. 94.

18   Edwin Chadwick, *Report on the Sanitary Condition of the Labouring Population of Great Britain* (1842), republished by Edinburgh University Press 1965, pp. 423–4.

19   Finer, op. cit., p. 215.

20   Hilton, op. cit., p. 589, letter from Russell to Chadwick.

21 Hilton, op. cit., p. 593, letter from Nassau senior to Brougham, 9 March 1833.

22 The fullest account is in Ian Anstruther, *The Scandal of the Andover Workhouse* (Geoffrey Bles 1973), p. 134.

23 Finer, op. cit., p. 257.

24 Anstruther, op. cit., p. 151.

25 Brenda Colloms, *Victorian Country Parsons* (Book Club Associates 1977), pp. 196–209.

26 'The Home of the Rick Burner', cartoon in *Punch* (1845), vol. vii, p. 17.

27 Eric Hobsbawm and George Rude, *Captain Swing* (Penguin 1973), p. 73.

28 'The Game Laws, or the Sacrifice of the peasant to the hare', cartoon in *Punch* (1844), vol. vii, p. 197.

29 See Harry Hopkins, *The Long Affray: The Poaching Wars in Britain* (Papermac 1986), pp. 213–31, for a full account of the 1846 Game Laws inquiry.

30 Hopkins, op. cit., p. 179.

31 Trinder, op. cit., pp. 196–7.

32 Hopkins, op. cit., p. 224

33 Hopkins, op. cit., p. 225.

34 Hopkins, op. cit., p. 229.

35 Douglas Hurd, *Robert Peel: A Biography* (Phoenix 2007), p. 257, letter of 20 August 1842.

CHAPTER 3: ALAS! THE FOUL AND FATAL BLIGHT

1 Douglas Hurd, *Robert Peel: A Biography* (Phoenix 2007), p. 337. Gash also states this in his biography of Peel (p. 609).

2 Cecil Woodham-Smith, *The Great Hunger* (New English Library 1968), p. 70.

3 Norman Gash, *Sir Robert Peel* (Longman 1972), p. 610.

4 See, for example, John Kelly, *The Graves are Walking* (Faber 2012), pp. 40–2, which dismisses Peel as foppish and seems to

think that Drayton Manor, his Staffordshire estate, is in Yorkshire
– a bit like referring to Chicago, Indiana.

5   Woodham-Smith, op. cit., p. 59.

6   E. Margaret Crawford, 'Food and Famine', in Cathal Poirteir
(ed.), *The Great Irish Famine* (Mercier Press 1995), p. 64.

7   Woodham-Smith, op. cit., p. 174.

8   Charles Chenevix Trench, *The Great Dan* (Triad Books 1986),
pp. 273–97.

9   Robert Kee, *The Most Distressful Country* (Quartet 1976),
p. 243.

10 *Punch* (1846), vol. xi, pp. 159 and 203.

11 Woodham-Smith, op. cit., pp. 66–7.

12 Woodham-Smith, op. cit., pp. 67.

13 Woodham-Smith, op. cit., pp. 67.

14 Woodham-Smith, op. cit., p. 59.

15 Irene Whelan, 'The Stigma of Souperism', in Poirteir, op. cit.,
pp. 135–55.

16 Poirteir, op. cit., p. 148.

17 Woodham-Smith, op. cit., p. 101.

18 A. N. Wilson, *The Victorians* (Hutchinson 2002), p. 82.

19 Wilson, op. cit., p. 77.

20 Mary E. Daly, 'The Operations of Famine Relief', in Cathal
Poirteir (ed.), *The Great Irish Famine* (Mercier Press 1995),
p. 113, quoting *The Times* editorial, 4 January 1847.

21 Wilson, op. cit., p. 82.

22 Chenevix Trench, op. cit., p. 288.

23 Ian Bradley, *The Call to Seriousness* (Lion 2006), p. 160.

24 Woodham-Smith, op., cit., p. 54.

25 Woodham-Smith, op. cit., pp. 53–4.

26 Laura Trevelyan, *A Very British Family* (I. B. Tauris 2006), p. 24.

27 Hurd, op. cit., p. 337.

28 Woodham-Smith, op. cit., p. 84.

29 Kee, op. cit., p. 256.

30 Edward Pearce (ed.), *The Diaries of Charles Greville* (Pimlico 2006), pp. 250–1, entry for 4 December 1846.

31 Chenevix Trench, op. cit., pp. 296–7.

32 Kee, op. cit., p. 257.

CHAPTER 4: A DAMNED DISHONEST ACT

1 Norman Gash, *Sir Robert Peel* (Longman 1972), p. 564.

2 Benjamin Disraeli, *Lord George Bentinck* (Constable 1905), p. 24.

3 Robert Blake, *Disraeli* (Methuen 1966), pp. 81–2.

4 Queen Victoria's journal, 22 January 1846. See http://www. queenvictoriasjournals.org/home.do.

5 *Manchester Guardian*, 24 January 1846.

6 See Caroline Shenton, *The Day Parliament Burned Down* (OUP 2012).

7 Hansard parliamentary archive: http://hansard.millbanksystems. com/sittings/1846/jan/22.

8 Edward Pearce (ed.), *The Diaries of Charles Greville* (Pimlico 2006), p. 242, entry for 23 January 1846.

9 Queen Victoria's journal, 23 January 1846.

10 *Observer*, 1 February 1846.

11 *Manchester Guardian*, 24 January 1846.

12 Roy Jenkins, *Gladstone* (Macmillan 1995), p. 70.

13 See Jenkins, op. cit., chapter 7.

14 Blake, op. cit., p. 234.

15 Pearce, op. cit., p. 245, entry for 21 March 1846.

16 See Mary Lawson-Tancred, 'The Anti-League and the Crisis of 1846', *Historical Journal*, vol. iii, 2 (1960), pp. 162–83.

17 Jenkins, op. cit., p. 85.

18 Hansard parliamentary archive, 16 February 1846.

19 Douglas Hurd, *Robert Peel: A Biography* (Phoenix 2007), p. 359.

20 Elizabeth Longford, *Wellington: Pillar of State* (Panther 1975), p. 482.

21 Christopher Hibbert, *Wellington: A Personal History* (Harper Collins 1997), p. 344.

CHAPTER 5: FUSTIAN JACKETS, BLISTERED HANDS AND UNSHORN CHINS

1 Feargus O'Connor speech, January 1846; see J.T. Ward, *Chartism* (Batsford 1973) p. 176.

2 Norman Gash, *Politics in the Age of Peel* (Longman 1953), p. 122.

3 Gash, op. cit., p. 147.

4 Edward Pearce (ed.), *The Diaries of Charles Greville* (Pimlico 2006), p. 139, entry for 1 January 1835.

5 Asa Briggs, *The Age of Improvement* (Longman 1971), p. 305.

6 Ward, op. cit., p. 112.

7 See Jemima Thackray, 'The Battle Hymns of the Public', *Church Times*, 4 October 2013.

8 Donald Read, *Peel and the Victorians* (Blackwell 1987), pp. 38–42.

9 See www.chartists.net.

10 Briggs, op. cit., p. 320.

11 Ward, op. cit., pp. 189–99.

12 Elizabeth Longford, *Victoria* (Abacus 2011), p. 211.

13 Ward, op. cit., p. 205.

14 See entry 'Chartism' in Wikipedia (http://en.wikipedia.org), where Kilburn's photograph is reproduced.

15 Queen Victoria's journal, 10 April 1848. See http://www.queenvictoriasjournals.org/home.do.

16 *Manchester Guardian*, 15 April 1848.

17 *The Times*, 4 December 1845.

18 *Morning Chronicle*, 13 April 1843. This and the following newspaper references are cited in Mary Lawson-Tancred, 'The Anti-League and the Crisis of 1846', *Historical Journal*, vol. iii, 2 (1960), pp. 162–83.

19 Briggs, op. cit., p. 313.

20 www.chartists.net (see section on relations with Anti-Corn Law League).

21 Read, op. cit., p. 233.

22 Briggs, op. cit., p. 316

23 Stephen Koss, *The Rise and Fall of the Political Press in Britain* (Fontana 1984), p. 62.

24 Read, op. cit., p. 49.

25 Asa Briggs, *Victorian People* (Pelican 1970), p. 218.

26 Briggs, op. cit., p. 216.

27 Lawson-Tancred, op. cit.

28 *Morning Post*, 27 July 1846 (HJ).

29 Lawson-Tancred, op. cit.

30 *Morning Herald*, 30 January 1844 (HJ).

31 Speech in Brighton, 6 January 1846, cited in Lawson-Tancred, op. cit.

32 *The Times*, 10 January 1846.

33 Robert Blake, *Disraeli* (Methuen 1966), p. 225.

34 Gash, op. cit., chapter 15.

35 Gash, op. cit., p. 418.

36 Gash, op. cit., pp. 414–18.

37 Gash, op. cit., p. 42.

38 Gash, op. cit., p. 426.

39 Briggs, op. cit., p. 129.

40 David Ayerst, *Guardian: Biography of a Newspaper* (Collins 1971), chapters 5 and 6.

41 Ayerst, op. cit., p. 73.

42 Ayerst, op. cit., p. 140.

43 Koss, op. cit., p. 64.

44 *Manchester Guardian*, 27 June 1846.

CHAPTER 6: THE WHOLE WORLD RAILWAY MAD

1 Christian Wolmar, *Fire and Steam: How the Railways Transformed Britain* (Atlantic 2007), p. 80.

2   Nicholas Faith, *The World the Railways Made* (Pimlico 1990), pp. 33–4.

3   Charles Dickens, *Dombey and Son*, chapter 20.

4   Wolmar, op. cit., p. 93.

5   L.T.C. Rolt, *Isambard Kingdom Brunel* (Penguin 1989), pp. 171–2.

6   Rolt, op. cit., p. 185.

7   Terry Coleman, *The Railway Navvies* (Pelican 1972), p. 23.

8   See kilsbyvillage.co.uk.

9   Coleman, op. cit., p. 24.

10 Coleman, op. cit., p. 24.

11 Coleman, op. cit., p. 125.

12 Coleman, op. cit., p. 31.

13 www.carlyleletters.dukejournals.org.

14 Coleman, op. cit., p. 60.

15 Rolt, op. cit., p. 249.

16 Rolt, op. cit., p. 272.

17 Faith, op. cit., p. 19.

18 Wolmar, op. cit., p. 72.

19 Matthew Engel, *Eleven Minutes Late* (Macmillan 2009), p. 98.

20 Article on the 1845 railway mania in the *British Quarterly Review* (1872), reprinted in the *Manchester Guardian*, 11 October 1872.

21 Faith, op. cit., pp. 24–5.

22 *Punch* (1845), vol. ix, p. 47.

23 *British Quarterly Review*, 1872 (see note 20 above).

24 Wolmar, op. cit., p. 105.

25 Mark Bills and Vivien Knight, *William Powell Frith: Painting the Victorian Age* (Yale 2006), pp. 63–5.

26 *Punch* (1844), vol. vii, p. 258.

27 Engel, op. cit., p. 102.

28 Judith Flanders, *The Invention of Murder* (Harper Press 2011), pp. 329–31.

29 Lawrence James, *The Middle Class: A History* (Little Brown 2006), p. 236.

30 Faith, op. cit., p. 38.

31 Faith, op. cit., pp. 38–9.

32 James Hamilton, *Turner: A Life* (Sceptre 1997), pp. 300–10.

33 Hamilton, op. cit., p. 305.

CHAPTER 7: AN AGREEABLE SIGHT TO A MERCIFUL CREATOR

1 Saul David, *Victoria's Wars* (Penguin 2007), chapter 3.

2 Norman Gash, *Sir Robert Peel* (Longman 1972), p. 482.

3 Gash, op. cit., p. 497.

4 Gash, op. cit., pp. 496–7.

5 David, op. cit., p. 102.

6 Richard Holmes, *Sahib: The British Soldier in India* (Harper Collins 2005), p. 15.

7 Holmes, op. cit., p. 17.

8 See the St Margaret's Community website (www.stmgrts.org.uk) for an account of 'the disgraceful affair at Hounslow'.

9 David, op. cit., p. 109.

10 Douglas Hurd, *Robert Peel: A Biography* (Phoenix 2007), p. 365.

11 Sam W. Haynes, *James K. Polk and the Expansionist Impulse* (Pearson Longman 2006) is the only recent biography.

12 Haynes, op. cit., p. 132.

13 Haynes, op. cit., pp. 150–1.

14 Nigel Cliff, *The Shakespeare Riots: Revenge, Drama and Death in 19th-Century America* (Random House 2007), p. 151.

15 Amanda Foreman, *A World on Fire* (Penguin 2011), pp. 23–8.

16 Margaret C.S. Christman, *1846: Portrait of a Nation* (Smithsonian Institution Press 1996) tells the story of the US debate about the Smithson bequest.

CHAPTER 8: LEAD THOU ME ON

1 Owen Chadwick, *The Victorian Church: Part One, 1829–1859* (Adam and Charles Black 1966), p. 160.

2   Charlotte Brontë, *Jane Eyre*, chapter 4.

3   Edward Carpenter, *Cantuar: The Archbishops in their Office* (Mowbray 1997), p. 293.

4   Boyd Hilton, *A Mad, Bad and Dangerous People? England 1783–1846* (OUP 2006), p. 524.

5   Douglas Hurd, *Robert Peel: A Biography* (Phoenix 2007), p. 184.

6   Norman Gash, *Sir Robert Peel* (Longman 1972), p. 186.

7   Chadwick, op. cit., p. 169.

8   Diarmaid MacCulloch, *A History of Christianity* (Allen Lane 2009), p. 841.

9   *Punch* (1850), vol. xix, p. 207.

10   Chadwick, op. cit., p. 292.

11   Raymond Chapman, *Godly and Righteous, Peevish and Perverse: Clergy and Religious in Literature and Letters* (Canterbury Press 2002), p. 160.

12   Ian Bradley, *The Call to Seriousness: The Evangelical Impact on the Victorians* (Lion 2006), p. 19.

13   G. F. A. Best, *Shaftesbury* (New English Library 1964), p. 103.

14   June Bridgeman, *Canon Edward Hoare* (booklet published by Friends of Woodbury Park Cemetery, Tunbridge Wells).

15   Bradley, op. cit., p. 70.

16   Bradley, op. cit., p. 101.

17   Bradley, op. cit., p. 109.

18   Chadwick, op. cit., p. 532.

19   Frederick Karl, *George Eliot: A Biography* (HarperCollins 1995), p. 76.

20   Hilton, op. cit., pp. 524–38.

21   Judith Flanders, *The Invention of Murder* (Harper Press 2011), p. 219.

22   Asa Briggs, *Victorian People* (Pelican 1970), p. 150.

23   Jonathan Gathorne-Hardy, *The Public School Phenomenon* (Penguin 1977), p. 81.

24   Thomas Hughes, *Tom Brown's Schooldays* (Oxford World's Classics 1999), chapters 3 and 4.

25 Briggs, op. cit., p. 157.

26 Hilton, op. cit., p. 467.

27 Jan Morris, *The Oxford Book of Oxford* (OUP 1984), p. 238.

28 John Buxton and Penry Williams, *New College Oxford 1379–1979* (New College 1979), pp. 66–8.

29 Morris, op. cit., p. 244.

CHAPTER 9: THE NOBLEST AND WEALTHIEST OF THE LAND

1 Ronald Pearsall, *The Worm in the Bud: The World of Victorian Sexuality* (Pimlico edition 1993), p. 40.

2 Lawrence James, *Aristocrats: Power, Grace and Decadence* (Abacus 2009), p. 301.

3 Norman Gash, *Sir Robert Peel* (Longman 1972), pp. 678–82.

4 Highclere Castle guidebook (2012).

5 Mark Girouard, *Life in the English Country House* (Yale 1978), pp. 260–8.

6 Jeremy Musson, *Up and Down Stairs: The History of the Country House Servant* (John Murray 2009), p. 148.

7 Musson, op. cit., p. 149.

8 James, op. cit., p. 295.

9 Edward Pearce (ed.), *The Diaries of Charles Greville* (Pimlico 2006), pp. 165–6, entry for 4 January 1838.

10 James, op. cit., pp. 296–7.

11 Girouard, op. cit., p. 285.

12 Pearce, op. cit., p. 210, entry for 19 March 1842.

13 James, op. cit., pp. 286–7.

14 Mark Adkin, *The Charge: The Real Reason Why the Light Brigade was Lost* (Pimlico 2000)

15 Girouard, op. cit., p. 274.

16 Benjamin Disraeli, *Sybil*, book 2, chapter 5.

17 Robert Blake, *Disraeli* (Methuen 1966), p. 168.

18 Rosemary Hill, *God's Architect: Pugin and the Building of Romantic Britain* (Penguin 2007), pp. 155–7.

19   Clive Aslet and Alan Powers, *The National Trust Book of the English House* (Penguin 1985), p. 156.

20   Mark Girouard, *The Return to Camelot: Chivalry and the English Gentleman* (Yale 1981), chapter 7.

21   *The Pre-Raphaelites*, Tate Gallery exhibition catalogue (1984).

22   Judith Flanders, *The Victorian House* (Harper Perennial 2003), p. 94.

23   Liza Picard, *Victorian London* (Weidenfeld and Nicolson 2005), p. 155.

24   Picard, op. cit., p. 148.

25   Musson, op. cit., p. 187.

26   Flanders, op. cit., p. 113.

27   See the Carlyle letters online: www.carlyleletters.dukejournals.org.

28   Judith Flanders, *The Invention of Murder* (Harper Press 2011), pp. 200–13.

29   Reay Tannahill, *Sex in History* (Abacus 1980), p. 352.

30   Pearsall, op. cit., p. 293.

31   Pearsall, op. cit., pp. 272–6.

32   Musson, op. cit., pp. 181–2.

33   Cecil Woodham-Smith, *Queen Victoria: Her Life and Times*, vol. 1, 1819–61 (Book Club Associates 1972), pp. 250–76.

34   Woodham-Smith, op. cit.

35   Woodham-Smith, op. cit.

CHAPTER 10: THE SILVER BULLET

1   Norman Gash, *Sir Robert Peel* (Longman 1972), p. 585.

2   See Hansard parliamentary archive (http://hansard. millbanksystems.com) for 27 March 1846.

3   Queen Victoria's journal, 28 March 1846. See http://www. queenvictoriasjournals.org/home.do.

4   Edward Pearce (ed.), *The Diaries of Charles Greville* (Pimlico 2006), entry for 28 March 1846.

5   See Hansard archive for 15 May 1846.

6   Pearce, op. cit., entry for 21 May 1846.

7   Douglas Hurd, *Robert Peel: A Biography* (Phoenix 2007), p. 240.

8   Robert Blake, *Disraeli* (Methuen 1966), p. 178.

9   Blake, op. cit., p. 238.

10 Donald Read, *Peel and the Victorians* (Blackwell 1987), p. 239.

11 See Hansard archive for 15 May 1846.

12 Gash, op. cit., p. 594.

13 Alethea Hayter, *A Sultry Month: Scenes of London Literary Life in 1846* (Robin Clark 1992), pp. 47–8.

14 See Hansard archive for 8 June 1846.

15 Gash, op. cit., p. 596.

16 See Hansard archive for 19 June 1846.

17 Pearce, op. cit., entry for 20 June 1846.

18 G.F.A. Best, *Shaftesbury* (New English Library 1964), p. 114.

19 Gash, op. cit., p. 601.

20 See the Carlyle letters online: www.carlyleletters.dukejournals.org. Carlyle wrote two slightly different versions of the letter, so he was clearly choosing his words carefully. Peel's reply is also in the Duke University collection.

21 Benjamin Disraeli, *Lord George Bentinck* (Constable 1905), pp. 194–7.

22 Gash, op. cit., p. 602.

23 Queen Victoria's journal, 26 June 1846.

24 Queen Victoria's journal, 27–29 June 1846.

25 Hurd, op. cit., p. 369.

26 Read, op. cit., p. 231.

27 *Punch*, vol. x, 11 July 1846.

28 See Hansard archive for 29 June 1846.

29 Read, op. cit., p. 237.

30 Read, op. cit., p. 239.

31 Pearce, op. cit., entry for 4 July 1846.

32 Richard A. Gaunt, *Sir Robert Peel: The Life and Legacy*, p. 106.

33 Hayter, op. cit., p. 133.

34 Read, op. cit., p. 239.

CHAPTER 11: A FEW PALTRY POUNDS

1 Alethea Hayter, *A Sultry Month: Scenes of London Literary Life in 1846* (Robin Clark 1992), p. 22. The events of Haydon's last months are taken from this book.

2 Hayter, op. cit., p. 196.

3 Rebecca Fraser, *Charlotte Brontë* (Methuen 1989), p. 263.

4 Juliet Barker, *The Brontës* (Phoenix 1994), p. 507.

5 Juliet Barker, *The Brontës: A Life in Letters* (Folio Society 2006), pp. 164–5.

6 Helen Martens, *Felix Mendelssohn: Out of the Depths of his Heart* (Annotation Press 2009), pp. 293–5.

7 Derek Birley, *A Social History of English Cricket* (Aurum Press 1999), pp. 82–3.

8 A.W. Pullin, *Talks with Old English Cricketers* (Blackwood and Sons 1900), p. 88.

9 Patrick Morrah, *Alfred Mynn and the Cricketers of his Time* (Constable 1986), p. 165.

10 Margaret Forster, *Elizabeth Barrett Browning* (Vintage 1998), pp. 179–80.

11 Reay Tannahill, *Sex in History* (Abacus 1980), p. 347.

12 Paul Schlicke, *Oxford Companion to Charles Dickens* (OUP 2011), pp. 33–4.

13 Claire Tomalin, *Charles Dickens: A Life* (Viking 2011), pp. 189–90.

14 *Manchester Guardian*, 30 December 1846.

CHAPTER 12: A VOTE MORE OR LESS IS NOTHING TO YOU

1 Norman Gash, *Sir Robert Peel* (Longman 1972), p. 616.

2 Cited in Winston Churchill, *History of the English Speaking Peoples* (Cassell 1956); see book 10, chapter 3.

3 John Prest, *Lord John Russell* (Macmillan 1972), p. 233.

4 Prest, op. cit., p. 231.

5 Jasper Ridley, *Lord Palmerston* (Panther 1970), p. 408.

6 Prest, op. cit., p. 240.

7   Queen Victoria's journal, 31 December 1846. See http://www. queenvictoriasjournals.org/home.do.

8   Gash, op. cit., p. 617.

9   Robert Blake, *Disraeli* (Methuen 1966), pp. 249–50.

10   Blake, op. cit., p. 247.

11   Prest, op. cit., p. 210.

12   Ridley, op. cit., pp. 506–9.

13   Douglas Hurd, *Robert Peel: A Biography* (Phoenix 2007), p. 382.

14   *The Times*, 2 July 1850.

15   Donald Read, *Peel and the Victorians* (Blackwell 1987), pp. 297–8.

16   Terry Coleman, *Passage to America* (Penguin 1974), pp. 22–3.

17   *The Pre-Raphaelites*, Tate Gallery exhibition catalogue (1984), p. 124.

18   Queen Victoria's journal, 31 December 1846.

Bibliography

Ackroyd, Peter, *Dickens* (Sinclair Stevenson 1990)

Ackroyd, Peter, *Wilkie Collins* (Chatto and Windus 2012)

Adkin, Mark, *The Charge: The Real Reason Why the Light Brigade was Lost* (Pimlico 2000)

Altick, Richard A., *Victorian Studies in Scarlet* (Norton 1970)

Annan, Noel, *The Dons* (Chicago Press 2001)

Anstruther, Ian, *The Scandal of the Andover Workhouse* (Geoffrey Bles 1973)

Aslet, Clive and Powers, Alan, *The National Trust Book of the English House* (Penguin 1985)

Avery-Quash, Susanna and Sheldon, Julie, *Art for the Nation: The Eastlakes and the Victorian Art World* (National Gallery 2011)

Ayerst, David, *Guardian: Biography of a Newspaper* (Collins 1971)

Ayerst, David, *The Guardian Omnibus 1821–1971* (Collins 1973)

Barker, Juliet, *The Brontës* (Phoenix 1994)

Barker, Juliet, *The Brontës: A Life in Letters* (Folio Society 2006)

Barret-Ducrocq, Françoise, *Love in the Time of Victoria* (Penguin 1991)

Beattie, Owen and Geiger, John, *Frozen in Time: The Fate of the Franklin Expedition* (Bloomsbury 1987)

Best, G.F.A., *Shaftesbury* (New English Library 1964)

Bills, Mark and Knight, Vivien, *William Powell Frith: Painting the Victorian Age* (Yale 2006)

Birley, Derek, *A Social History of English Cricket* (Aurum Press 1999)

Blake, Robert, *The Conservative Party from Peel to Thatcher* (Fontana 1985)

Blake, Robert, *Disraeli* (Methuen 1966)

Bradley, Ian, *The Call to Seriousness: The Evangelical Impact on the Victorians* (Lion 2006)

Bradley, Ian, *The Penguin Book of Hymns* (Penguin 1990)

Brandt, Anthony, *The Man Who Ate His Boots: Sir John Franklin and the Tragic History of the Northwest Passage* (Jonathan Cape 2011)

Bridgeman, June, *Canon Edward Hoare* (monograph produced by the Friends of Woodbury Park Cemetery, Tunbridge Wells)

Briggs, Asa, *The Age of Improvement* (Longman 1971)

Briggs, Asa, *Victorian Cities* (Pelican 1975)

Briggs, Asa, *Victorian People* (Pelican 1970)

Briggs, Asa, *Victorian Things* (Penguin 1990)

Briggs, Asa and Susan, *Cap and Bell: Punch's Chronicle of English History 1841–61* (History Book Club 1972)

Brock, Michael, *The Great Reform Act* (Hutchinson 1973)

Buxton, John and Williams, Penry, *New College, Oxford 1379–1979* (New College 1979)

Carpenter, Edward, *Cantuar: The Archbishops in their Office* (Mowbray 1997)

Chadwick, Edwin, *Report on the Sanitary Condition of the Labouring Population of Great Britain 1842* (Edinburgh University Press 1965)

Chadwick, Owen, *The Victorian Church: Part One, 1829–1859* (Adam and Charles Black 1966)

Chandos, John, *Boys Together: English Public Schools 1800–1864* (OUP 1985)

Chapman, Raymond, *Godly and Righteous, Peevish and Perverse: Clergy and Religious in Literature and Letters* (Canterbury Press 2002)

Chenevix Trench, Charles, *The Great Dan* (Triad Books 1986)

Christman, Margaret C.S., *1846: Portrait of the Nation* (Smithsonian Institution Press 1996)

Churchill, Winston, *A History of the English Speaking Peoples*, vol. 4 (Cassell 1956)

Cliff, Nigel, *The Shakespeare Riots: Revenge, Drama and Death in 19th-Century America* (Random House 2007)

Coleman, Terry, *Passage to America* (Penguin 1974)

Coleman, Terry, *The Railway Navvies* (Pelican 1972)

Colloms, Brenda, *Victorian Country Parsons* (Book Club Associates 1977)

Crowley, John, Smyth, William and Murphy, Mike (eds.), *Atlas of the Great Irish Famine* (Cork University Press 2012)

Curl, James Stevens, *The Victorian Celebration of Death* (Sutton 2000)

David, Saul, *Victoria's Wars* (Penguin 2007)

Desmond, Adrian and Moore, James, *Darwin* (Penguin 1991)

Diamond, Michael, *Victorian Sensation* (Anthem Press 2003)

Dickens, Charles, *Dombey and Son* (Wordsworth Classics 2002)

Dickens, Charles, *Little Dorrit* (Penguin Classics, 1986)

Disraeli, Benjamin, *Coningsby* (Nonsuch Classics 2007)

Disraeli, Benjamin, *Lord George Bentinck* (Constable 1905)

Disraeli, Benjamin, *Sybil* (OUP 1998)

Douglas-Fairhurst, Robert, *Becoming Dickens* (Harvard University Press 2011)

Dyos, H.J. and Wolff, Michael, *The Victorian City: Images and Realities*, 2 vols (Routledge 1978)

Ellmann, Richard, *Oscar Wilde* (Penguin 1988)

Engel, Matthew, *Eleven Minutes Late* (Macmillan 2009)

Engels, Friedrich, *The Condition of the Working Class in England* (OUP 1999)

Faith, Nicholas, *The World the Railways Made* (Pimlico 1994)

Finer, S.E., *The Life and Times of Sir Edwin Chadwick* (Methuen 1952)

Flanders, Judith, *The Invention of Murder* (Harper Press 2011)

Flanders, Judith, *The Victorian House* (Harper Perennial 2003)

Foreman, Amanda, *A World on Fire* (Penguin 2011)

Forster, Margaret, *Elizabeth Barrett Browning* (Vintage 1988)

Foster, R.F., *Paddy and Mr Punch* (Allen Lane 1993)

Fraser, Rebecca, *Charlotte Brontë* (Methuen 1989)

Gash, Norman, *Politics in the Age of Peel* (Longman 1953)

Gash, Norman, *Sir Robert Peel* (Longman 1972)

Gaskell, Elizabeth, *Mary Barton* (OUP 2006)

Gathorne-Hardy, Jonathan, *The Public School Phenomenon* (Penguin 1977)

Gatrell, V.A.C., *The Hanging Tree* (OUP 1994)

Gaunt, Richard A., *Sir Robert Peel: The Life and Legacy* (I. B. Tauris 2010)

Girouard, Mark, *Life in the English Country House* (Yale 1978)

Girouard, Mark, *The Return to Camelot: Chivalry and the English Gentleman* (Yale 1981)

Gross, John, *The Rise and Fall of the Man of Letters* (Pelican 1973)

Hamilton, James, *Faraday* (HarperCollins, 2002)

Hamilton, James, *Turner: A Life* (Sceptre 1997)

Haynes, Sam W., *James K. Polk and the Expansionist Impulse* (Pearson Longman 2006)

Hayter, Alethea, *A Sultry Month: Scenes of London Literary Life in 1846* (Robin Clark 1992)

Hayward, John, *The Penguin Book of English Verse* (Penguin 1970)

Hibbert, Christopher, *London* (Penguin 1987)

Hibbert, Christopher, *Wellington: A Personal History* (HarperCollins 1997)

Hill, Rosemary, *God's Architect: Pugin and the Building of Romantic Britain* (Penguin 2007)

Hilton, Boyd, *A Mad, Bad and Dangerous People? England 1783–1846* (OUP 2006)

Hinde, Wendy, *George Canning* (Purnell 1973)

Hobsbawm, Eric and Rude, George, *Captain Swing* (Penguin 1973)

Holmes, Richard, *Sahib: The British Soldier in India* (HarperCollins 2005)

Holmes, Richard, *Soldiers* (Harper Press 2012)

Hopkins, Harry, *The Long Affray: The Poaching Wars in Britain* (Papermac 1986)

Hughes, Thomas, *Tom Brown's Schooldays* (OUP 1989)

Hurd, Douglas, *Robert Peel: A Biography* (Phoenix 2007)

James, Lawrence, *Aristocrats: Power, Grace and Decadence* (Abacus 2009)

James, Lawrence, *The Middle Class: A History* (Little Brown 2006)

Jenkins, Roy, *Gladstone* (Macmillan 1995)

Karl, Frederick, *George Eliot: A Biography* (HarperCollins 1995)

Kee, Robert, *The Most Distressful Country* (Quartet 1976)

Kelly, John, *The Graves are Walking: The History of the Great Irish Famine* (Faber 2012)

Kitson, Clark G., *The Making of Victorian England* (Routledge 1994)

Koss, Stephen, *The Rise and Fall of the Political Press in Britain* (Fontana 1984)

Leapman, Michael, *The World for a Shilling* (Hodder Headline 2002)

Longford, Elizabeth, *Victoria* (Abacus 2011)

Longford, Elizabeth, *Wellington: Pillar of State* (Panther 1975)

Lubenow, William C., *The Politics of Government Growth: Early Victorian Attitudes toward State Intervention 1833–1848* (David and Charles 1971)

MacCulloch, Diarmaid, *A History of Christianity* (Allen Lane 2009)

Martens, Helen, *Felix Mendelssohn: Out of the Depths of his Heart* (Annotation Press 2009)

Mayhew, Henry, *London Labour and the London Poor* (OUP 2010)

Morley, John, *The Life of Gladstone* (Hodder and Stoughton 1904)

Morrah, Patrick, *Alfred Mynn and the Cricketers of his Time* (Constable 1986)

Morris, Jan, *The Oxford Book of Oxford* (OUP 1978)

Musson, Jeremy, *Up and Down Stairs: The History of the Country House Servant* (John Murray 2010)

Paterson, Michael, *Voices from Dickens' London* (David and Charles 2006)

Pearce, Edward (ed.), *The Diaries of Charles Greville* (Pimlico 2006)

Pearsall, Ronald, *The Worm in the Bud: The World of Victorian Sexuality* (Pimlico 1993)

Pearson, Geoffrey, *Hooligan: A History of Respectable Fears* (Macmillan 1983)

Picard, Liza, *Victorian London* (Weidenfeld and Nicolson 2005)

Poirteir, Cathal (ed.), *The Great Irish Famine* (Mercier Press 1995)

Pool, Bernard (ed.), *The Croker Papers* (B.T. Batsford 1967)

Porter, Roy, *London: A Social History* (Hamish Hamilton 1994)

Prest, John, *Lord John Russell* (Macmillan 1972)

Pullin, A. W., *Talks with Old English Cricketers* (Blackwood and Sons 1900)

Read, Donald, *Peel and the Victorians* (Blackwell 1987)

Reynolds, Graham, *Victorian Painting* (Guild Publishing 1987)

Richardson, John, *The Annals of London* (Cassell, 2000)

Richardson, Ruth, *Death, Dissection and the Destitute* (Penguin 1988)

Richardson, Ruth, *Dickens and the Workhouse* (OUP 2012)

Ridley, Jasper, *Lord Palmerston* (Panther 1972)

Rolt, L.T.C., *Isambard Kingdom Brunel* (Penguin 1989)

Rosenblum, Naomi, *A World History of Photography* (Abbeville Press 1984)

Schlicke, Paul, *The Oxford Companion to Charles Dickens* (OUP 2011)

Shenton, Caroline, *The Day Parliament Burned Down* (OUP 2012)

Stamp, Gavin, *The Changing Metropolis* (Viking 1984)

Sweet, Matthew, *Inventing the Victorians* (Faber 2001)

Tannahill, Reay, *Sex in History* (Abacus 2001)

Thomson, David, *England in the Nineteenth Century* (Pelican 1969)

Thompson, E. P., *The Making of the English Working Class* (Pelican 1968)

Tomalin, Claire, *Charles Dickens: A Life* (Viking 2011)

Trevelyan, Laura, *A Very British Family* (I. B. Tauris 2006)

Trinder, Barrie, *The Making of the Industrial Landscape* (J. M. Dent 1982)

Ward, J.T., *Chartism* (B.T. Batsford 1973)

Weightman, Gavin and Humphries, Steve, *The Making of Modern London 1815–1914* (Sidgwick and Jackson 1983)

White, Jerry, *London in the 19th Century* (Vintage 2008)

Wilson, A.N., *The Victorians* (Hutchinson 2002)

Wilson, Colin and Pitman, Pat, *Encyclopaedia of Murder* (Pan Books 1964)

Witheridge, John, *Excellent Dr Stanley: The Life of Dean Stanley of Westminster* (Michael Russell 2013)

Wolmar, Christian, *Fire and Steam: How the Railways Transformed Britain* (Atlantic 2007)

Woodham-Smith, Cecil, *The Great Hunger* (New English Library 1968)

Woodham-Smith, Cecil, *Queen Victoria: Her Life and Times*, vol. 1 (1819–61) (Book Club Associates 1973)

NEWSPAPER ARCHIVES

Manchester Guardian

Observer

Punch

The Times

MOST CONSULTED WEBSITES

www.carlyletters.dukejournals.org

www.chartists.net

www.queenvictoriasjournals.org/home.do

www.victorianweb.org/history

http://hansard.millbanksystems.com/sittings/1846

http://homepage.ntlworld.com/hitch/gendocs/pop.html

Acknowledgements

As will have become evident to the attentive reader, I rather admire Sir Robert Peel, who has become a somewhat over-shadowed and distant figure in nineteenth-century politics. I first became interested in him nearly forty years ago when I studied his government for a special-subject finals paper as an undergraduate at Oxford. It was the era of Edward Heath and Harold Wilson, the three-day week, industrial upheaval, Irish turmoil, profound economic policy divisions and the looming prospect of a referendum on the Common Market as a harbinger of Britain's future place in the world, so the great debates of the 1840s had a certain contemporary resonance. There were even some superficial resemblances between Peel and Heath, another stiff and rectitudinous leader drawn from the purple of trade – albeit from a much lower social level than Peel – rather than the ranks of the aristocracy; both prone to U-turns and ultimately doomed to internal over-throw and exile within their own party. The analogy goes even further since each was supplanted in due course by the unlikeliest of outsider candidates: Benjamin Disraeli and Margaret Thatcher, both of whom would in their turn profoundly alter the character of the Conservative party.

While it is an exaggeration to say that Peel made me inter-ested in politics, I was certainly conscious of him and his contemporaries when I later became a parliamentary reporter at the BBC and then a political correspondent at Westminster for the *Daily Telegraph* and latterly the *Guardian* and sat looking down on the chamber below. Few speeches matched the rhetoric and dramatic tension of the Corn Law debates, but I was there to watch a benighted John Major struggling to overcome the Maastricht rebels and facing similar attacks from his own side as those that had confronted Peel.

I owe thanks for the suggestion that I should write this book to my friend (even if he does support UKIP) the historian and fellow journalist Nigel Jones; to Jane Shaw, former chaplain of New College, Oxford, now dean of San Francisco Cathedral, who read, commented on and improved the church chapter; to Tom Webber and Richard Milbank at Head of Zeus who commissioned this book; to Ben Dupré, who valiantly, tolerantly and courteously edited the text; and to Charlie Viney, my gallant agent, who has championed and supported me in my writing. Any mistakes are, of course, my responsibility.

My wife Alice and children, Helena, Tim and Philip, have also had to put up with Robert Peel, perhaps more than they would have wished. Finally, this book is dedicated to John King, for many years a teacher at St Bartholomew's School, Newbury, who steered many of his students towards the study of history and inspired our lifelong fascination for the subject. Even though he used to claim to be sceptical of the great person theory of historiography – to the shock and consternation of some of his adolescent pupils – he might yet politically approve of Sir Robert Peel.

Tunbridge Wells, Kent
August 2013

Index

Pratt, Rev. Josiah 212–13
Pre-Raphaelite brotherhood 237
prisons 56
professions 47
prostitution 243–5
protectionists/protectionism 50, 74,
    93–4, 97–8, 103, 108–9, 113, 118,
    139–40, 143, 147, 224, 251–3,
    255–7, 260, 262, 267–9, 303
Protestant Ascendancy 21–2
public schools 217–18
Pugin, Augustus Welby 234–5
Punch 51, 64, 65, 81, 99, 171, 175,
    207, 273
Pusey, Edward 205, 207, 221
Pycroft, Rev. James 292

Quakers 85, 213

Ragged Schools Union 216
Railway Regulation Act (1844) 177
railways 1–2, 39, 157–81
    building of 159–61
    classes 175–6
    costs and financing of 169–71
    death of navvies during building of
    165
    expansion of 157, 159
    gauges 167
    impact on countryside and society
    174
    investing in 171–3
    and navvies 160–6
    obstacles to building of 170
    people working on the 173–4
    and Turner's *Rain, Steam and
    Speed* 160, 179
Rebecca agricultural riots 121–2
Reform Act (1832) *see* Great Reform
    Act
Reform Club 148, 150
religion 46, 199–215
    church attendance 200
    and evangelicals 208–14
    threats to certainties of 215

see also Catholics/Catholicism;
    Church of England
revivalist movement 209
Richmond, Duke of 106, 108, 144,
    146–7, 232
riots 121–2
Robarts, Abraham 124–5
Rocket 159
Roman Catholic Relief Act (1829) 201
Ronalds, Francis 2
Routh, Sir Randolph 77
Royal Academy 237
royal commissions 2
Royal Society for the Prevention of
    Cruelty to Animals (RSPCA) 212
Rugby school 218
Ruskin, John 176–7
Russell, Lord John 10–11, 14, 16, 17,
    19, 58, 73, 86, 96, 251, 262, 275,
    297, 299–300
Russell, Lord William 88, 242–3
Rutland, Duke of 229–30

St Giles-in-the-Fields 43–4
sanitation 44, 56
    improvements in 57
Scotland
    clearances of the Highlands 224–5
Scott, Gilbert 233
seaside resorts 174
self-improvement 150
servants 226–8, 229, 238–44
    cost of keeping 228, 238
    housemaid's day 240–1
    life of 238–9
    living conditions in houses of
    aristocracy 226–7
    number of 238
    relationship with employers
    229–30, 242–3
sewage system 44
sex 244–5
Seymour, Edward 124
Shadwell Park (Norfolk) 226
Shaftesbury, Lord *see* Ashley, Lord